HYPERTEXT

Parallax: Re-visions of Culture and Society

Stephen G. Nichols,

Gerald Prince, and

Wendy Steiner,

Series Editors

HYPER

The Convergence of

Contemporary Critical Theory

and Technology

TEXT

George P. Landow

The Johns Hopkins

University Press

Baltimore and London

Originally published, hardcover and paperback, 1992
Second printing, paperback, 1992

The Johns Hopkins University Press
701 West 40th Street
Baltimore, Maryland 21211-2190
The Johns Hopkins Press Ltd., London

Library of Congress Cataloging-in-Publication Data

Landow, George P.
  Hypertext: the convergence of contemporary critical theory and technology / George P. Landow.
      p.   cm.
  Includes bibliographical references and index.
  ISBN 0-8018-4280-8.—ISBN 0-8018-4281-6 (pbk.)
  1. Criticism. 2. Literature and technology. 3. Hypertext systems. I. Title.
PN81.L28 1992
801′.95—dc20   91-20068

Apple, HyperCard, and Macintosh are registered trademarks of Apple Computer, Inc. CD Word is a trademark of CD Word Library, Inc. CMS is a trademark of International Business Machines, Inc. Guide is a trademark of OWL International Ltd. InterLex and Intermedia are copyrighted by Brown University. MacDraw is a registered trademark of Claris Corp. Microsoft is a registered trademark of Microsoft Corp. On Location is a trademark of ON Technology, Inc. Storyspace is a trademark of Eastgate Systems, Inc.

For Shoshana, Serena, and Noah

Contents

Acknowledgments

I would like to thank the past and present staff of Brown University's Institute for Research in Information and Scholarship (IRIS), with special thanks to its founding director, William G. Shipp, and its current co-directors, Norman K. Meyrowitz and Marty J. Michel. Nicole Yankelovich, IRIS project coordinator during the initial stages of development and application of Intermedia, and Paul D. Kahn, project coordinator during the *Dickens Web* and later Intermedia projects, have proved to be enormously resourceful, helpful, and good humored even during periods of crisis, as has Julie Launhardt, assistant project coordinator. The IRIS facilities engineers, Todd VanderDoes and Larry Larrivee, maintained the hardware and software during conditions of continual change.

Since 1988, when Brown University's Computing and Information Services in the Center for Information Technology took over responsibility for the Intermedia lab from the IRIS team, Steve Andrade, Chris Chung, and Vic Nair have made teaching and research with Intermedia possible. I owe an especial debt to my enthusiastic and talented graduate and undergraduate research assistants, particularly Randall Bass, David C. Cody, Kathryn Stockton, Shoshana M. Landow, and Gary Weissman, and to my undergraduate students at Brown University. The development of Intermedia was funded in part by grants and contracts from International Business Machines, Apple Computer, and the Annenberg/Corporation for Public Broadcasting Project, and I am grateful to them for their support.

I also owe a debt of gratitude to many colleagues and students who shared their work with me: Stuart Moulthrop for letting me have his Storyspace version of "Forking Paths," and J. David Bolter, Robert Coover, Terence Harpold, Paul D. Kahn, and Gary Marchionini for kindly providing me with draft or prepublication versions of their writings. I would also like to thank for their advice and encouragement William Crossgrove, Sheila Emerson, William Keach, Neil Lazarus, J. Hillis Miller, Elli Mylonas, Allen Renear, Ellen Rooney, Gregory Ulmer, and the members of CHUG.

I am particularly indebted to the staff at the Johns Hopkins University Press, first of all to Eric Halpern, editor in chief, who was open-minded enough to have enthusiasm for a project that other editors at other presses thought too strange or too unintelligible to consider. Anne Whitmore, my copyeditor, knows how much I owe to her rare combination of knowledge, rigor, and skepticism, and I want to emphasize that she has contributed greatly to whatever grace, clarity, and accuracy this book may possess. Jim Johnston and Glen Burris, of design and production, deserve thanks for daring to tackle something new in a new way.

Finally, I must acknowledge the support and encouragement of my wife, Ruth, and my children, to whom this volume is dedicated. They have all listened for years to my effusions about links, webs, lexias, Web Views, and Local Tracking Maps, and they have responded with enthusiasm and understanding. Of all the debts I have incurred while writing this book, I enjoy most acknowledging the one to them.

HYPERTEXT

Hypertext and

Critical Theory

The problem of causality. It is not always easy to
determine what has caused a specific change
in a science. What made such a discovery
possible? Why did this new concept appear?
Where did this or that theory come from?
Questions like these are often highly embarrass-
ing because there are no definite methodological
principles on which to base such an analysis.
The embarrassment is much greater in the case
of those general changes that alter a science
as a whole. It is greater still in the case of
several corresponding changes. But it probably
reaches its highest point in the case of the
empirical sciences: for the role of instruments,
techniques, institutions, events, ideologies,
and interests is very much in evidence; but one
does not know how an articulation so complex
and so diverse in composition actually operates.

MICHEL FOUCAULT
The Order of Things

■ ■ ■ ■ ■ ■ ■

Hypertextual Derrida,

Poststructuralist Nelson?

When designers of computer software examine the pages of *Glas* or *Of Grammatology*, they encounter a digitalized, hypertextual Derrida; and when literary theorists examine *Literary Machines*, they encounter a deconstructionist or poststructuralist Nelson. These shocks of recognition can occur because over the past several decades literary theory and computer hypertext, apparently unconnected areas of inquiry, have increasingly converged. Statements by theorists concerned with literature, like those by theorists concerned with computing, show a remarkable convergence. Working often, but not always, in ignorance of each other, writers in these areas offer evidence that provides us a way into the contemporary *episteme* in the midst of major changes. A paradigm shift, I suggest, has begun to take place in the writings of Jacques Derrida and Theodor Nelson, of Roland Barthes and Andries van Dam. I expect that one name in each pair will be unknown to most of my readers. Those working in computing will know well the ideas of Nelson and van Dam; those working in literary and cultural theory will know equally well the ideas of Derrida and Barthes.[1] All four, like many others who write on hypertext or literary theory, argue that we must abandon conceptual systems founded upon ideas of center, margin, hierarchy, and linearity and replace them with ones of multilinearity, nodes, links, and networks. Almost all parties to this paradigm shift, which marks a revolution in human thought, see electronic writing as a direct response to the strengths and weaknesses of the printed book. This response has profound implications for literature, education, and politics.

The many parallels between computer hypertext and critical theory have many points of interest, the most important of which, perhaps, lies in the fact that critical theory promises to theorize hypertext and hypertext promises to embody and thereby test aspects of theory, particularly those concerning textuality, narrative, and the roles or functions of reader and writer. Using hypertext, critical theorists will have, or now already have, a new laboratory, in addition to the conventional library of printed texts, in which to test their ideas. Most important, perhaps, an experience of reading hypertext or reading with hypertext greatly clarifies many of the most significant ideas of critical theory. As J. David Bolter points out in the course of explaining that hypertextuality embodies poststructuralist conceptions of the open text, "what is unnatural in print becomes natural in the electronic medium and will soon no longer need saying at all, because it can be shown."[2]

■ ■ ■ ■ ■ ■ ■

The Definition of Hypertext and

Its History as a Concept

In *S/Z*, Roland Barthes describes an ideal textuality that precisely matches that which has come to be called computer hypertext — text composed of blocks of words (or images) linked electronically by multiple paths, chains, or trails in an open-ended, perpetually unfinished textuality described by the terms *link, node, network, web,* and *path:*
"In this ideal text," says Barthes, "the networks [*réseaux*] are many and interact, without any one of them being able to surpass the rest; this text is a galaxy of signifiers, not a structure of signifieds; it has no beginning; it is reversible; we gain access to it by several entrances, none of which can be authoritatively declared to be the main one; the codes it mobilizes extend *as far as the eye can reach,* they are indeterminable . . . ; the systems of meaning can take over this absolutely plural text, but their number is never closed, based as it is on the infinity of language" (emphasis in original).[3]

Like Barthes, Michel Foucault conceives of text in terms of network and links. In *The Archeology of Knowledge,* he points out that the "frontiers of a book are never clear-cut," because "it is caught up in a system of references to other books, other texts, other sentences: it is a node within a network . . . [a] network of references."[4] Like almost all structuralists and poststructuralists, Barthes and Foucault describe text, the world of letters, and the power and status relations they involve in terms shared by the field of computer hypertext.

Hypertext, a term coined by Theodor H. Nelson in the 1960s, refers also to a form of electronic text, a radically new information technology, and a mode of publication. "By 'hypertext,' " Nelson explains, "I mean *nonsequential writing* — text that branches and allows choices to the reader, best read at an interactive screen. As popularly conceived, this is a series of text chunks connected by links which offer the reader different pathways."[5] Hypertext, as the term will be used in the following pages, denotes text composed of blocks of text — what Barthes terms a *lexia* — and the electronic links that join them. *Hypermedia* simply extends the notion of the text in hypertext by including visual information, sound, animation, and other forms of data. Since hypertext, which links a passage of verbal discourse to images, maps, diagrams, and sound as easily as to another verbal passage, expands the notion of text beyond the solely verbal, I do not distinguish between hypertext and hypermedia. *Hypertext* denotes an information medium that links verbal and nonverbal information. In the following pages, I shall use the terms *hypermedia* and *hypertext* interchangeably. Electronic links connect lexias "external" to a work — say, commentary on it by another author or parallel or contrasting texts — as well as within it and thereby create text that is experienced as nonlinear, or, more properly, as multilinear or multisequential. Although conventional reading habits apply within each lexia, once one leaves the shadowy bounds of any text unit, new rules and new experience apply.

The standard scholarly article in the humanities or physical sciences perfectly embodies the underlying notions of hypertext as multisequentially read text. For example, in reading an article on, say, James Joyce's *Ulysses,* one reads through what is conventionally known as the main text, encounters a number or symbol that indicates the presence of a foot- or endnote, and leaves the main text to read that note, which can contain a citation of passages in *Ulysses* that supposedly support the argument in question or information about the scholarly author's indebtedness to other authors, disagreement with them, and so on. The note can also summon up information about sources, influences, and parallels in other literary texts. In each case, the reader can follow the link to another text indicated by the note and thus move entirely outside the scholarly article itself. Having completed reading the note or having decided that it does not warrant a careful reading at the moment, one returns to the main text and continues reading until one encounters another note, at which point one again leaves the main text.

This kind of reading constitutes the basic experience and starting point of hypertext. Suppose now that one could simply touch the page where the symbol of a note, reference, or annotation appeared, and thus instantly bring into view the material contained in a note or even the entire other text — here all of *Ulysses* — to which that note refers. Scholarly articles situate themselves within a field of relations, most of which the print medium keeps out of sight and relatively difficult to follow, because in print technology the referenced (or linked) materials lie spatially distant from the references to them. Electronic hypertext, in contrast, makes individual references easy to follow and the entire field of interconnections obvious and easy to navigate. Changing the ease with which one can orient oneself within such a context and pursue individual references radically changes both the experience of reading and ultimately the nature of that which is read. For example, if one possessed a hypertext system in which our putative Joyce article was linked to all the other materials it cited, it would exist as part of a much larger system, in which the totality might count more than the individual document; the article would now be woven more tightly into its context than would a printed counterpart.

As this scenario suggests, hypertext blurs the boundaries between reader and writer and therefore instantiates another quality of Barthes's ideal text. From the vantage point of the current changes in information technology, Barthes's distinction between readerly and writerly texts appears to be essentially a distinction between text based on print technology and electronic hypertext, for hypertext fulfills

the goal of literary work (of literature as work) [which] is to make the reader no longer a consumer, but a producer of the text. Our literature is characterized by the pitiless divorce which the literary institution maintains between the producer of the text and its user, between its owner and its customer, between its author and its reader. This reader is thereby plunged into a kind of idleness—he is intransitive; he is, in short, *serious:* instead of functioning himself, instead of gaining access to the magic of the signifier, to the pleasure of writing, he is left with no more than the poor freedom either to accept or reject the text: reading is nothing more than a *referendum.* Opposite the writerly text, then, is its countervalue, its negative, reactive value: what can be read, but not written: the *readerly.* We call any readerly text a classic text. (*S/Z,* 4)

Compare the way the designers of Intermedia, one of the most advanced hypertext systems thus far developed, describe the active reader that hypertext requires and creates:

Both an author's tool and a reader's medium, a hypertext document system allows authors or groups of authors to *link* information together, create *paths* through a corpus of related material, *annotate* existing texts, and create notes that point readers to either bibliographic data or the body of the referenced text. . . . Readers can browse through linked, cross-referenced, annotated texts in an orderly but nonsequential manner.[6]

To get an idea of how hypertext produces Barthes's readerly text, let us examine how you, the reader of this book, would read it in a hypertext version. In the first place, instead of encountering it in a paper copy, you would begin to read it on a computer screen. Contemporary screens, which have neither the portability nor the tactility of printed books, make the act of reading somewhat more difficult. For people like me who do a large portion of their reading reclining on a bed or couch, screens also appear less convenient. At the same time, reading on Intermedia, the hypertext system with which I work, offers certain important compensations. Reading an Intermedia version of this book, for example, you could change the size and even style of font to make reading easier. Although you could not make such changes permanently in the text as seen by others, you could make them whenever you wished.

More important, since you would read this hypertext book on a large two-page graphics monitor, you would have the opportunity to place several texts next to one another. Thus, upon reaching the first note in the main text, which follows the passage just quoted from *S/Z,* you would activate the hypertext equivalent of a reference mark (button, link marker), and this action would bring the endnote into view. A hypertext version of a note differs from that in a printed book in several ways. First, it links directly to the reference symbol and does not reside in some sequentially numbered list at the rear of the main text. Second, once opened and either superimposed upon the main text or placed along side it, it appears as an independent, if connected, document in its own right and not as some sort of subsidiary, supporting, possibly parasitic text.

The note in question contains the following information: "Roland Barthes, *S/Z*, trans. Richard Miller (New York: Hill and Wang, 1974), 5–6." A hypertext lexia equivalent to this note could include this same information, or, more likely, take the form of the quoted passage, a longer section or chapter, or the entire text of Barthes's work. Furthermore, that passage could in turn link to other statements by Barthes of similar import, comments by students of Barthes, and passages by Derrida and Foucault that also concern this notion of the networked text. As a reader, you would have to decide whether to return to my argument, pursue some of the connections I have suggested by links, or, using other capacities of the system, search for connections I had not suggested. The multiplicity of hypertext, which appears in multiple links to individual blocks of text, calls for an active reader.

In addition, a full hypertext system, unlike a book and unlike some of the first approximations of hypertext currently available (Hyper-Card, Guide), offers the reader and writer the same environment. Therefore, by opening the text-processing program, or editor, as it is known, you can take notes, or you can write against my interpretations, against my text. Although you cannot change my text, you can write a response and then link it to my document. You thus have read the readerly text in two ways not possible with a book: You have chosen your reading path — and since you, like all readers, will choose individualized paths, the hypertext version of this book might take a very different form in your reading, perhaps suggesting the values of alternate routes and probably devoting less room in the main text to quoted passages. You might also have begun to take notes or produce responses to the text as you read, some of which might take the form of texts that either support or contradict interpretations proposed in my texts.

■ ■ ■ ■ ■ ■ ■ ■ Like Barthes, Foucault, and Mikhail Bakhtin,
Jacques Derrida continually uses the terms *link*

Other Convergences: *(liaison), web (toile), network (réseau),* and *interwoven
(s'y tissent),* which cry out for hypertextuality;[7]

Intertextuality, Multivocality, but in contrast to Barthes, who emphasizes the
readerly text and its nonlinearity, Derrida empha-

and De-centeredness sizes textual openness, intertextuality, and the
irrelevance of distinctions between inside and out-
side a particular text. These emphases appear
with particular clarity when he claims that "like any text, the text of
'Plato' couldn't not be involved, at least in a virtual, dynamic, lateral
manner, with all the worlds that composed the system of the Greek
language" (129). Derrida in fact here describes extant hypertext systems in which the active reader in the process of exploring a text,
probing it, can call into play dictionaries with morphological analyzers
that connect individual words to cognates, derivations, and opposites.
Here again something that Derrida and other critical theorists
describe as part of a seemingly extravagant claim about language turns
out precisely to describe the new economy of reading and writing
with electronic virtual, rather than physical, forms.

Derrida properly acknowledges (in advance, one might say) that a
new, freer, richer form of text, one truer to our potential experience,
perhaps to our actual if unrecognized experience, depends upon
discrete reading units. As he explains, in what Gregory Ulmer terms
"the fundamental generalization of his writing,"[8] there also exists "the
possibility of disengagement and citational graft which belongs to
the structure of every mark, spoken and written, and which constitutes
every mark in writing before and outside of every horizon of semio-
linguistic communication. . . . Every sign, linguistic or nonlinguistic,
spoken or written . . . can be *cited*, put between quotation marks." The
implication of such citability and separability appears in the fact,
crucial to hypertext, that, as Derrida adds, "in so doing it can break
with every given context, engendering an infinity of new contexts in a
manner which is absolutely illimitable."[9]

Like Barthes, Derrida conceives of text as constituted by discrete
reading units. Derrida's conception of text relates to his "methodology
of decomposition" that might transgress the limits of philosophy.
"The organ of this new philosopheme," as Gregory Ulmer points out,
"is the mouth, the mouth that bites, chews, tastes. . . . The first step

of decomposition is the bite" (57). Derrida, who describes text in terms of something close to Barthes's lexias, explains in *Glas* that "the object of the present work, its style too, is the 'mourceau,' " which Ulmer translates as "bit, piece, morsel, fragment; musical composition; snack, mouthful." This *mourceau*, adds Derrida, "is always detached, as its name indicates and so you do not forget it, with the teeth," and these teeth, Ulmer explains, refer to "quotation marks, brackets, parentheses: when language is cited (put between quotation marks), the effect is that of releasing the grasp or hold of a controlling context" (58).

Derrida's groping for a way to foreground his recognition of the way text operates in a print medium — he is, after all, the fierce advocate of writing as against orality — shows the position, possibly the dilemma, of the thinker working with print who sees its shortcomings but for all his brilliance cannot think his way outside this *mentalité*. Derrida, the experience of hypertext shows, gropes toward a new kind of text: he describes it, he praises it, but he can present it only in terms of the devices — here those of punctuation — associated with a particular kind of writing. As the Marxists remind us, thought derives from the forces and modes of production, though, as we shall see, few Marxists or Marxians ever directly confront the most important mode of literary production — that dependent upon the *techne* of writing and print.

From this Derridean emphasis upon discontinuity comes the conception of hypertext as a vast assemblage, what I have elsewhere termed the *metatext* and what Nelson calls the "docuverse." Derrida in fact employs the word *assemblage* for cinema, which he perceives as a rival, an alternative, to print. Ulmer points out that "the gram or trace provides the 'linguistics' for collage/montage" (267), and he quotes Derrida's use of *assemblage* in *Speech and Phenomena:* "The word 'assemblage' seems more apt for suggesting that the kind of bringing-together proposed here has the structure of an interlacing, a weaving, or a web, which would allow the different threads and different lines of sense or force to separate again, as well as being ready to bind others together." [10] To carry Derrida's instinctive theorizing of hypertext further, one may also point to his recognition that such a montagelike textuality marks or foregrounds the writing process and therefore rejects a deceptive transparency.

Hypertext and Intertextuality

Hypertext, which is a fundamentally intertextual system, has the capacity to emphasize intertextuality in a way that page-bound text in books cannot. As we have already observed, scholarly articles and books offer an obvious example of *explicit* hypertextuality in nonelectronic form. Conversely, any work of literature — which for the sake of argument and economy I shall here confine in a most arbitrary way to mean "high" literature of the sort we read and teach in universities — offers an instance of *implicit* hypertext in nonelectronic form. Again, take Joyce's *Ulysses* as an example. If one looks, say, at the Nausicaa section, in which Bloom watches Gerty McDowell on the beach, one notes that Joyce's text here "alludes" or "refers" (the terms we usually employ) to many other texts or phenomena that one can treat as texts, including the Nausicaa section of the *Odyssey*, the advertisements and articles in the women's magazines that suffuse and inform Gerty's thoughts, facts about contemporary Dublin and the Catholic Church, and material that relates to other passages within the novel. Again, a hypertext presentation of the novel links this section not only to the kinds of materials mentioned but also to other works in Joyce's career, critical commentary, and textual variants. Hypertext here permits one to make explicit, though not necessarily intrusive, the linked materials that an educated reader perceives surrounding it.

Thaïs Morgan suggests that intertextuality, "as a structural analysis of texts in relation to the larger system of signifying practices or uses of signs in culture," shifts attention from the triad constituted by author/work/tradition to another constituted by text/discourse/culture. In so doing, "intertextuality replaces the evolutionary model of literary history with a structural or synchronic model of literature as a sign system. The most salient effect of this strategic change is to free the literary text from psychological, sociological, and historical determinisms, opening it up to an apparently infinite play of relationships."[11] Morgan well describes a major implication of hypertext (and hypermedia) intertextuality: such opening up, such freeing one to create and perceive interconnections, obviously occurs. Nonetheless, although hypertext intertextuality would seem to devalue any historic or other reductionism, it in no way prevents those interested in reading in terms of author and tradition from doing so. Experiments thus far with Intermedia, HyperCard, and other hypertext systems suggest that hypertext does not necessarily turn one's attention away from such approaches. What is perhaps most interesting about hypertext, though, is not that it may fulfill certain claims of structuralist and poststructuralist criticism but that it provides a rich means of testing them.

Hypertext and Multivocality

In attempting to imagine the experience of reading and writing with (or within) this new form of text, one would do well to pay heed to what Mikhail Bakhtin has written about the dialogic, polyphonic, multivocal novel, which he claims "is constructed not as the whole of a single consciousness, absorbing other consciousness as objects into itself, but as a whole formed by the interaction of several consciousnesses, none of which entirely becomes an object for the other." [12] Bakhtin's description of the polyphonic literary form presents the Dostoevskian novel as a hypertextual fiction in which the individual voices take the form of lexias.

If Derrida illuminates hypertextuality from the vantage point of the "bite" or "bit," Bakhtin illuminates it from the vantage point of its own life and force — its incarnation or instantiation of a voice, a point of view, a Rortyian conversation. [13] Thus, according to Bakhtin, "in the novel itself, nonparticipating 'third persons' are not represented in any way. There is no place for them, compositionally or in the larger meaning of the work" (*Problems*, 18). In terms of hypertextuality this points to an important quality of this information medium: hypertext does not permit a tyrannical, univocal voice. Rather the voice is always that distilled from the combined experience of the momentary focus, the lexia one presently reads, and the continually forming narrative of one's reading path.

Hypertext and De-centering

As readers move through a web or network of texts, they continually shift the center — and hence the focus or organizing principle — of their investigation and experience. Hypertext, in other words, provides an infinitely re-centerable system whose provisional point of focus depends upon the reader, who becomes a truly active reader in yet another sense. One of the fundamental characteristics of hypertext is that it is composed of bodies of linked texts that have no primary axis of organization. In other words, the metatext or document set — the entity that describes what in print technology is the book, work, or single text — has no center. Although this absence of a center can create problems for the reader and the writer, it also means that anyone who uses hypertext makes his or her own interests the de facto organizing principle (or center) for the investigation at the moment. One experiences hypertext as an infinitely de-centerable and re-centerable system, in part because hypertext transforms any document that has more than one link into a transient center, a directory document that one can employ to orient oneself and to decide where to go next.

Western culture imagined such quasi-magical entrances to a networked reality long before the development of computing technology. Biblical typology, which played such a major role in English culture during the seventeenth and nineteenth centuries, conceived sacred history in terms of types and shadows of Christ and his dispensation.[14] Thus, Moses, who existed in his own right, also existed as Christ, who fulfilled and completed the prophet's meaning. As countless seventeenth-century and Victorian sermons, tracts, and commentaries demonstrate, any particular person, event, or phenomenon acted as a magical window into the complex semiotic of the divine scheme for human salvation. Like the biblical type, which allows significant events and phenomena to participate simultaneously in many realities or levels of reality, the individual lexia inevitably provides a way into the network of connections. Given that evangelical Protestantism in America preserves and extends these traditions of biblical exegesis, one is not surprised to discover that some of the first applications of hypertext involved the Bible and its exegetical tradition.[15]

Not only do lexia work much in the manner of types, they also become Borgesian Alephs, points in space that contain all other points, because from the vantage point each provides one can see everything else — if not exactly simultaneously, then a short way distant, one or two jumps away, particularly in systems that have full text searching. Unlike Jorge Luis Borges's Aleph, one does not have to view it from a single site, neither does one have to sprawl in a cellar resting one's head on a canvas sack.[16] The hypertext document becomes a traveling Aleph.

Such capacity has an obvious relation to the ideas of Derrida, who emphasizes the need to shift vantage points by de-centering discussion. As Derrida points out in "Structure, Sign, and Play in the Discourse of the Human Sciences," the process or procedure he calls de-centering has played an essential role in intellectual change. He says, for example, that "ethnology could have been born as a science only at the moment when a de-centering had come about: at the moment when European culture — and, in consequence, the history of metaphysics and of its concepts — had been *dislocated*, driven from its locus, and forced to stop considering itself as the culture of reference."[17] Derrida makes no claim that an intellectual or ideological center is in any way bad, for, as he explains in response to a query from Serge Doubrovsky, "I didn't say that there was no center, that we could get along without the center. I believe that the center is a function, not a being — a reality, but a function. And this function is absolutely indispensable" (271).

All hypertext systems permit the individual reader to choose his or her own center of investigation and experience. What this principle means in practice is that the reader is not locked into any kind of particular organization or hierarchy. Experiences with Intermedia reveal that for those who choose to organize a session on the system in terms of authors — moving, say, from Keats to Tennyson — the system represents an old-fashioned, traditional, and in many ways still useful author-centered approach. On the other hand, nothing constrains the reader to work in this manner, and readers who wish to investigate the validity of period generalizations can organize their sessions in terms of such periods by using the Victorian and Romantic overviews as starting or midpoints while yet others can begin with ideological or critical notions, such as feminism or the Victorian novel. In practice most readers employ the materials developed at Brown University as a text-centered system, since they tend to focus upon individual works, with the result that even if they begin sessions by entering the system to look for information about an individual author, they tend to spend most time with lexias devoted to specific texts, moving between poem and poem (Swinburne's "Laus Veneris" and Keats's "La Belle Dame Sans Merci" or works centering on Ulysses by Joyce, Tennyson, and Soyinka) and between poem and informational texts ("Laus Veneris" and files on chivalry, medieval revival, courtly love, Wagner, and so on).

· · · · · · ·

Vannevar Bush and the Memex

Writers on hypertext trace the concept to a pioneering article by Vannevar Bush, in a 1945 issue of *Atlantic Monthly*, that called for mechanically linked information-retrieval machines to help scholars and decision makers faced with what was even then becoming an explosion of information.[18] Struck by the "growing mountain of research" that confronted workers in every field, Bush realized that the number of publications had already "extended far beyond our present ability to make real use of the record. The summation of human experience is being expanded at a prodigious rate, and the means we use for threading through the consequent maze to the momentarily important item is the same as was used in the days of square-rigged ships" (17–18). As he emphasized, "there may be millions of fine thoughts, and the account of the experience on which they are based, all encased within stone walls of acceptable architectural form; but if the scholar can get at only one a week by diligent search, his syntheses are not likely to keep up with the current scene" (29).

According to Bush, the main problem lies with what he termed "the matter of selection" — information retrieval — and the primary reason that those who need information cannot find it lies in turn with inadequate means of storing, arranging, and tagging information:

Our ineptitude in getting at the record is largely caused by the artificiality of systems of indexing. When data of any sort are placed in storage, they are filed alphabetically or numerically, and information is found (when it is) by tracing it down from subclass to subclass. It can be in only one place, unless duplicates are used; one has to have rules as to which path will locate it, and the rules are cumbersome. Having found one item, moreover, one has to emerge from the system and re-enter on a new path. (31)

As Ted Nelson, one of Bush's most prominent disciples, points out, "there is nothing wrong with categorization. It is, however, by its nature transient: category systems have a half-life, and categorizations begin to look fairly stupid after a few years. . . . The army designation of 'Pong Balls, Ping' has a certain universal character to it (*Literary Machines*, 2/49).

In contrast to the rigidity and difficulty of access produced by present means of managing information based on print and other physical records, one needs an information medium that better accommodates to the way the mind works. After describing present methods of storing and classifying knowledge, Bush complains, "The human mind does not work that way" ("As We May Think," 31) but by association. With one fact or idea "in its grasp," the mind "snaps instantly to the next that is suggested by the association of thoughts, in accordance with some intricate web of trails carried by the cells of the brain" (32).

To liberate us from the confinements of inadequate systems of classification and to permit us to follow natural proclivities for "selection by association, rather than by indexing," Bush therefore proposes a device, the "memex," that would mechanize a more efficient, more human, mode of manipulating fact and imagination. "A memex," he explains, "is a device in which an individual stores his books, records, and communications, and which is mechanized so that it may be consulted with exceeding speed and flexibility. It is an enlarged intimate supplement to his memory" (32). Writing in the days before digital computing (the first idea for a memex came to him in the mid-1930s), Bush conceived of his device as a desk with translucent screens, levers, and motors for rapid searching of microform records.

In addition to thus searching for and retrieving information, the memex would also permit the reader to "add marginal notes and comments, taking advantage of one possible type of dry photography, and it could even be arranged so that he can do this by a stylus scheme, such as is now employed in the telautograph seen in railroad waiting rooms, just as though he had the physical page before him" (33). Two things about this crucial aspect of Bush's conception of the memex demand attention: First, he believes that while reading one needs to append one's own individual, transitory thoughts and reactions to texts. With this emphasis Bush in other words reconceives reading as an active process that involves writing. Second, his remark that this active, intrusive reader can annotate a text "just as though he had the physical page before him" recognizes the need for a conception of a virtual, rather than a physical, text. One of the things that is so intriguing about Bush's proposal is the way he thus allows the shortcomings of one form of text to suggest a new technology, and that leads, in turn, to an entirely new conception of text.

The "essential feature of the memex," however, lies not only in its capacities for retrieval and annotation but also in those involving "associative indexing" — what present hypertext systems term a *link* — "the basic idea of which is a provision whereby any item may be caused at will to select immediately and automatically another" (34). Bush then provides a scenario of how readers would create "endless trails" of such links:

> When the user is building a trail, he names it, inserts the name in his code book, and taps it out on his keyboard. Before him are the two items to be joined, projected onto adjacent viewing positions. At the bottom of each there are a number of blank code spaces, and a pointer is set to indicate one of these on each item. The user taps a single key, and the items are permanently joined. In each code space appears the code word. Out of view, but also in the code space, is inserted a set of dots for photocell viewing; and on each item these dots by their positions designate the index number of the other item.
>
> Thereafter, at any time, when one of these items is in view, the other can be instantly recalled merely by tapping a button below the corresponding code space. (34)

Bush's remarkably prescient description of how the memex user creates and then follows links joins his major recognition that trails of such links themselves constitute a new form of textuality and new form of writing. As he explains, "when numerous items have been thus joined together to form a trail . . . it is exactly as though the physical items had been gathered together from widely separated sources and bound together to form a new book." In fact, "it is more than this," Bush adds, "for any item can be joined into numerous trails" (34), and thereby any block of text, image, or other information can participate in numerous books.

These new memex books themselves, it becomes clear, *are* the new book, or one additional version of the new book, and, like books, these trail sets or webs can be shared. Bush proposes, again quite accurately, that "wholly new forms of encyclopedias will appear, ready-made with a mesh of associative trails running through them, ready to be dropped into the memex and there amplified" (35). Equally important, individual reader-writers can share document sets and apply them to new problems.

Bush, an engineer interested in technical innovation, provides the example of a memex user

> studying why the short Turkish bow was apparently superior to the English long bow in the skirmishes of the Crusades. He has dozens of possibly pertinent books and articles in his memex. First he runs through an encyclopedia, finds an interesting but sketchy article, leaves it projected. Next, in a history, he finds another pertinent item, and ties the two together. Thus he goes, building a trail of many items. Occasionally he inserts a comment of his own,

either linking it into the main trail or joining it by a side trail to a particular item. When it becomes evident that the elastic properties of available materials had a great deal to do with the bow, he branches off on a side trail which takes him through textbooks on elasticity and tables of physical constants. He inserts a page of longhand analysis of his own. Thus he builds a trail of his interest through the maze of materials available to him. (34–35)

And, Bush adds, his researcher's memex trails, unlike those in his mind, "do not fade," so when he and a friend several years later discuss "the queer ways in which a people resist innovations, even of vital interest" (35), he can reproduce the trails he created to investigate one subject or problem and then apply them to another.

Bush's idea of the memex, to which he occasionally turned his thoughts for three decades, directly influenced Nelson, Douglas Englebart, Andries van Dam, and other pioneers in computer hypertext, including the group at Brown University's Institute for Research in Information and Scholarship (IRIS) who created Intermedia. In "As We May Think" and "Memex Revisited" Bush proposed the notion of blocks of text joined by links, and he also introduced the terms *links, linkages, trails,* and *web* to describe his new conception of textuality.[19] Bush's description of the memex contains several other seminal, even radical, conceptions of textuality. It demands, first of all, a radical reconfiguration of the practice of reading and writing, in which both activities draw closer together than is possible with book technology. Second, despite the fact that he conceived of the memex before the advent of digital computing, Bush perceives that something like virtual textuality is essential for the changes he advocates. Third, his reconfiguration of text introduces three entirely new elements — associative indexing (or links), trails of such links, and sets or webs of such trails. These new elements in turn produce the conception of a flexible, customizable text, one that is open — and perhaps vulnerable — to the demands of each reader. They also produce a concept of multiple textuality, since within the memex world *texts* refers to (a) individual reading units that make up a traditional "work," (b) those entire works, (c) sets of documents created by trails, and perhaps (d) those trails themselves without accompanying documents.

Perhaps most interesting to one considering the relation of Bush's ideas to contemporary critical and cultural theory is that this engineer began by rejecting some of the fundamental assumptions of the information technology that had increasingly dominated — and some would say largely created — Western thought since Gutenberg. Moreover, Bush wished to replace the essentially linear fixed methods that had produced the triumphs of capitalism and industrialism with what are essentially poetic machines — machines that work according to analogy and association, machines that capture the anarchic brilliance of human imagination. Bush, we perceive, assumed that science and poetry work in essentially the same way.

▪ ▪ ▪ ▪ ▪ ▪ ▪

Virtual Text, Virtual Authors, and Literary Computing

The characteristic effects of computing upon the humanities all derive from the fact that computing stores information in electronic codes rather than in physical marks on a physical surface. Since the invention of writing and printing, information technology has concentrated on the problem of creating and then disseminating static, unchanging records of language. As countless authors since the inception of writing have proclaimed, such fixed records conquer time and space, however temporarily, for they permit one person to share data with people in other times and places. Printing adds the absolutely crucial element of multiple copies of the same text; this multiplicity, which preserves a text by dispersing individual copies of it, permits readers separated in time and space to refer to the same information.[20] As Elizabeth Eisenstein, Marshall McLuhan, William M. Ivins, J. David Bolter, and other students of the history of the cultural effects of print technology have shown, Gutenberg's invention produced what we today understand as scholarship and criticism in the humanities. No longer primarily occupied by the task of preserving information in the form of fragile manuscripts that degraded with frequent use, scholars, working with books, were able to develop new conceptions of scholarship, originality, and authorial property.

Although the fixed multiple text produced by print technology has had enormous effects on modern conceptions of literature, education, and research, it still, as Bush and Nelson emphasize, confronts the knowledge worker with the fundamental problem of an information retrieval system based on physical instantiations of text — namely, that preserving information in a fixed, unchangeable linear format makes information retrieval difficult.

We may state this problem in two ways. First, no one arrangement of information proves convenient for all who need that information.

Second, although both linear and hierarchical arrangements provide information in some sort of order, that order does not always match the needs of individual users of that information. Over the centuries scribes, scholars, publishers, and other makers of books have invented a range of devices to increase the speed of what today are called information processing and information retrieval. Manuscript culture gradually saw the invention of individual pages, chapters, paragraphing, and spaces between words. The technology of the book found enhancement by pagination, indices, and bibliographies. Such devices have made scholarship possible, if not always easy or convenient to carry out.

Electronic text processing marks the next major shift in information technology after the development of the printed book. It promises (or threatens) to produce effects on our culture, particularly on our literature, education, criticism, and scholarship, just as radical as those produced by Gutenberg's movable type.

Text-based computing provides us with electronic rather than physical texts, and this shift from ink to electronic code — what Jean Baudrillard calls the shift from the "tactile" to the "digital" — produces an information technology that combines fixity and flexibility, order and accessibility — but at a cost.[21] Since electronic text processing is a matter of manipulating computer-manipulated codes, all texts that the reader-writer encounters on the screen are virtual texts. Using an analogy to optics, computer scientists speak of "virtual machines" created by an operating system that provides individual users the experience of working on their own individual machines when they in fact share a system with as many as several hundred others.[22] Similarly, all texts the reader and the writer encounter on a computer screen exist as versions created specifically for them while an electronic primary version resides in the computer's memory. One therefore works on an electronic copy until both versions converge when one commands the computer to "save" one's own version of the text by placing it in memory. At this point the text on screen and in the computer's memory briefly coincide, but the reader always encounters a virtual image of the stored text and not the original version itself; in fact, in descriptions of electronic word processing, such terms and such distinctions do not make much sense.

As Bolter explains, the most "unusual feature" of electronic writing is that it is "not directly accessible either to the writer or to the reader.

The bits of the text are simply not on a human scale. Electronic technology removes or abstracts the writer and reader from the text. If you hold a magnetic or optical disk up to the light, you will not see text at all. . . . In the electronic medium several layers of sophisticated technology must intervene between the writer or reader and the coded text. There are so many levels of deferral that the reader or writer is hard put to identify the text at all: is it on the screen, in the transistor memory, or on the disk?" (*Writing Space*, 42–43).

Jean Baudrillard, who presents himself as a follower of Walter Benjamin and Marshall McLuhan, is someone who seems both fascinated and appalled by what he sees as the all-pervading effects of such digital encoding, though his examples suggest that he is often confused about which media actually employ it. The strengths and weaknesses of Baudrillard's approach appear in his remarks on the digitization of knowledge and information. Baudrillard correctly perceives that movement from the tactile to the digital is the primary fact about the contemporary world, but then he misconceives — or rather only partially perceives — the implications of his point. According to him, digitality involves binary opposition: "Digitality is with us. It is that which haunts all the messages, all the signs of our societies. The most concrete form you see it in is that of the test, of the question/answer, of the stimulus/response" (*Simulations*, 115). Baudrillard most clearly posits this equivalence, which he mistakenly takes to be axiomatic, in his statement that "the true generating formula, that which englobes all the others, and which is somehow the stabilized form of the code, is that of binarity, of digitality" (145). From this he concludes that the primary fact about digitality is its connection to "cybernetic control . . . the new *operational* configuration," since "digitalization is its metaphysical principle (the God of Leibnitz), and DNA its prophet" (103).

True, at the most basic level of machine code and at the far higher one of programming languages, the digitization, which constitutes a fundamental of electronic computing, does involve binarity. But from this fact one cannot so naively extrapolate, as Baudrillard does, a complete thought world or *episteme*. Baudrillard, of course, may well have it partially right; he might have perceived one key connection between the stimulus/response model and digitality. The fact of hypertext, however, demonstrates quite clearly that digitality does not necessarily lock one into either a linear world or one of binary oppositions.

Unlike Derrida, who emphasizes the role of the book, writing, and writing technology, Baudrillard never considers verbal text, whose absence glaringly runs through his argument and reconstitutes it in ways that he obviously did not expect. Part of Baudrillard's theoretical difficulty, I suggest, derives from the fact that he bypasses digitized verbal text and moves with too easy grace directly from the fact of digital encoding of information in two directions: (1) to his stimulus/response, either/or model, and (2) to other nonalphanumeric (or nonwriting) media, such as photography, radio, and television. Interestingly enough, when Baudrillard correctly emphasizes the role of digitality in the postmodern world, he generally derives his examples of digitization from media that, particularly at the time he wrote, for the most part depended upon analogue rather than digital technology — and the differences between the qualities and implications of each are great. Whereas analogue recording of sound and visual information requires serial, linear processing, digital technology removes the need for sequence by permitting one to go directly to a particular bit of information. Thus, if one wishes to find a particular passage in a Bach sonata on a tape cassette, one must scan through the cassette sequentially, though modern tape decks permit one to speed the process by skipping from space to space between sections of music. In contrast, if one wishes to locate a passage in digitally recorded music, one can instantly travel to that passage, note it for future reference, and manipulate it in ways impossible with analogue technologies — for example, one can instantly replay passages without having to scroll back through them.

In concentrating on nonalphanumeric media, and in apparently confusing analogue and digital technology, Baudrillard misses the opportunity to encounter the fact that digitalization also has the potential to prevent, block, and bypass linearity and binarity, which it replaces with multiplicity, true reader activity and activation, and branching through networks. Baudrillard has described one major thread or constituent of contemporary reality that is potentially at war with the multilinear, hypertextual one.

In addition to hypertext, several aspects of humanities computing derive from virtuality of text. First of all, the ease of manipulating individual alphanumeric symbols produces simpler word processing. Simple word processing in turn makes vastly easier old-fashioned, traditional scholarly editing — the creation of reliable, supposedly authoritative texts from manuscripts or published books — at a time when the very notion of such single, unitary, univocal texts may be changing or disappearing.

Second, this same ease of cutting, copying, and otherwise manipulating texts permits different forms of scholarly composition, ones in which the researcher's notes and original data exist in experientially closer proximity to the scholarly text than ever before. According to Michael Heim, as electronic textuality frees writing from the constraints of paper-print technology, "vast amounts of information, including further texts, will be accessible immediately below the electronic surface of a piece of writing. . . . By connecting a small computer to a phone, a professional will be able to read 'books' whose footnotes can be expanded into further 'books' which in turn open out onto a vast sea of data bases systemizing all of human cognition." [23] The manipulability of the scholarly text, which derives from the ability of computers to search data bases with enormous speed, also permits full-text searches, printed and dynamic concordances, and other kinds of processing that allow scholars in the humanities to ask new kinds of questions. Moreover, as one writes, "the text in progress becomes interconnected and linked with the entire world of information" (161).

Third, the electronic virtual text, whose appearance and form readers can customize as they see fit, also has the potential to add an entire new element — the electronic or virtual link that reconfigures text as we who have grown up with books have experienced it. Electronic linking creates hypertext, a form of textuality composed of blocks and links that permits multilinear reading paths. As Heim has argued, electronic word processing inevitably produces linkages, and these linkages move text, readers, and writers into a new writing space:

The distinctive features of formulating thought in the psychic framework of word processing combine with the automation of information handling and produce an unprecedented linkage of text. By *linkage* I mean not some loose physical connection like discrete books sharing a common physical space in the library. *Text* derives originally from the Latin word for weaving and for interwoven material, and it has come to have extraordinary accuracy of meaning in the case of word processing. Linkage in the electronic element is interactive, that is, texts can be brought instantly into the same psychic framework. (160–61)

The presence of multiple reading paths, which shift the balance between reader and writer, thereby creating Barthes's readerly text, also creates a text that exists far less independently of commentary, analogues, and traditions than does printed text. This kind of democratization not only reduces the hierarchical separation between the so-called main text and the annotation, which now exist as independent texts, reading units, or lexias, but it also blurs the boundaries of individual texts. In so doing, electronic linking reconfigures our experience of both author and authorial property, and this reconception of these ideas promises to affect our conceptions of both the authors (and authority) of texts we study and of ourselves as authors.

Equally important, all these changes take place in an electronic environment, the Nelsonian docuverse, in which publication changes meaning. Hypertext, far more than any other aspect of computing, promises to make publication a matter of gaining access to electronic networks. For the time being scholars will continue to rely on books, and one can guess that continuing improvements in desktop publishing and laser printing will produce a late efflorescence of the text as a physical object. Nonetheless, these physical texts will be produced (or rather reproduced) from electronic texts; and as readers increasingly become accustomed to the convenience of electronically linked texts, books, which now define the scholar's tools and end-products, will gradually lose their primary role in humanistic scholarship.

■ ■ ■ ■ ■ ■ ■

The Nonlinear Model of

the Network in

Current Critical Theory

Discussions and designs of hypertext share with contemporary critical theory an emphasis upon the model or paradigm of the network. At least four meanings of *network* appear in descriptions of actual hypertext systems and plans for future ones. First, individual print works when transferred to hypertext take the form of blocks, nodes, or lexias joined by a network of links and paths. *Network*, in this sense, refers to one kind of electronically linked electronic equivalent to a printed text. Second, any gathering of lexias, whether assembled by the original author of the verbal text or by someone gathering together texts created by multiple authors, also takes the form of a network; thus document sets, whose shifting borders make them in some senses the hypertextual equivalent of a work, are called in some present systems a web.

Third, the term *network* also refers to an electronic system involving additional computers as well as cables or wire connections that permit individual machines, workstations, and reading-and-writing-sites to share information. These networks can take the form of contemporary local area networks (LANs), such as Ethernet, that join sets of machines within an institution or a part of one, such as a department or administrative unit.[24] Networks also take the form of wide area networks (WANs) that join multiple organizations in widely separated geographical locations. Early versions of such wide area national and international networks include JANET (in the U.K.), ARPANET (in the U.S.A.), the proposed National Research and Education Network (NREN), and BITNET, which links universities, research centers, and laboratories in North America, Europe, Israel, Australia, New Zealand, and Japan.[25] Such networks, which have thus far been used chiefly for electronic mail and transfer of individual files, have also supported international electronic bulletin boards, such as Humanist. More powerful networks that transfer large quantities of information at great speed will be necessary before such networks can fully support hypertext.

The fourth meaning of *network* in relation to hypertext comes close to matching the use of the term in critical theory. *Network* in this fullest sense refers to the entirety of all those terms for which there is no term and for which other terms stand until something better comes along, or until one of them gathers fuller meanings and fuller acceptance to itself: "literature," "infoworld," "docuverse," in fact "all writing" in the alphanumeric as well as Derridean senses. The future wide area networks necessary for large scale, interinstitutional and intersite hypertext systems will instantiate and reify the current information worlds, including that of literature. To gain access to information, in other words, will require access to some portion of the network. To publish in a hypertextual world requires gaining access, however limited, to the network.

The analogy, model, or paradigm of the network so central to hypertext appears throughout structuralist and poststructuralist theoretical writings. Related to the model of the network and its components is a rejection of linearity in form and explanation, often in unexpected applications. One example of such antilinear thought will suffice. Although narratologists have almost always emphasized the essential linearity of narrative, critics have recently begun to find it to be nonlinear. Barbara Herrnstein Smith, for example, argues that, "by virtue of the very nature of discourse, nonlinearity is the rule rather than the exception in narrative accounts."[26] Since I shall return to the question of linear and nonlinear narrative in a later chapter, I wish here only to remark that nonlinearity has become so important in contemporary critical thought, so fashionable, one might say, that Smith's observation, whether accurate or not, has become almost inevitable.

The general importance of non- or antilinear thought appears in the frequency and centrality with which Barthes and other critics employ the terms *link*, *network*, *web*, and *path*. More than almost any other contemporary theorist, Derrida uses the terms *link*, *web*, *network*, *matrix*, and *interweaving*, associated with hypertextuality; and Bakhtin similarly employs *links* (*Problems*, 9, 25), *linkage* (9), *interconnectedness* (19), and *interwoven* (72).

Like Barthes, Bakhtin, and Derrida, Foucault conceives of text in terms of the network, and he relies precisely upon this model to describe his project, "the archaeological analysis of knowledge itself." Arguing in *The Order of Things* that his project requires rejecting the "celebrated controversies" that occupy his contemporaries, he claims that "one must reconstitute the general system of thought whose network, in its positivity, renders an interplay of simultaneous and apparently contradictory opinions possible. It is this network that defines the conditions that make a controversy or problem possible, and that bears the historicity of knowledge."[27] Order, for Foucault, is in part "the inner law, the hidden network" (xx); and according to him a "network" is the phenomenon "that is able to link together" (127) a wide range of often contradictory taxonomies, observations, interpretations, categories, and rules of observation.

Heinz Pagels's description of a network in *The Dreams of Reason* suggests why it has such appeal to those leery of hierarchical or linear models. According to Pagels, "a network has no 'top' or 'bottom.' Rather it has a plurality of connections that increase the possible interactions between the components of the network. There is no central executive authority that oversees the system."[28] Furthermore, as Pagels also explains, the network functions in various physical sciences as a powerful theoretical model capable of describing — and hence offering research agenda for — a range of phenomena at enormously different temporal and spatial scales. The model of the network has captured the imaginations of those working on subjects as apparently diverse as immunology, evolution, and the brain.

> The immune system, like the evolutionary system, is thus a powerful pattern-recognition system, with capabilities of learning and memory. This feature of the immune system has suggested to a number of people that a dynamical computer model, simulating the immune system, could also learn and have memory. . . . The evolutionary system works on the time scale of hundreds of thousands of years, the immune system in a matter of days, and the brain in milliseconds. Hence if we understand how the immune system recognizes and kills antigens, perhaps it will teach us about how neural nets recognize and can kill ideas. After all, both the immune system and the neural network consist of billions of highly specialized cells that excite and inhibit one another, and they both learn and have memory. (134–35)

The network model has also inspired the connectionism movement in computing, which has drawn upon a hypothesized "neural architecture for the network design" of its radically different machines. Connectionists propose that "the connections, the very design of the network" provide "the key to its functioning, not some internal program like those in a conventional computer" (125). Connectionists also offer a "representation of knowledge," in which "*knowledge is distributed throughout the network*; it is not localized in a specific magnetic memory core or the position of a microswitch. The representation of knowledge, according to connectionists, is distributed among the strengths of the connections [links!] between the units" (126). As Pagels demonstrates, contemporary science and critical theory offer converging theories of human thought and the thought world based on the network paradigm.

Terry Eagleton and other Marxist theorists who draw upon poststructuralism frequently employ this kind of network model or image.[29] In contrast, more orthodox Marxists, who have a vested interest (or sincere belief) in linear narrative and metanarrative, tend to use *network* and *web* chiefly to characterize error. Pierre Machery might therefore at first appear slightly unusual in following Barthes, Derrida, and Foucault in situating novels within a network of relations to other texts. According to Machery, "the novel is initially situated in a *network* of books which replaces the complexity of real relations by which a world is effectively constituted." Machery's next sentence, however, makes clear that unlike most poststructuralists and postmodernists who employ the network as a paradigm of an open-ended, nonconfining situation, he perceives a network as something that confines and limits: "Locked within the totality of a corpus, within a complex system of relationships, the novel is, in its very letter, allusion, repetition and resumption of an object which now begins to resemble an inexhaustible world."[30]

Fredric Jameson, who in *The Political Unconscious* attacks Althusser for creating impressions of "facile totalization" and of "a seamless web of phenomena," himself more explicitly and more frequently makes these network models the site of error.[31] For example, when he criticizes the "anti-speculative bias" of the liberal tradition, in *Marxism and Form*, he notes "its emphasis on the individual fact or item at the expense of the network of relationships in which that item may be imbedded" as liberalism's means of keeping people from "drawing otherwise unavoidable conclusions at the political level."[32] The network model here represents a full, adequate contextualization, one suppressed by an other-than-Marxist form of thought, but it is still only necessary in describing pre-Marxian society. Jameson repeats this paradigm in his chapter on Herbert Marcuse when he explains that "genuine desire risks being dissolved and lost in the vast network of pseudosatisfactions which make up the market system" (100–101). Once again, the concept of the network provides a paradigm apparently necessary for describing the complexities of a fallen society. It does so again when in the Sartre chapter he discusses Marx's notion of fetishism, which, according to Jameson, presents "commodities and the 'objective' network of relationships which they entertain with each other" as the illusory appearance masking the "reality of social life," which "lies in the labor process itself" (296).

■ ■ ■ ■ ■ ■ ■ ■ What relation obtains between electronic computing, hypertext in particular, and literary theory

Cause or Convergence,   of the past three or four decades? At the May 1990 Elvetham Hall conference on technology

Influence or Confluence?   and the future of scholarship in the humanities, J. Hillis Miller proposed that "the relation . . . is multiple, non-linear, non-causal, non-dialectical, and heavily overdetermined. It does not fit most traditional paradigms for defining 'relationship.' "[33]

Miller himself provides a fine example of the convergence of critical theory and technology. Before he discovered computer hypertext, he wrote about text and (interpretative) text processing in ways that sound very familiar to anyone who has read or worked with hypertext. Here, for example, is the way *Fiction and Repetition* describes the way he reads a novel by Hardy in terms of what I would term a Bakhtinian hypertextuality: "Each passage is a node, a point of intersection or focus, on which converge lines leading from many other passages in the novel and ultimately including them all." No passage has any particular priority over the others, in the sense of being more important or as being the "origin or end of the others."[34]

Similarly, in providing "an 'example' of the deconstructive strategy of interpretation," in "The Critic as Host" (1979), he describes the dispersed, linked text block whose paths one can follow to an ever-widening, enlarging metatext or universe. He applies deconstructive strategy "to the cited fragment of a critical essay containing within itself a citation from another essay, like a parasite within its host." Continuing the microbiological analogy, Miller next explains that "the 'example' is a fragment like those miniscule bits of some substance which are put into a tiny test tube and explored by certain techniques of analytical chemistry. [One gets] so far or so much out of a little piece of language, context after context widening out from these few phrases to include as their necessary milieux all the family of Indo-European languages, all the literature and conceptual thought within these languages, and all the permutations of our social structures of household economy, gift-giving and gift receiving."[35]

Miller does, however, point out that Derrida's "*Glas* and the personal computer appeared at more or less the same time. Both work self-consciously and deliberately to make obsolete the traditional codex linear book and to replace it with the new multilinear multimedia hypertext that is rapidly becoming the characteristic mode of expression both in culture and in the study of cultural forms. The 'triumph of theory' in literary studies and their transformation by the digital revolution are aspects of the same sweeping change" ("Literary Theory," 19–20). This sweeping change has many components, to be sure, but one theme appears in both writings on hypertext (and the memex) and in contemporary critical theory — the limitations of print culture, the culture of the book. Bush and Barthes, Nelson and Derrida, like all theorists of these perhaps unexpectedly intertwined subjects, begin with the desire to enable us to escape the confinements of print. This common project requires that one first recognize the enormous power of the book, for only after we have made ourselves

conscious of the ways it has formed and informed our lives can we
seek to pry ourselves free from some of its limitations.

Looked at within this context, Claude Lévi-Strauss's explanations
of preliterate thought in *The Savage Mind* and in his treatises on
mythology appear in part as attempts to de-center the culture of the
book — to show the confinements of our literate culture by getting
outside of it, however tenuously and briefly. In emphasizing electronic,
noncomputer media, such as radio, television, and film, Baudrillard,
Derrida, Jean-François Lyotard, McLuhan, and others similarly argue
against the future importance of print-based information technology,
often from the vantage point of those who assume that analogue
media employing sound and motion as well as visual information will
radically reconfigure our expectations of human nature and human
culture.

Among major critics and critical theorists, Derrida stands out as
the one who most realizes the importance of free-form information
technology based upon digital, rather than analogue, systems. As
he points out, "the development of the *practical methods* of information
retrieval extends the possibilities of the 'message' vastly, to the point
where it is no longer the 'written' translation of a language, the trans-
porting of a signified which could remain spoken in its integrity."[36]
Derrida, more than any other major theorist, understands that electronic computing and other changes in media have eroded the power
of the linear model and the book as related culturally dominant paradigms. "The end of linear writing," Derrida declares, "is indeed the
end of the book," even if, he continues, "it is within the form of a
book that the new writings — literary or theoretical — allow themselves
to be, for better or worse, encased" (*Of Grammatology*, 86). Therefore,
as Ulmer points out, "grammatological writing exemplifies the struggle
to break with the investiture of the book" (*Applied Grammatology*, 13).

According to Derrida, "the form of the 'book' is now going
through a period of general upheaval, and while that form appears less
natural, and its history less transparent, than ever . . . the book form
alone can no longer settle . . . the case of those writing processes
which, in *practically* questioning that form, must also dismantle it."
The problem, too, Derrida recognizes, is that "one cannot tamper"
with the form of the book "without disturbing everything else" (*Dissemination*, 3) in Western thought. Always a tamperer, Derrida does
not find that much of a reason for not tampering with the book, and

his questioning begins in the chain of terms that appear as more-or-less the title at the beginning of *Dissemination:* "Hors Livres: Outwork, Hors D'oeuvre, Extratext, Foreplay, Bookend, Facing, and Prefacing." He does so willingly because, as he announced in *Of Grammatology,* "all appearances to the contrary, this death of the book undoubtedly announces (and in a certain sense always has announced) nothing but a death of speech (of a *so-called* full speech) and a new mutation in the history of writing, in history as writing. Announces it at a distance of a few centuries. It is on that scale that we must reckon it here" (8).

In conversation with me, Ulmer mentioned that since Derrida's gram equals link, grammatology is the art and science of linking — the art and science, therefore, of hypertext.[37] One may add that Derrida also describes dissemination as a description of hypertext: "Along with an ordered extension of the concept of text, dissemination inscribes a different law governing effects of sense or reference (the interiority of the 'thing,' reality, objectivity, essentiality, existence, sensible or intelligible presence in general, etc.), a different relation between writing, in the metaphysical sense of the word, and its 'outside' (historical, political, economical, sexual, etc.)" (*Dissemination*, 42).

▪ ▪ ▪ ▪ ▪ ▪ ▪

Analogues to

the Gutenberg Revolution

If we find ourselves in a period of fundamental technological and cultural change analogous to the Gutenberg revolution, this is the time to ask what we can learn from the past. In particular, what can we predict about the future by understanding the "logic" of a particular technology or set of technologies? According to Alvin Kernan, "the 'logic' of a technology, an idea, or an institution is its tendency consistently to shape whatever it affects in a limited number of definite forms or directions."[38] The work of Kernan and others, such as Roger Chartier and Eisenstein, who have studied the complex transitions from manuscript to print culture suggest three clear lessons or rules for anyone anticipating similar transitions.

First of all, such transitions take a long time, certainly much longer than early studies of the shift from manuscript to print culture led one to expect. Students of technology and reading practice point to several hundred years of gradual change and accommodation, during which different reading practices, modes of publication, and conceptions of literature obtained. According to Kernan, not until about 1700 did print technology "transform the more advanced countries of Europe from oral into print societies, reordering the entire social world, and restructuring rather than merely modifying letters" (9). How long, then, will it take computing, specifically, computer hypertext to effect similar changes? How long, one wonders, will the change to electronic language take until it becomes culturally pervasive? And what byways, transient cultural accommodations, and the like will intervene and thereby create a more confusing, if culturally more interesting, picture?

The second chief rule is that studying the relations of technology to literature and other aspects of humanistic culture does not produce any mechanical reading of culture, such as that feared by Jameson and others. As Kernan makes clear, understanding the logic of a particular technology cannot permit simple prediction because under varying conditions the same technology can produce varying, even contradictory, effects. J. David Bolter and other historians of writing have pointed out, for example, that initially writing, which served priestly and monarchical interests in recording laws and records, appeared purely elitist, even hieratic; later, as the practice diffused down the social and economic scale, it appeared democratizing, even anarchic. To a large extent, printed books had similarly diverse effects, though it took far less time for the democratizing factors to triumph over the hieratic — a matter of centuries, perhaps decades, instead of millennia!

Similarly, as Marie-Elizabeth Ducreux and Roger Chartier have shown, both printed matter and manuscript books functioned as instruments of "religious acculturation controlled by authority, but under certain circumstances [they] also supported resistance to a faith rejected, and proved an ultimate and secret recourse against forced conversion." Books of hours, marriage charters, and so-called evangelical books all embodied a "basic tension between public, ceremonial, and ecclesiastical use of the book or other print object, and personal, private, and internalized reading."[39]

Kernan himself points out that "knowledge of the leading principles of print logic, such as fixity, multiplicity, and systematization, makes it possible to predict the tendencies but not the *exact* ways in which they were to manifest themselves in the history of writing and in the world of letters. The idealization of the literary text and the attribution to it of a stylistic essence are both developments of latent print possibilities, but there was, I believe, no precise necessity beforehand that letters would be valorized in *these* particular ways" (181). Kernan also points to the "tension, if not downright contradiction, between two of the primary energies of print logic, multiplicity and fixity — what we might call 'the remainder house' and the 'library' effects" (55), each of which comes into play, or becomes dominant, only under certain economic, political, and technological conditions.

The third lesson or rule one can derive from the work of Kernan and other historians of the relations among reading practice, information technology, and culture is that transformations have political contexts and political implications. Considerations of hypertext, critical theory, and literature have to take into account what Jameson calls the basic "recognition that there is nothing that is not social and historical — indeed, that everything is 'in the last analysis' political" (*Political Unconscious*, 20).

■ ■ ■ ■ ■ ■ ■ If the technology of printing radically changed the world in the manner that Kernan convincingly

Predictions explains, what then will be the effects of the parallel shift from print to computer hypertext?

Although the changes associated with the transition from print to electronic technology may not parallel those associated with that from manuscript to print, paying attention to descriptions of the most recent shift in the technology of alphanumeric text provides areas for investigation.

One of the most important changes involved fulfilling the democratizing potential of the new information technology. During the shift from manuscript to print culture "an older system of polite or courtly letters — primarily oral, aristocratic, authoritarian, court-centered — was swept away . . . and gradually replaced by a new print-based, market-centered, democratic literary system" whose fundamental values "were, while not strictly determined by print ways, still indirectly in accordance with the actualities of print" (*Printing Technology*, 4). If hypertextuality and associated electronic information technologies have similarly pervasive effects, what will they be? Nelson, Miller, and almost all authors on hypertext who touch upon the political implications of hypertext assume that the technology is essentially democratizing and that it therefore supports some sort of decentralized, liberated existence.

Kernan offers numerous specific instances of ways that technology "actually affects individual and social life." For example, "by changing their work and their writing, [print] forced the writer, the scholar, and the teacher — the standard literary roles — to redefine themselves, and if it did not entirely create, it noticeably increased the importance and number of critics, editors, bibliographers, and literary historians." Print technology similarly redefined the audience for literature by transforming it from

a small group of manuscript readers or listeners . . . to a group of readers . . . who bought books to read in the privacy of their homes. Print also made literature objectively real for the first time, and therefore subjectively conceivable as a universal fact, in great libraries of printed books containing large collections of the world's writing. . . . Print also rearranged the relationship of letters to other parts of the social world by, for example, freeing the writer from the need for patronage and the consequent subservience to wealth, by challenging and reducing established authority's control of writing by means of state censorship, and by pushing through a copyright law that made the author the owner of his own writing. (*Printing Technology*, 4–5)

Electronic linking shifts the boundaries between one text and another as well as between the author and the reader and between the teacher and the student. As we shall observe below, it also has radical effects upon our experience of author, text, and work, redefining each. Its effects are so basic, so radical, that it reveals that many of our most cherished, most commonplace ideas and attitudes toward literature and literary production turn out to be the result of that particular form of information technology and technology of cultural memory that has provided the setting for them. This technology — that of the printed book and its close relations, which include the typed or printed page — engenders certain notions of authorial property, authorial uniqueness, and a physically isolated text that hypertext makes untenable. The evidence of hypertext, in other words, historicizes many of our most commonplace assumptions, thereby forcing them to descend from the ethereality of abstraction and appear as corollaries to a particular technology rooted in specific times and places.

In making available these points, hypertext has much in common with some major points of contemporary literary and semiological

HYPERTEXT theory, particularly with Derrida's emphasis on de-centering and with Barthes's conception of the readerly versus the writerly text. In fact, hypertext creates an almost embarrassingly literal embodiment of both concepts, one that in turn raises questions about them and their interesting combination of prescience and historical relations (or embeddedness).

Reconfiguring

the Text

From Text to Hypertext

Although in some distant, or not-so-distant, future all individual texts will be electronically linked to one another, thus creating metatexts and metametatexts of a kind only partly imaginable at present, less far-reaching forms of hypertextuality have already appeared. Translations into hypertextual form already exist of poetry, fiction, and other materials originally conceived for book technology. The simplest, most limited form of such translation preserves the linear text with its order and fixity and then appends various kinds of texts to it, including critical commentary, textual variants, and chronologically anterior and later texts.[1] In such a case, the original text, which retains its old form, becomes an unchanging axis from which radiate linked texts that surround it, modifying the reader's experience of this original text-in-a-new-context.

Hypertext corpora that employ a single text, originally created for print dissemination, as an unbroken axis off which to hang annotation and commentary appear in educational presentations of canonical literary texts. Paul Delany at Simon Fraser University has, for example, used Apple's HyperCard to create such a hypermedia translation and amplification of Henry Fielding's *Joseph Andrews*, and at Brown University we have used Intermedia similarly to present individual short stories by Kipling and Lawrence.[2]

A second case appears when one adapts for hypertextual presentation material originally conceived for book technology that divides into discrete lexias, particularly if it has multilinear elements that call for the kind of multisequential reading associated with hypertext. An example of this form of hypertext appears in *CD Word: The Interactive Bible Library*, which a team based at Dallas Theological Seminary created using an enhanced version of Guide. This hypertext Bible corpus, intended for the "student, theologian, pastor, or lay person" rather than for the historian of religion, includes the King James, New International, New American Standard, and Revised Standard versions of the Bible, as well as Greek texts for the New Testament and the Septuagint. These materials are supplemented by three Greek lexica, two Bible dictionaries, and three Bible commentaries.[3] Using this system, which stores the electronic texts on a compact disc, the Bible reader can juxtapose passages from different versions and compare variants, examine the original Greek, and receive rapid assistance on Greek grammar and vocabulary.

A similar kind of corpus that uses a more sophisticated hypertext system is Paul D. Kahn's *Chinese Literature* web, which offers different versions of the poetry of Tu Fu (712–770), ranging from the Chinese text, Pin-yin transcriptions, and literal translations to much freer ones by Kenneth Rexroth and others.[4] *Chinese Literature* also includes abundant secondary materials that support interpreting Tu Fu's poetry. Like *CD Word*, Kahn's corpus permits both beginning and advanced students to approach a canonical text in a foreign language through various versions, and like the hypertext Bible on compact disc, it also situates its primary text within a network of links to both varying translations and reference materials.

Before considering other kinds of hypertext, we should note the implicit justifications or rationales for these two successful projects. *CD Word* offers its readers a technological presentation of the Bible that is particularly appropriate, because they habitually handle this text in terms of brief passages — or, as writers on hypertext might put it, as if it had "fine granularity." Because the individual poems of Tu Fu are fairly brief, a body of them invites similar conversion to hypertext.

In contrast to these two instances of hypertext materials, which support study chiefly by electronically linking multiple parallel texts, the *In Memoriam* web, another Intermedia corpus created at Brown University, uses electronic links to map and hence reify a text's internal and external allusions and references — its inter- and *intra*textuality.[5]

Tennyson's radically experimental *In Memoriam* provides an exem-

plification of the truth of Benjamin's remark that "the history of
every art form shows critical epochs in which a certain art form aspires
to effects which could be fully obtained only with a changed technical
standard, that is to say, in a new art form."[6] Another manifestation
of this principle appears in Victorian word painting, particularly in the
hands of Ruskin and Tennyson, which anticipates in abundant detail
the techniques of cinematography.[7] Whereas word painting anticipates
a future medium (cinema) by using narrative to structure description,
In Memoriam anticipates electronic hypertextuality precisely by challenging narrative and the literary form based upon it. Convinced
that the thrust of elegiac narrative, which drives the reader and the
mourner relentlessly from grief to consolation, falsified real experience, the poet constructed a poem of 131 fragments to communicate
the ebb and flow of emotion, particularly the way the aftershocks
of grief irrationally intrude long after the mourner has supposedly
recovered.

Arthur Henry Hallam's death in 1833 forced Tennyson to question
his faith in nature, God, and poetry. *In Memoriam* reveals that Tennyson, who found that brief lyrics best embodied the transitory emotions
that buffeted him after his loss, rejected conventional elegy and narrative because both presented the reader with a too unified — and hence
too simplified — version of the experiences of grief and acceptance.
Creating an antilinear poetry of fragments, Tennyson leads the reader
of *In Memoriam* from grief and despair through doubt to hope and
faith; but at each step stubborn, contrary emotions intrude, and one
encounters doubt in the midst of faith, and pain in the midst of resolution. Instead of the elegiac plot found in "Lycidas," "Adonais,"
and "Thyrsis," *In Memoriam* offers fragments interlaced by dozens of
images and motifs and informed by an equal number of minor and
major resolutions, the most famous of which is section 95's representation of Tennyson's climactic, if wonderfully ambiguous, mystical
experience of contact with Hallam's spirit. In addition, individual sections, like 7 and 119 or 28, 78, and 104, variously resonate with one
another.

The proto-hypertextuality of *In Memoriam* atomizes and disperses
Tennyson the man. He is to be found nowhere, except possibly in
the epilogue, which appears after and outside the poem itself. Tennyson, the real, once-existing man, with his actual beliefs and fears,
cannot be extrapolated from within the poem's individual sections, for

each presents Tennyson only at a particular moment. Traversing these individual sections, the reader experiences a somewhat idealized version of Tennyson's moments of grief and recovery. *In Memoriam* thus fulfills Paul Valéry's definition of poetry as a machine that reproduces an emotion. It also fulfills another of Benjamin's observations, one he makes in the course of contrasting the painter and the cameraman: "The painter maintains in his work a natural distance from reality, the cameraman penetrates deeply into its web. There is a tremendous difference between the pictures they obtain. That of the painter is a total one, that of the cameraman consists of multiple fragments which are assembled under a new law" ("Work of Art," 233–34). Although speaking of a different information medium, Benjamin here captures some sense of the way hypertext, when compared to print, appears atomized; and in doing so, he also conveys one of the chief qualities of Tennyson's antilinear, multisequential poem.

The *In Memoriam* web attempts to capture the nonlinear organization of the poem by linking sections, such as 7 and 119, 2 and 39, or the Christmas poems, which echo across the poem to one another (figure 1). More important, using the capacities of Intermedia, the web permits the reader to trace from section to section several dozen leitmotifs that thread through the poem. Working with section 7, for example, readers who wish to move through the poem following a linear sequence can do so by using links to previous and succeeding sections, but they can also look up any word in a linked electronic dictionary or follow links to variant readings, critical commentary (including a comparison of this section and 119), and discussions of the poem's intertextual relations. Furthermore, activating indicated links near the words *dark, house, doors, hand,* and *guilty* produces a choice of several kinds of materials. Choosing *hand* instantly generates a menu that lists all the links to that word, and these include a graphic directory of *In Memoriam*'s major images, critical commentary on the image of the hand, and, most important, a concordancelike list of each use of the word in the poem and the phrase in which it appears; choosing any one item in the list produces the linked document, the graphic overview of imagery, a critical comment, or the full text of the section in which a particular use of *hand* appears.

Using Intermedia's capacities to create bidirectional links and to join an indefinite number of them to any passage (or block) of text, the reader can move through the poem along many different axes.

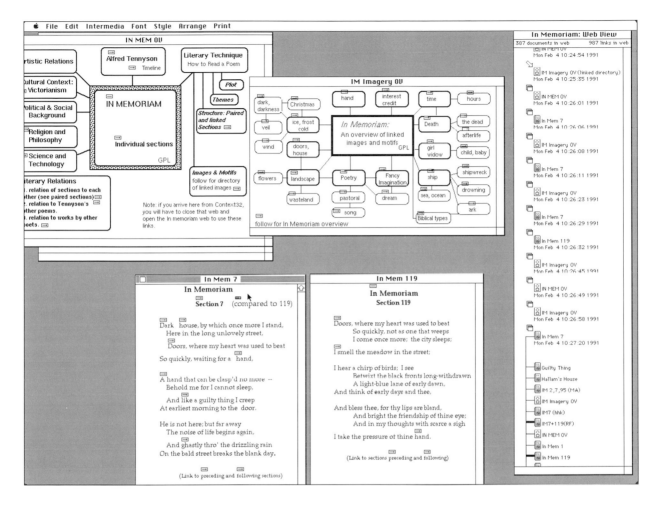

Figure 1. The *In Memoriam* Web. In this snapshot of a typical screen during a session on Intermedia, the active document, *In Memoriam*, section 7 ("In Mem 7"), appears at the lower left center of the screen with a darkened strip across its top to indicate its status. Using the capacities of hypertext to navigate the poem easily, a reader has juxtaposed sections 119 and 7, which echo and complete each other. The *In Memoriam* overview (IN MEM OV), which appears at the upper left, is a graphic document that serves as a directory; it organizes linked materials under generalized headings, such as "Cultural Context: Victorianism" or "Images and Motifs." The *In Memoriam* imagery overview (IM IMAGERY OV), a second visual index document, overlies the right border of the overview for the entire poem. On the right appears the Web View, which the system automatically creates for each document as the document becomes active either by being opened or, if it is already open on the desktop, by being clicked upon. In contrast to the hierarchically organized overviews the author creates, the Web View shows titled icons representing all documents connected electronically to the active document, in this case section 7 of the poem. Touching any link marker with the arrow-shaped cursor darkens the icons representing the documents linked to it; in this case, the reader has activated the marker above the phrase "compared to 119" and thereby darkened icons representing both the text of section 7 and a student essay comparing it to section 119.

Although, like the previously mentioned hypertext materials, the *In Memoriam* web contains reference materials and variant readings, its major difference appears in its use of link paths that permit the reader to organize the poem by means of its network of leitmotifs and echoing sections.[8] Although my co-workers, who included undergraduate and graduate students, and I created these links, they represent a form of objective links that could have been created automatically by a full-text search. Here, as in other respects, the Intermedia version of *In Memoriam* represents an adaptive form of hypertext.

In contrast to thus adapting texts whose printed versions already divide into sections analogous to lexias, one may, in the manner of Barthes's treatment of "Sarrasine" in *S/Z*, impose one's own divisions upon a work. Obvious examples of possible projects of this sort include hypertext versions either of "Sarrasine" alone or of it and Barthes's *S/Z*.[9] Stuart Moulthrop's *Forking Paths: An Interaction after Jorge Luis Borges* (1987), which runs in Storyspace, a hypertext system created by J. David Bolter, Michael Joyce, and John B. Smith, adapts Jorge Luis Borges's "Forking Paths" in an electronic version that activates much of the work's potential for variation.[10]

These instances of adaptive hypertext exemplify forms of transition between textuality and hypertextuality. In addition, works originally conceived for hypertext already exist. These electronically link blocks of text, that is lexias, to one another and to various graphic supplements, such as illustrations, maps, diagrams, and visual directories and overviews, some of which are foreign to print technology. In the future there will be more metatexts formed by linking individual sections of individual works, although the notion of an individual, discrete work becomes increasingly undermined and untenable within this form of information technology, as it already has within much contemporary critical theory. Such materials include hypertextual poetry and fiction, which I shall discuss later in this volume, and the hypertextual equivalent of scholarly and critical work in print.

One of the first such works in this new medium — certainly the first on Intermedia — was Barry J. Fishman's "The Works of Graham Swift: A Hypertext Thesis," a 1989 Brown University honors thesis on the contemporary British novelist. Fishman's thesis takes the form of sixty-two lexias, of which fifty-five are text documents and seven diagrams or digitized photographs. The fifty-five text documents he created, which range from one-half to three single-spaced pages in length, include discussions of Swift's six published book-length works, the reviews each received, correspondence with the novelist, and essays on themes, techniques, and intertextual relations of both each individual book and Swift's entire *oeuvre*. Although Fishman created his hypermedia corpus as a relatively self-contained set of documents, he linked his materials to several dozen documents already present on the system, including materials by faculty members in at least three different departments and comments by other students.

■ ■ ■ ■ ■ ■ ■

Problems with Terminology:

What Is the Object We Read and

What Is a Text in Hypertext?

As the opening sentences of this chapter may already have suggested, writing about hypertext in a print medium immediately produces terminological problems much like those Barthes, Derrida, and others encountered when trying to describe a textuality neither instantiated by the physical object of the printed book nor limited to it. Since hypertext radically changes the experiences that *reading*, *writing*, and *text* signify, how, without misleading, can one employ these terms, so burdened with the assumptions of print technology, when referring to electronic materials? We still read *according to* print technology, and we still direct almost all of what we write toward print modes of publication, but we can already glimpse the first appearances of hypertextuality and begin to ascertain some aspects of its possible futures. Terms so implicated with print technology necessarily confuse unless handled with great care. Two examples will suffice.

An instance of the kind of problem we face appears when we try to decide what to call the object with which one reads. The object with which one reads the production of print technology is, of course, the book. In our culture the term *book* can refer to three very different entities — the object itself, the text, and the instantiation of a particular technology. Calling the machine one uses to read hypertext an "electronic book," however, would be misleading, since the machine with which one reads (and writes, and carries out other operations, including sending and receiving mail) does not itself constitute a book, that is, a text: it does not coincide either with the virtual text or with a physical embodiment of it.

Additional problems arise because hypertext involves a more active reader, one who not only chooses his or her reading paths but also has the opportunity of reading as an author; that is, at any time the person reading can assume an authorial role and either attach links or add text to the text being read. Therefore, to employ the term *reader*, as some computer systems do in their electronic mailboxes or message spaces, does not seem appropriate either.[11]

One solution has been to call this reading-and-writing site a workstation by analogy to the engineer's workstation, the term assigned to relatively high-powered machines, often networked, that have far more computing power, memory, and graphics capacities than the personal computer.[12] However, because *workstation* seems to suggest that such objects will exist only in the work place and find application only for gainful labor or employment, this term also misleads. Nonetheless, I shall employ it occasionally, if only because it seems closer to what hypertext demands than any of the other terms thus far suggested. The problem with terminology arises, as has now become obvious, because the roles of reader and author change so much in hypermedia technology that our current vocabulary does not have much appropriate to offer.

Whatever one wishes to call the reading-and-writing site, one should not think of the actual mechanism that one will use to work (and play) in hypertext as a free-standing machine, like today's personal computer. Rather, the "object one reads" must be seen as the entrance, the magic doorway, into the docuverse, since it is the individual reader's and writer's means of participating in — of being linked to — the world of linked hypermedia documents.

A similar terminological problem appears in what to do with the term *text*, which I have already employed so many times in this study. More than any other term crucial to this discussion, *text* has ceased to inhabit a single world. Existing in two very different worlds, it gathers contradictory meanings to itself, and one must find some way of avoiding confusion when using it. Frequently, in trying to explain certain points of difference, I have found myself forced to blur old and new definitions or have discovered myself using the old term in an essentially anachronistic sense. For example, in discussing that hypertext systems permit one to link a passage "in" the "text" to other passages "in" the "text" as well as to those "outside" it, one confronts precisely such anachronism. The kind of text that permits one to write, however incorrectly, of insides and outsides belongs to print, whereas we are here considering a form of electronic virtual textuality for which these already suspect terms have become even more problematic and misleading. One solution has been to use *text* as an anachronistic shorthand for the bracketed material in the following expression: "If one were to transfer a [complete printed] text (work), say, Milton's *Paradise Lost*, into electronic form, one could link passages within [what had been] the [original] text (Milton's poem) to each other and one could also link passages to a wide range of materials outside the original text to it." The problem is, of course, that as soon as one converts the printed text to an electronic one, it no longer possesses the same kind of textuality. In the following pages, references to text must therefore be understood to mean "the electronic version of a printed text."

■ ■ ■ ■ ■ ■ ■   The question what to call "text" in the medium of hypertext leads directly to the question what to

Verbal and Nonverbal Text   include under that rubric in the first place. This question in turn immediately forces us to recognize that hypertext reconfigures the text in a fundamental way not immediately suggested by the fact of linking. Hypertextuality inevitably includes a far higher percentage of nonverbal information than does print; the comparative ease with which such material can be appended encourages its inclusion. Hypertext, in other words, implements Derrida's call for a new form of hieroglyphic writing that can avoid some of the problems implicit and therefore inevitable in Western writing systems and their printed versions. Derrida argues for the inclusion of visual elements in writing as a means of escaping the constraints of linearity. Commenting on this thrust in Derrida's argument, Gregory Ulmer explains that grammatology thereby "confronts" four millennia during which anything in language that "resisted linearization was suppressed. Briefly stated, this suppression amounts to the denial of the pluridimensional character of symbolic thought originally evident in the 'mythogram' (Leroi-Gourhan's term), or nonlinear writing (pictographic and rebus writing)" (*Applied Grammatology*, 8). Derrida, who asks for a new pictographic writing as a way out of logocentrism, has to a large extent had his requests answered in hypertext.

Because hypertext systems link passages of verbal text with images as easily as they link two or more passages of text, hypertext includes hypermedia. Moreover, since computing digitizes both alphanumeric symbols and images, electronic text in theory easily integrates the two. In practice, popular word-processing programs, such as Microsoft Word, have increasingly featured the capacity to include graphic materials in text documents. Linking, which permits an author to send the reader to an image from many different portions of the text, makes such integration of visual and verbal information even easier.

In addition to expanding the quantity and diversity of alphabetic and nonverbal information included in the text, hypertext provides visual elements not found in printed work. Perhaps the most basic of these is the cursor, the blinking arrow, line, or other graphic element that represents the reader-author's presence in the text. The cursor, which the user moves either from the keypad by pressing arrow-marked keys or with devices like a "mouse" or a rollerball, provides a moving intrusive image of the reader's presence in the text. From this position the reader can actually change the text: Using the mouse, one can position the cursor between the letters in a word, say between *t* and *h* in *the*. Pressing a button on the mouse inserts a vertical blinking line at this point; pressing the backspace or delete key removes the *t*; typing will insert characters at this point. In a book one can always move one's finger or pencil across the printed page, but one's intrusion always remains physically separate from the text. One may make a mark on the page, but one's intrusion does not affect the text itself.

The cursor, which adds reader presence, activity, and movement, combines in most extant hypertext systems with another graphic element, a symbol that indicates the presence of linked material. To indicate the presence of one or more links, Intermedia places a link marker, which takes the form of a small horizontal rectangle containing an arrow, at the beginning of a passage. Apple's HyperCard permits a wide range of graphic symbols ("buttons") to indicate the unidirectional links that characterize that program. *CD Word*, which is based upon an amplification of Guide, employs an ingenious combination of cursor shapes to indicate linked material. For example, if one moves the cursor over a word and the cursor changes into a horizontal outline of an arrow, one knows the cursor is on a reference button, and clicking the mouse will produce the linked text. Following this procedure on the title page and clicking the mouse when the cursor is on *Bibles* produces a list of abbreviations of included versions of the Scriptures. Then, moving the cursor over *RSV* changes it to a crosshair shape, which indicates the presence of a replacement button; clicking the mouse button produces the phrase "Revised Standard Version." All these graphic devices remind readers that they are processing and manipulating a new kind of text, in which graphic elements play an important part.

A second major visual component appears in those hypertext systems that utilize either static or dynamic devices to orient readers navigating through hyperspace. HyperCard's home card represents such a static graphic device, as does Intermedia's use of graphic overviews, which are discussed below. Storyspace and Intermedia both provide forms of dynamically created concept maps. Intermedia automatically generates the Web View, a dynamic graphic concept map that informs the reader by means of labeled icons which documents "surround" the document one is currently reading. When beginning a session, the reader chooses a particular metatext's web — say, that for *In Memoriam*, for Wole Soyinka, or for English literature between 1700 and the present — by placing the cursor on that web's icon, and opens it by double clicking the mouse button or by first activating it and then choosing "open" from the Intermedia menu. Once the Web View opens, the reader moves it to one side of the screen (conventionally the right). Now the reader can work with an individual document and the tracking map it generates open side by side. Each time the reader opens a new document or activates a previously opened one, the Web View transforms itself, thus providing information about where one can go next. Clicking twice on any icon in the Web View opens the document represented by that icon. The Web View also presents a graphic history of the reader's path by means of a vertical array of icons that indicate the titles of documents previously opened; additional smaller icons show whether the document was opened from a folder, by following a link, or by reactivating a document previously opened on the desktop.[13]

The hypertext system, not the author, generates such devices as the Web View. In contrast, hypertext authors employ important visual elements in the form of graphic overviews or directories that they create to assist readers in navigating through the metatext. Such overviews, which bear the generic moniker OV, take a variety of forms, probably the most important of which is the concept map (e.g., IN CUSTODY OV, shown in figure 2), which informs readers about linked material and provides clear, convenient access to it. The overview efficiently organizes a body of complex ideas in relation to some central phenomenon, which can be an author (Tennyson, Derrida), chronological or period term (eighteenth century, postmodern), idea or movement (realism, feminism), or other concept (biblical typology, deconstruction). In true hypertextual fashion, overviews imply that any idea that the reader makes the center of his or her investigations exists situated within a field of other phenomena, which may or may not relate to it causally.

A second kind of graphic concept overview, a flow chart suggesting vector forces, uses arrows to show lines of influence or causal connection. "Dickens Literary Relations" (figure 3), for example, uses arrows to show his relation to authors who influenced him, those he influenced, and those with whom he shared mutual influence. This form of graphic overview proves particularly useful when it is presenting clear historical relationships. Images of objects, such as photographs of a cell or the moon, can constitute a third kind of graphic overview, as do maps and technical diagrams.

Although Intermedia's Web View succeeds well in orienting the reader, it works even better when combined with author-generated overview files or other forms of intellectual mapping. The Web View presents a nonhierarchical image of all documents attached to the overview (or other active document). In contrast, the overview has a hierarchical organization, but it does not reveal the nature or number of documents linked to each link marker. Intermedia provides two ways of obtaining this information — the Web View and a menu that is activated by following links attached to a particular link marker. Clicking upon a particular link and thus activating it darkens all the links attached to that block in the Web View. Thus, working together, individual documents and the Web View continually inform the reader what information lies one jump away from the current text. This combination of materials generated by authors and Intermedia well exemplifies the way hypertext authors employ visual devices rhetorically to supplement system design and to work synergistically with it.[14]

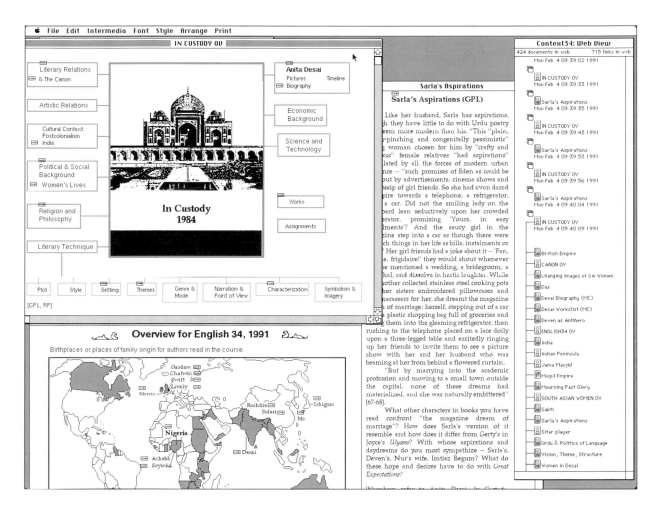

Figure 2. IN CUSTODY OV. This graphic overview for Anita Desai's novel *In Custody* appears at upper left and surrounds an image relevant to the novel with a range of topic headings, including "Literary Relations," "The Canon," "Cultural Context: India," "Postcolonialism," and "Anita Desai." Across the bottom of this graphic directory extend headings indicating materials on literary techniques, including plot, style, setting, themes, genre and mode, narration and point of view, and so on. At the right of the screen the reader has placed the system-generated Web View, which provides both a record of the reader's recent reading path and an indication of the names and types of documents linked to the currently active one, in this case the overview for Desai's novel. Below the overview appears another, in the form of a map of the British Empire, which serves as a directory for a Brown University course on recent postcolonial fiction. Between these two graphic documents and the system-created Web View appears "Sarla's Aspirations," a typical text document that follows a brief section of the novel with reading questions that compare it to works read in this and other courses.

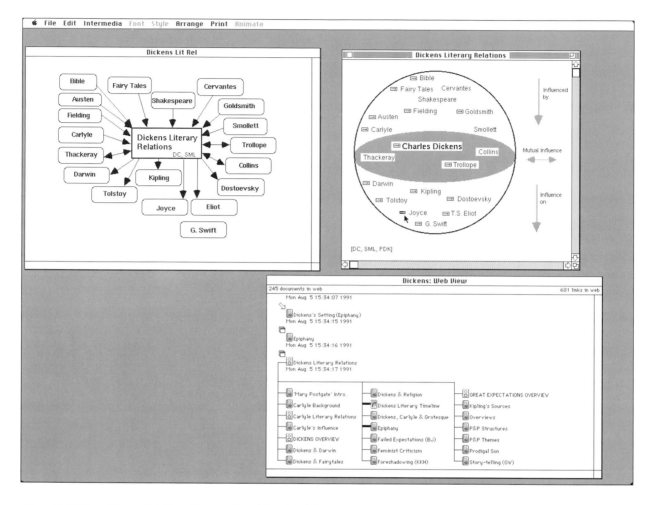

Figure 3. "Dickens Literary Relations," two versions. The original form of this kind of visual directory appears at the left and Paul D. Kahn's more recent one at the right. The Web View at the lower right tells the reader that the directory for Dickens's literary relations links to twenty-two other documents, some written by students (identified as such by the presence of the author's initials within parentheses following the document title), including "Dickens and Darwin," "Epiphany," and "Dickens, Carlyle, and Grotesque."

■ ■ ■ ■ ■ ■ ■ This description of visual elements of hypertext reminds one that print also employs more visual information than people usually take into account: visual information is not limited, as one might at first think, merely to the obvious instances, such as illustrations, maps, diagrams, flow charts, or graphs.[15] Even printed text without explicitly visual supplementary materials already contains a good bit of visual information in addition to alphanumeric code. The visual components of writing and print technology include spacing between words, paragraphing, changes of type style and font size, formatting to indicate passages quoted from other works, assigning specific locations on the individual page or at the end of sections or of the entire document to indicate reference materials (foot- and endnotes).

Visual Elements in Print Text

Despite the considerable presence of visual elements in print text, they tend to go unnoticed when contemporary writers contemplate the nature of text in an electronic age. Like other forms of change, the expansion of writing from a system of verbal language to one that centrally involves nonverbal information — visual information in the form of symbols and representational elements as well as other forms of information, including sound — has encountered stiff resistance, often from those from whom one is least likely to expect it, namely, from those who already employ computers for writing. Even those who advocate a change frequently find the experience of advocacy and of change so tiring that they resist the next stage, even if it appears implicit in changes they have themselves advocated.

This resistance appears particularly clearly in the frequently encountered remark that writers should not concern themselves with typesetting or desktop publishing but ought to leave those activities to the printer. Academics and other writers, we are told, do not design well; and even if they did, the argument continues, such activities are a waste of their time. Such advice, which has recently become an injunction, should make us ask why. After all, when told that one should not avail oneself of some aspect or form of empowerment, particularly as a writer, one should ask why. What if someone told us: "Here is a pencil. Although it has a rubber apparatus at the opposite end from that with which you write, you should not use it. Real writers don't use it"? At the very least we should wonder why anyone had included such capacity to do something; experimenting with it would show that it erases; and very likely, given human curiosity and perversity, which may be the same thing in certain circumstances, we would be tempted to try it out. Thus a capacity would evolve into a guilty pleasure!

Anyone with the slightest interest in design who has even casually surveyed the output of commercial and university presses has noticed a high percentage of appallingly designed or obviously undesigned books. Despite the exemplary work of designers like P. J. Conkwright and Richard Eckersley, many presses continue to produce nasty-looking books with narrow margins and gutters, type too small or too coarse for a particular layout, and little sense of page design. Financial constraints are usually offered as the sole determinant of the situation, though good design does not have to produce a more costly final product, particularly in an age of computer typesetting. In several cases of which I am aware publishers have assigned book design to beginning manuscript editors who confessed they had no training or experience in graphic design. As one who has been fortunate enough to have benefited from the efforts of first-rate, talented designers far more than I have suffered from those of poor ones, I make these observations not as a complaint but as a preparation for inquiring why authors are told they should not concern themselves with the visual appearance of their texts and why authors readily accept such instruction.

They do so in part because this injunction clearly involves matters of status and power. In particular, it involves a particular interpretation — that is, a social construction — of the idea of writer and writing. According to this conception, the writer's role and function is just to write. Writing, in turn, is conceived solely as a matter of recording (or creating) ideas by means of language. On the surface, such an approach seems neutral and obvious enough, and that in itself should warn one that it has been so naturalized as to include cultural assumptions that might be worth one's while to examine.

The injunction "just to write," which is based upon this purely verbal conception of writing, obviously assumes the following: first, that only verbal information has value, at least for the writer as a writer and probably for the reader as reader;[16] second, that visual information has less value. Making use of such devalued or lesser-valued forms of information (or does visual material deserve the

description "real information" at all?) in some way reduces the status
of the writer, making him or her less of a real writer. This matter
of status again raises its head when one considers another reason for
the injunction "just to write," one tied more tightly to conceptions
of division of labor, class, and status. In this view of things, it is
thought that authors should not concern themselves with matters that
belong to the printer. Although troubled by this exclusion, I accepted
this argument until I learned that until recently (say, in the 1930s)
authors routinely wandered around the typesetting shop at Oxford
University Press while their books were being set and were permitted
to render advice and judgment, something we are now told is none
of our business, beneath us, and so on. The ostensible reason for
instructing authors to refuse the power offered them by their writing
implement also includes the idea that authors do not have the expertise, the sheer know-how to produce good design. Abundant papers
by beginning undergraduates and beginning Macintosh users, clut-
tered with dissonant typefaces and font sizes, are thrust forward to
support this argument, one that we receive too readily without additional information.

Much of our prejudice against the inclusion of visual information
in text derives from print technology. Looking at the history of writing, one sees that it has a long connection with visual information, not

The fact that beginners in any field of endeavor do a relatively
poor quality job at this new activity hardly argues forcefully for their
abandoning that activity. If it did, we would similarly advise beginning
students immediately to abandon their attempts at creative and discursive writing, at drawing and philosophy, and at mathematics and
chemistry. One reason we do not offer such instructions is because we
feel the skills involved in those endeavors are important — apparently
in contrast to those involved in visual ones. Another reason of course is
that teaching involves our livelihood and status. The question that
arises, then, is why is visual information less important? The very fact
that people experiment with graphic elements of text on their computers shows the obvious pleasure they receive in manipulating visual
effects. This pleasure suggests in turn that by forbidding the writer
visual resources, we deny an apparently innocent source of pleasure,
something that apparently must be cast aside if one is to be a true
writer and a correct reader.

Much of our prejudice against the inclusion of visual information
in text derives from print technology. Looking at the history of writing, one sees that it has a long connection with visual information, not

least the origin of many alphabetic systems in hieroglyphics and other originally graphic forms of writing. Medieval manuscripts present a sort of hypertext combination of font sizes, marginalia, and illustrations, and visual embellishment, in the form of both calligraphy and pictorial additions.

■ ■ ■ ■ ■ ■ ■ Hypertext linking, reader control, and variation not only militate against the modes of argumenta-

Dispersed Text tion to which we have become accustomed but have other, far more general effects, one of which is to add what may be seen as a kind of randomness to the reader's text. Another is that the writer, as we shall see, loses certain basic controls over his text, particularly over its edges and borders. Yet a third is that the text appears to fragment, to atomize, into constituent elements (into lexias or blocks of text), and these reading units take on a life of their own as they become more self-contained, because they become less dependent on what comes before or after in a linear succession.

When compared to text as it exists in print technology, forms of hypertext evince varying combinations of atomization and dispersal. Unlike the spatial fixity of text reproduced by means of book technology, electronic text always has variation, for no one state or version is ever final; it can always be changed. Compared to a printed text, one in electronic form appears relatively dynamic, since it always permits correction, updating, and similar modification. Even without linking, therefore, electronic text abandons the fixity that characterizes print and that provides some of its most important effects on Western culture. Without fixity one cannot have a unitary text.

Hypertext, which adds a second fundamental form of variation, further disperses or atomizes text. Electronic links permit individual readers to take different paths through a given body of lexias. This quality of hypertext, which produces its characteristic avoidance of unilinearity, has obvious major effects upon conceptions of textuality and upon rhetorical structures. In explaining his procedure in *S/Z*, Barthes announces: "We shall therefore star the text, separating, in the manner of a minor earthquake, the blocks of signification of which reading grasps only the smooth surface, imperceptibly soldered by the movement of sentences, the flowing discourse of narration, the 'naturalness' of ordinary language. The tutor signifier will be cut up into a series of brief, contiguous fragments, which we shall call *lexias*, since they are units of reading" (13). However self-dramatizing and over-heated Barthes's presentation of his method in *S/Z* might appear from the perspective of print, it accurately describes the way an attempt to move beyond print in the direction of hypertextuality disturbs the text and the reading experience as we know them. Text — or, more properly, passages of text — that had followed one another in an apparently inevitable seamless linear progression now fracture, break apart, assume more individual identities.

At the same time that the individual hypertext lexia has looser, or less determining, bonds to other lexias from the *same work* (to use a terminology that now threatens to become obsolete), it also associates itself with text created by other authors. In fact, it associates with whatever text links to it, thereby dissolving notions of the intellectual separation of one text from others in the way that some chemicals destroy the cell membrane of an organism: destroying the cell membrane destroys the cell; it kills. In contrast, similarly destroying now-conventional notions of textual separation may destroy certain attitudes associated with text, but it will not necessarily destroy text. It will, however, reconfigure it and our expectations of it.

Another related effect of electronic linking: it disperses "the" text into other texts. As an individual lexia loses its physical and intellectual separation from others when linked electronically to them, it finds itself dispersed into them. The necessary contextuality and intertextuality produced by situating individual reading units within a network of easily navigable pathways weaves texts, including those by different authors and those in nonverbal media, tightly together. One effect of this process is to weaken and perhaps destroy any sense of textual uniqueness.

Such notions are hardly novel to contemporary literary theory, but here, as in so many other cases, hypertext creates an almost embarrassingly literal embodiment of a principle that had seemed particularly abstract and difficult when read from the vantage point of print. Since much of the appeal, even charm, of these theoretical insights lies in their difficulty and even preciousness, this more literal presentation promises to disturb theoreticians, in part, of course, because it greatly disturbs status and power relations within their field of expertise.

Hypertext fragments, disperses, or atomizes text in two related ways. First, by removing the linearity of print, it frees the individual passages from one ordering principle — sequence — and threatens to transform the text into chaos. Second, hypertext destroys the notion of a fixed unitary text. Considering the "entire" text in relation to its component parts produces the first form of fragmentation; considering it in relation to its variant readings and versions produces the second.

Loss of a belief in unitary textuality could produce many changes in Western culture, many of them quite costly, when judged from our present print-based attitudes. Not all these changes are necessarily costly or damaging, however, particularly to the world of scholarship, where this conceptual change would permit us to redress some of the distortions of naturalizing print culture. Accustomed to the standard scholarly edition of canonical texts, we conventionally suppress the fact that such twentieth-century print versions of works originally created within a manuscript culture are bizarrely fictional idealizations that produce a vastly changed experience of text. To begin with, the printed scholarly edition of Plato, Vergil, or Augustine provides a text far easier to negotiate and decipher than any available to contemporary readers. They encountered texts so different from ours that even to suggest that we share common experiences of *reading* misleads. Contemporary readers of Plato, Vergil, or Augustine processed texts without interword spacing, capitalization, or punctuation. Had you read these last few sentences fifteen hundred years ago, they would have taken the following form:

theyencounteredtextssodifferentfromoursthateventosuggestthatwesharecommonexperience
sofreadingmisleadscontemporaryreadersofplatovergiloraugustineprocessedtextswithouti
nterwordspacingcapitalizationorpunctuationhadyoureadtheselasttwosentencesfifteenhundr
edyearsagotheywouldhavetakenthefollowingform

Such unbroken streams of alphabetic characters made even phonetic literacy a matter of great skill. Since deciphering such texts heavily favored reading aloud, almost all readers experienced texts not only as an occasion for strenuous acts of code breaking but also as a kind of public performance.

The very fact that the text we would have read fifteen hundred years ago appeared in a manuscript form also implies that to read it in the first place we would have had to gain access to a rare, even unique object — assuming, that is, that we could have discovered the existence of the manuscript and made an inconvenient, expensive, and often dangerous trip to see it. Having gained access to this manuscript, we would also have approached it much differently from the way we today approach the everyday encounter with a printed book. We would probably have taken the encounter as a rare privileged opportunity, and we would also have approached the experience of reading this unique object with a very different set of assumptions than would a modern scholar. As Elizabeth Eisenstein has shown, the first role of the scholar in a manuscript culture was simply to preserve the text, which doubly threatened to degrade with each reading: each time someone physically handled the fragile object its longevity was reduced, and each time someone copied the manuscript to preserve and transmit its text, the copyist inevitably introduced textual drift.

Thus, even without taking into account the alien presence of pagination, indices, references, title pages, and other devices of book technology, the encounter and subsequent reading of a manuscript constituted a very different set of experiences than those which we now take for granted. Equally important, whereas the significance of scholarly editions lies precisely in their appearance in comparatively large numbers, each manuscript of texts by Plato, Vergil, or Augustine existed as a unique object. We do not know which particular version of a text by these authors any reader encountered. Presenting the history and relation of texts created within a manuscript culture in terms of the unitary text of modern scholarship certainly fictionalizes — and falsifies — their intertextual relations.

Modern scholarly editions and manuscripts combine both uniqueness and multiplicity, but they do so in different ways. A modern edition of Plato, Vergil, or Augustine begins by assuming the existence of a unique, unitary text, but it is produced in the first place because it can disseminate that text in a number of identical copies. In contrast, each ancient or medieval manuscript, which embodies only one of many potential variations of "a text," exists as a unique object. A new conception of text is needed by scholars trying to determine not some probably mythical and certainly long-lost master text but the ways individual readers actually encountered Plato, Vergil, or Augustine in a manuscript culture. In fact, we must abandon the notion of a unitary text and replace it with conceptions of a dispersed text. We must do, in other words, what some art historians working with analogous medieval problems have done — take the conception of a unique type embodied in a single object and replace it with a conception of a type as a complex set of variants. For example, trying to determine the thematic, iconological, and compositional antecedents of early fourteenth-century ivory Madonnas, Robert Suckale and other recent students of the Court Style have abandoned linear derivations and the notion of a unitary type. Instead, they emphasize that sculptors chose among several sets of fundamental forms or "ground plans" as points of departure.[17] Some sort of change in basic attitudes toward the creations of manuscript culture seems necessary.

The capacity of hypertext to link all the versions or variants of a particular text might offer a means of somewhat redressing the balance between uniqueness and variation in preprint texts. Of course, even in hypertext presentations, both modern printing convention and scholarly apparatus will still infringe upon attempts to recreate the experience of encountering these texts, and nothing can restore the uniqueness and corollary aura of the individual manuscript. Nonetheless, hypertext offers the possibility of presenting a text as a dispersed field of variants and not as a falsely unitary entity. High resolution screens and other technological capacities should some day also permit presenting all the individual manuscripts. An acquaintance with hypertext systems might by itself sufficiently change assumptions about textuality to free students of preprint texts from some of their biases.

■ ■ ■ ■ ■ ■ ■

Argumentation, Organization,

and Rhetoric

Electronic linking, which gives the reader a far more active role than is possible with books, has certain major effects. Considered from the vantage point of a literature intertwined with book technology, these effects appear harmful and dangerous, as indeed they must be to a cultural hegemony based, as ours is, on a different technology of cultural memory. In particular, the numerating linear rhetoric of "first, second, third" so well suited to print will continue to appear within individual blocks of text but cannot be used to structure arguments in a medium that encourages readers to choose different paths rather than following a linear one. The shift away from linearization might seem a major change, and it is, but we should remind ourselves that it is not an abandonment of the natural.

"The structuring of books," Tom McArthur reminds us, "is anything but 'natural' — indeed, it is thoroughly *un*natural and took all of 4,000 years to bring about. The achievement of the Scholastics, preeminently among the world's scribal elites, was to conventionalize the themes, plot and shapes of books in a truly rigorous way, as they also structured syllabuses, scripture and debate."[18] Their conventions of book structure, however, changed fundamentally with the advent of the printing press, which encouraged alphabetic ordering, a procedure that had never before caught on. Why?

One reason must certainly be that people had already become accustomed over too many centuries to thematically ordered material. Such material bore a close resemblance to the "normal" organization of written work: . . . Alphabetization may also have been offensive to the global Scholastic view of things. It must have seemed a perverse, disjointed and ultimately meaningless way of ordering material to men who were interested in neat frames for the containing of all knowledge. Certainly, alphabetization poses problems of fragmentation that may be less immediately obvious with word lists but can become serious when dealing with subject lists. (76–77)

McArthur's salutary remarks, which remind us that we always naturalize the social constructions of our world, also suggest that from one point of view, the Scholastics', the movement from manuscript to print and then to hypertext appears one of increasing fragmentation. As long as a thematic or other culturally coherent means of ordering is available to the reader, the fragmentation of the hypertext document docs not imply the kind of entropy that such fragmentation would have in the world of print. Capacities such as full-text searching, automatic linking, agents, and conceptual filtering potentially have the power to retain the benefits of hypertextuality while insulating the reader from the ill effects of abandoning linearity.

Beginnings and Endings in the Open Text

The concepts (and experiences) of beginning and ending imply linearity. What happens to them in a form of textuality not governed chiefly by linearity? If we assume that hypertextuality possesses multiple sequences rather than that it has an entire absence of linearity and sequence, then one answer to this query must be that it provides multiple beginnings and endings rather than single ones. Drawing upon Edward W. Said's work on origins and openings, one can suggest that, in contrast to print, hypertext offers at least two different kinds of beginnings. The first concerns the individual lexia, the second a gathering of them into a metatext. Whenever one has a body of hypertext materials that stands alone — either because it occupies an entire system or because it exists, however transiently, within a frame, the reader has to begin reading at some point, and for the reader that point is a beginning. Writing of print, Said explains that "a work's beginning is, practically speaking, the main entrance to what it offers."[19] But what happens when a work offers many "main" entrances — in fact, offers as many entrances as there are linked passages by means of which one can arrive at the individual lexia (which, from one perspective, becomes equivalent to a work)? Said provides materials for an answer when he argues that a " 'beginning' is designated in order to indicate, clarify, or define a *later* time, place, or action. In short, the designation of a beginning generally involves also the designation of a consequent *intention*" (5). In Said's terms, therefore, even atomized text can make a beginning when the link site, or point of departure, assumes the role of the beginning of a chain or path. According to Said, "we see that the beginning is the first point (in time, space, or action) of an accomplishment or process that has duration and meaning. *The beginning, then, is the first step in the intentional production of meaning*" (5).

Said's quasi-hypertextual definition of a beginning suggests that "in retrospect we can regard a beginning as the point at which, in a given work, the writer departs from all other works; a beginning immediately establishes relationships with works already existing, relationships of either continuity or antagonism or some mixture of both" (3).

If hypertext makes determining the beginning of a text difficult because it both changes our conception of text and permits readers to "begin" at many different points, it similarly changes the sense of an ending. Readers cannot only choose different points of ending, they can also continue to add to the text, to extend it, to make it more than it was when they began to read. As Ted Nelson, one of the originators of hypertext, points out: "There is no Final Word. There can be no final version, no last thought. There is always a new view, a new idea, a reinterpretation. And literature, which we propose to electron-

ify, is a system for preserving continuity in the face of this fact. . . .
Remember the analogy between text and water. Water flows freely, ice
does not. The free-flowing, live documents on the network are subject to constant new use and linkage, and those new links continually
become interactively available. Any detached copy someone keeps
is frozen and dead, lacking access to the new linkage" (*Literary
Machines*, 2/61, 48). Here, as in several other ways, Bakhtin's conception of textuality anticipates hypertext. Caryl Emerson, his translator
and editor, explains that "for Bakhtin 'the whole' is not a finished
entity; it is always a relationship. . . . Thus, the whole can never be
finalized and set aside; when a whole is realized, it is by definition
already open to change" (*Problems*, xxxix).

Hypertext blurs the end boundaries of the metatext, and conventional notions of completion and a finished product do not apply
to hypertext, whose essential novelty makes difficult defining and
describing it in older terms, since they derive from another educational and informational technology and have hidden assumptions
inappropriate to hypertext. Particularly inapplicable are the related
notions of completion and a finished product. As Derrida recognizes,
a form of textuality that goes beyond print "forces us to extend . . .
the dominant notion of a 'text,' " so that it "is henceforth no longer a
finished corpus of writing, some content enclosed in a book or its
margins but a differential network, a fabric of traces referring endlessly
to something other than itself, to other differential traces."[20]

Hypertextual materials, which by definition are open-ended,
expandable, and incomplete, call such notions into question. If one
put a work conventionally considered complete, such as *Ulysses*, into a
hypertext format, it would immediately become "incomplete." Electronic linking, which emphasizes making connections, immediately
expands a text by providing large numbers of points to which other
texts can attach themselves. The fixity and physical isolation of book
technology, which permits standardization and relatively easy repro
duction, necessarily closes off such possibilities. Hypertext opens
them up.

Boundaries of the Open Text · · · · · · · Hypertext redefines not only beginnings and endings of the text but also its borders — its sides, as it were. Hypertext thus provides us with a means to escape what Gérard Genette terms a "sort of idolatry, which is no less serious, and today more dangerous" than idealization of the author, "namely, the fetishism of the work — conceived of as a closed, complete, absolute object."[21] When one moves from physical to virtual text, and from print to hypertext, boundaries blur — the blurring that Derrida works so hard to achieve in his print publications — and one therefore no longer can rely upon conceptions or assumptions of inside and out. As Derrida explains, "to keep the outside out . . . is the inaugural gesture of 'logic' itself, of good 'sense' insofar as it accords with the self-identity of *that which is:* being is what it is, the outside is outside and the inside inside. Writing must thus return to being what it *should never have ceased to be:* an accessory, an accident, an excess" (*Dissemination*, 128). Without linearity and sharp bounds between in and out, between absence and presence, and between self and other, philosophy will change. Working within the world of print, Derrida presciently argues, using Platonic texts as an example, that "the textual chain we must set back in place is thus no longer simply 'internal' to Plato's lexicon. But in going beyond the bounds of that lexicon, we are less interested in breaking through certain limits, with or without cause, than in putting in doubt the right to posit such limits in the first place. In a word, we do not believe that there exists, in all rigor, a Platonic text, closed upon itself, complete with its inside and outside" (130).

Derrida furthermore explains, with a fine combination of patience and wit, that in noticing that texts really do not have insides and outsides, one does not reduce them to so much mush: "Not that one must then consider that it [the text] is leaking on all sides and can be drowned confusedly in the undifferentiated generality of its element. Rather, provided the articulations are rigorously and prudently recognized, one should simply be able to untangle the hidden forces of attraction linking a present word with an absent word in the text of Plato" (130).

Another sign of Derrida's awareness of the limitations and confinements of contemporary attitudes, which arise in association with the technology of the printed book, is his hypertextual approach to

textuality and meaning, an approach that remains skeptical of "a fundamental or totalizing principle," since it recognizes that "the classical
system's 'outside' can no longer take the form of the sort of extratext which would arrest the concatenation of writing" (5).

Hypertext thus creates an open, open-bordered text, a text that
cannot shut out other texts and therefore embodies the Derridean text
in which blur "all those boundaries that form the running border of
what used to be called a text, of what we once thought this word could
identify, i.e., the supposed end and beginning of a work, the unity of
a corpus, the title, the margins, the signatures, the referential realm
outside the frame, and so forth." Hypertext therefore undergoes what
Derrida describes as "a sort of overrun [*débordement*] that spoils all
these boundaries and divisions" ("Living On," 83).

In hypertext systems, links within and without a text — intratextual
and intertextual connections between points of text (including
images) — become equivalent, thus bringing texts closer together and
blurring the boundaries among them. Consider the case of intertextual
links in Milton: Milton's various descriptions of himself as prophet
or inspired poet in *Paradise Lost* and his citations of Genesis 3:15
provide obvious examples. Extratextual and intratextual links, in contrast, are exemplified by links between a particular passage in which
Milton mentions prophecy and his other writings in prose or poetry
that make similar or obviously relevant points, as well as biblical texts,
commentaries throughout the ages, comparable or contrasting poetic
statements by others, and scholarly comment. Similarly, Miltonic
citations of the biblical text about the heel of man crushing the serpent's head and being in turn bruised by the serpent link obviously to
the biblical passage and its traditional interpretations as well as to
other literary allusions and scholarly comment upon all these subjects.
Hypertext linking simply allows one to speed up the usual process of
making connections while providing a means of graphing such transactions, if one can apply the word "simply" to such a radically trans-
formative procedure.

The speed with which one can move between passages and points
in sets of texts changes both the way we read and the way we write,
just as the high-speed number-crunching computing changed various
scientific fields by making possible investigations that before had
required too much time or risk. One change comes from the fact that
linking permits the reader to move with equal facility between points

within a text and those outside it. Once one can move with equal facility between, say, the opening section of *Paradise Lost* and a passage in Book 12 thousands of lines "away," and between that opening section and a particular anterior French text or modern scholarly comment, then, in an important sense, the discreteness of texts, which print culture creates, has radically changed and possibly disappeared. One may argue that, in fact, all that the hypertext linking of such texts does is embody the way one actually experiences texts in the act of reading; but if so, the act of reading has in some way gotten much closer to the electronic embodiment of text and in so doing has begun to change its nature.

These observations about hypertext suggest that computers bring us much closer to a culture some of whose qualities have more in common with that of preliterate man than even Walter J. Ong has been willing to admit. In *Orality and Literacy* he argues that computers have brought us into what he terms an age of "secondary orality" that has "striking resemblances" to the primary, preliterate orality "in its participatory mystique, its fostering of a communal sense, its concentration on the present moment, and even its use of formulas." [22] Nonetheless, although Ong finds interesting parallels between a computer culture and a purely oral one, he mistakenly insists: "The sequential processing and spatializing of the word, initiated by writing and raised to a new order of intensity by print, is further intensified by the computer, which maximizes commitment of the word to space and to (electronic) local motion and optimizes analytic sequentiality by making it virtually instantaneous" (136). In fact, hypertext systems, which insert every text into a web of relations, produce a very different effect, for they allow nonsequential reading and thinking.

One major effect of such nonsequential reading, the weakening of the boundaries of the text, can be thought of either as correcting the artificial isolation of a text from its contexts or as violating one of the chief qualities of the book. According to Ong, writing and printing produce the effect of discrete, self-contained utterance:

By isolating thought on a written surface, detached from any interlocutor, making utterance in this sense autonomous and indifferent to attack, writing presents utterance and thought as uninvolved with all else, somehow self-contained, complete. Print in the same way situates utterance and thought on a surface disengaged from everything else, but it also goes farther in suggesting self-containment. (132)

We have already observed the way in which hypertext suggests integration rather than self-containment. Another possible result of such hypertext may also be disconcerting. As Ong also points out, books, unlike their authors, cannot really be challenged:

> The author might be challenged if only he or she could be reached, but the author cannot be reached in any book. There is no way directly to refute a text. After absolutely total and devastating refutation, it says exactly the same thing as before. This is one reason why "the book says" is popularly tantamount to "it is true." It is also one reason why books have been burnt. A text stating what the whole world knows is false will state falsehood forever, so long as the text exists. (79)

The question arises, however, If hypertext situates texts in a field of other texts, can any individual work that has been addressed by another still speak so forcefully? One can imagine hypertext presentations of books (or the equivalent) in which the reader can call up all the reviews and comments on that book, which would then inevitably exist as part of a complex dialogue rather than as the embodiment of a voice or thought that speaks unceasingly. Hypertext, which links one block of text to myriad others, destroys that physical isolation of the text, just as it also destroys the attitudes created by that isolation. Because hypertext systems permit a reader both to annotate an individual text and to link it to other, perhaps contradictory texts, it destroys one of the most basic characteristics of the printed text — its separation and its univocality. Whenever one places a text within a network of other texts, one forces it to exist as part of a complex dialogue. Hypertext linking, which tends to change the roles of author and reader, also changes the limits of the individual text.

Electronic linking radically changes the experience of a text by changing its spatial and temporal relationship to other texts. Reading a hypertext version of Dickens's *Great Expectations* or Eliot's *Wasteland*, for example, one follows links to predecessor texts, variant readings, criticism, and so on. Following an electronic link to an image of, say, the desert or a wasteland in a poem by Tennyson, Browning, or Swinburne takes no more time than following one from a passage earlier in the poem to one near its end. Therefore, readers experience the texts outside *The Wasteland* and the passage inside the work as existing equally distant from the first passage. Hypertext thereby blurs the distinction between what is "inside" and what is "outside" a text.

64

It also makes all the texts connected to a block of text collaborate with that text.

The Status of the Text,

Status in the Text

Alvin Kernan claims that "Benjamin's general theory of the demystification of art through numerous reproductions explains precisely what happened when in the eighteenth century the printing press, with its logic of multiplicity, stripped the classical texts of the old literary order of their aura" (*Printing Technology*, 152), and it seems likely that hypertext will extend this process of demystification even further. Kernan convincingly argues that by Pope's time a "flood of books, in its accumulation both of different texts and identical copies of the same texts, threatened to obscure the few idealized classics, both ancient and modern, of polite letters, and to weaken their aura by making printed copies of them" (153). Any information medium that encourages rapid dissemination of texts and easy access to them will increasingly demystify individual texts. But hypertext has a second potentially demystifying effect: by making the borders of the text (now conceived as the individual lexia) permeable, it removes some of the text's independence and uniqueness.

Kernan further adds that, "since printed books were for the most part in the vernacular, they further desacralized letters by expanding its canon from a group of venerable texts written in ancient languages known only to an elite to include a body of contemporary writing in the native language understood by all who read" (153–54). Will electronic versions of the Bible, like *CD Word*, that seem to be essentially democratizing similarly desacralize the Scriptures? They have the potential to do so in two ways. First, by making some of the scholar's procedures easily available to almost any reader, this electronic Bible might demystify a text that possesses a talismanic power for many in its intended audience.

Second and more fundamental, the very fact that this hypertext Bible enforces the presence of multiple versions potentially undercuts belief in the possibility of a unique, unitary text. Certainly, the precedent of Victorian loss of belief in the doctrine of Verbal Inspiration of the Scriptures suggests that hypertext could have a potentially parallel effect (Landow, *Victorian Types*, 54–56). In Victorian England the wide-scale abandonment of belief that every word of the Bible was divinely inspired, even in its English translation, followed from a variety of causes including influence of the German Higher Criticism, independent British applications of rational approaches by those like Bishop Colenso, and the discoveries of geology, philology, and (later) biology. The discovery, for instance, that Hebrew did not possess the uniqueness as a language that some believers, particularly Evangelicals, had long assumed it did, eroded faith, in large part because believers became aware of unexpected multiplicity where they had assumed only unity. The discovery of multiple manuscripts of Scripture had parallel effects. Hypertext, which emphasizes multiplicity, may cause similar crises in belief.

Although the fundamental drive of the printed page is a linear, straight-ahead thrust that captures readers and forces them to read along if they are to read at all, specialized forms of text have developed that use secondary codes to present information difficult or impossible to include in linear text. The foot- or endnote, which is one of the prime ways that books create an additional space, requires some code, such as a superscript number or one within parentheses, that signals readers to stop reading what is conventionally termed the *main* text or the body of the text and begin reading some peripheral or appended patch of text that hangs off that part of the main text.

In both scholarly editing and scholarly prose such divisions of text partake of fixed hierarchies of status and power. The smaller size type that presents footnote and endnote text, like the placement of that text away from the normal center of the reader's attention, makes clear that such language is subsidiary, dependent, less important. In scholarly editing, such typographic and other encoding makes clear that the editor's efforts, no matter how lavish or long suffering, are obviously less important than the words being edited, for these appear in the main text. In scholarly and critical discourse that employs annotation, these conventions also establish the importance of the dominant argument in opposition to the author's sources, scholarly allies and opponents, and even the work of fiction or poetry upon which the critical text focuses.

One experiences hypertext annotation of a text very differently. In the first place, electronic linking immediately destroys the simple binary opposition of text and note that founds the status relations that inhabit the printed book. Following a link can bring the reader to a later portion of the text or to a text to which the first one alludes.

It may also lead to other works by the same author or to a range of critical commentary, textual variants, and the like. The assignment of text and annotation to what Tom Wolfe calls different "statuspheres" therefore becomes very difficult, and such text hierarchies tend quickly to collapse.

Hypertext linking situates the present text at the center of the textual universe, thus creating a new kind of hierarchy, in which the power of the center dominates that of the infinite periphery. But because in hypertext that center is always a transient, de-centerable virtual center — one created, in other words, only by one's act of reading that particular text — it never tyrannizes other aspects of the network in the way a printed text does.

Barthes, well aware of the political constraints of a text that makes a reader read in a particular way, himself manipulates the political relations of text in interesting ways. The entire procedure or construction of *S/Z*, for example, serves as a commentary on the political relationships among portions of the standard scholarly text, the problem of hierarchy. Barthes playfully creates his own version of complex footnote systems. Like Derrida in *Glas*, he creates a work or metatext that the reader accustomed to reading books finds either abrasively different or, on rare occasion, a wittily powerful commentary on the way books work — that is, on the way they force readers to see relationships between sections and thereby endow certain assemblages of words with power and value because they appear in certain formats rather than others.

Barthes, in other words, comments upon the footnote, and all of *S/Z* turns out to be a criticism of the power relations between portions of text. In a foot- or endnote, we recall, that portion of the text conventionally known as the main text has a value for both reader and writer that surpasses any of its supplementary portions, which include notes, prefaces, dedications, and so on, most of which supplements take the form of apparatuses designed to aid information retrieval. These devices, almost all of which derive directly from print technology, can function only in fixed, repeatable, physically isolated texts. They have great advantages and permit certain kinds of reading: one need not, for example, memorize the location of a particular passage if one has system features such as chapter titles, tables of contents, and indices. So the reference device has enormous value as a means of reader orientation, navigation, and information retrieval.

It comes at certain costs, costs that, like most paid by the reader of text, have become so much a part of our experience of reading that we do not notice them at all. Barthes makes us notice them. Barthes, like most late-twentieth-century critical theorists, is at his best seeing the invisible, breathing on it in hopes that the condensate will illuminate the shadows of what others have long missed and taken to be not there. What then does the footnote imply, and how does Barthes manipulate or avoid it? Combined with the physical isolation of each text, the division between main text and footnote establishes the primary importance of main text in its relation to other texts even when thinking about the subject instantly reveals that such relationship cannot in fact exist.

Take a scholarly article, the kind of article we academics all write. One wishes to write an article on some aspect of the Nausicaa section of Joyce's *Ulysses*, a text that by even the crudest quantitative measure appears to be more important, more powerful than our note identifying, say, one of the sources of Gerty McDowell's phrasing from a contemporary women's magazine. Joyce's novel, for example, exists in more copies than our article can or will and it therefore has an enormously larger readership and reputation — all problematic notions, I admit, all relying on certain ideologies; and yet most of us, I expect, will accede to them, for they are the values by which we work. Ostensibly, that is. Even deconstructionists privilege the text, the great work.

Once, however, one begins to write one's article, the conventions of print quickly call those assumptions into question, since anything in the main text is clearly more important than anything outside it. The physically isolated discrete text is very discreet indeed, for, as Ong makes clear, it hides obvious connections of indebtedness and qualification. When one introduces other authors into the text, they appear as attenuated, often highly distorted shadows of themselves. Part of this is necessary, since one cannot, after all, reproduce an entire article or book by another author in one's own. Part of this attenuation comes from authorial inaccuracy, slovenliness, or outright dishonesty. Nonetheless, such attenuation is part of the message of print, an implication one cannot avoid, or at least one cannot avoid since the advent of hypertext, which, by providing an alternative textual mode, reveals differences that turn out to be, no longer, inevitabilities and invisibilities.

In print when I provide the page number of an indicated or cited passage from Joyce, or even include that passage in text or note, that passage — that occasion for my article — clearly exists in a subsidiary, comparatively minor position in relation to my words, which appear, after all, in the so-called main text. What would happen, though, if one wrote one's article in hypertext? Assuming one worked in a fully implemented hypertextual environment, one would begin by calling up Joyce's novel and, on one side of a video screen, opening the passage or passages involved. Next, one would write one's comment, but where one would usually cite Joyce, one now does so in a very different way. Now one creates an electronic link between one's own text and one or more sections of the Joycean text. At the same time one also links passages in one's text to other aspects of one's own text, texts by others, and earlier texts by oneself. Several things have happened, things that violate our expectations. First, attaching my commentary to a passage from Joyce makes it exist in a far different, far less powerful relation to Joyce, the so-called original text, than it would in the world of physically isolated texts. Second, as soon as one attaches more than one text block or lexia to a single anchor (or block, or link marker), one destroys all possibility of the bipartite hierarchy of footnote and main text. In hypertext, the main text is that which one is presently reading. So one has a double revaluation: with the disolution of this hierarchy, any attached text gains an importance it might not have had before.

In Bakhtin's terms, the scholarly article, which quotes or cites statements by others — "some for refutation and others for confirmation and supplementation — is one instance of a dialogic interrelationship among directly signifying discourses within the limits of a single context. . . . This is not a clash of two ultimate semantic authorities, but rather an objectified (plotted) clash of two represented positions, subordinated wholly to the higher, ultimate authority of the author. The monologic context, under these circumstances, is neither broken nor weakened" (*Problems*, 188). Trying to evade the constraints, the logic, of print scholarship, Bakhtin himself takes an approach to quoting other authors that is more characteristic of hypertext or post-book technology than that of the book. According to his editor and translator, Emerson, when Bakhtin quotes other critics, "he does so at length, and lets each voice sound fully. He understands that the frame is always in the power of the framer, and that there is an outrageous privilege in the power to cite others. Thus Bakhtin's footnotes rarely serve to narrow down debate by discrediting totally, or (on the other hand) by conferring exclusive authority. They might identify, expand, illustrate, but they do not pull rank on the body of the text — and are thus more in the nature of a marginal gloss than an authoritative footnote" (xxxvii).

Derrida also comments upon the status relations that cut and divide texts, but unlike Barthes, he concerns himself with oppositions between preface and main text and main text and other texts. Recognizing that status that accrues to different portions of a text, Derrida examines the way each takes on associations with power or importance. In discussing Hegel's introduction to the *Logic*, Derrida points out, for example, that "the *preface* must be distinguished from the *introduction*. They do not have the same function, nor even the same dignity, in Hegel's eyes" (*Dissemination*, 17). Derrida's new textuality, or true textuality (which I have continually likened to hypertextuality), represents "an entirely other typology where the outlines of the preface and the 'main' text are blurred" (39).

■ ■ ■ ■ ■ ■ ■

Hypertext and De-centrality:

The Philosophical Grounding

One tends to think of text from within the position of the lexia under consideration. Accustomed to reading pages of print on paper, one tends to conceive of text from the vantage point of the reader experiencing that page or passage, and that portion of text assumes a centrality. Hypertext, however, makes such assumptions of centrality fundamentally problematic. In contrast, the linked text, the annotation, exists as the *other* text, and it leads to a conception (and experience) of text as Other.

In hypertext this annotation, or commentary, or appended text can be any linked text, and therefore the position of any lexia in hypertext resembles that of the Victorian sage. For like the sage, say, Carlyle, Thoreau, or Ruskin, the lexia stands outside, off center, and challenges. In other words, hypertext, like the sage, thrives on marginality. From that essential marginality, to which he stakes his claim by his skillful, aggressive use of pronouns to oppose his interests and views to those of the reader, he defines his discursive position or vantage point.

Hypertext similarly emphasizes that the marginal has as much to offer as does the central, in part because hypertext does not only redefine the central by refusing to grant centrality to anything, to any lexia, for more than the time a gaze rests upon it. In hypertext, centrality, like beauty and relevance, resides in the mind of the beholder. Like Andy Warhol's modern person's fifteen minutes of fame, centrality in hypertext exists only as a matter of evanescence. As one might expect from an information medium that changes our relations to data, thoughts, and selves so dramatically, that evanescence of this (ever-migrating) centrality is merely a given — that's the way things are — rather than an occasion for complaint or satire. It is simply the condition under which, or within which, we think, communicate, or record these thoughts and communications in the hypertextual docuverse.

This hypertextual dissolution of centrality, which makes the medium such a potentially democratic one, also makes it a model of a society of conversations in which no one conversation, no one discipline or ideology, dominates or founds the others. It is thus the instantiation of what Richard Rorty terms "edifying philosophy," the point of which "is to keep the conversation going rather than to find objective truth." It is a form of philosophy

having sense only as a protest against attempts to close off conversation by proposals for universal commensuration through the hypostatization of some privileged set of descriptions. The danger which edifying discourse tries to avert is that some given vocabulary, some way in which people might come to think of themselves, will deceive them into thinking that from now on all discourse could be, or should be, normal discourse. The resulting freezing-over of culture would be, in the eyes of edifying philosophers, the dehumanization of human beings. (*Philosophy,* 377)

Hypertext, which has a built-in bias against "hypostatization" and probably against privileged descriptions as well, therefore embodies the approach to philosophy that Rorty urges. The basic experience of text, information, and control, which moves the boundary of power away from the author in the direction of the reader, models such a postmodern, antihierarchical medium of information, text, philosophy, and society.

Reconfiguring

the Author

3

. . . .

Erosion of the Self

Like contemporary critical theory, hypertext reconfigures — rewrites — the author in several obvious ways. First of all, the figure of the hypertext author approaches, even if it does not entirely merge with, that of the reader; the functions of reader and writer become more deeply entwined with each other than ever before. This transformation and near merging of roles is but the latest stage in the convergence of what had once been two very different activities. Although today we assume that anyone who reads can also write, such was long not the case, and historians of reading point out that for millennia many people capable of reading could not even sign their own names. Today when we consider reading and writing, we probably think of them as serial processes or as procedures carried out intermittently by the same person: first one reads, then one writes, and then one reads some more. Hypertext, which creates an active, even intrusive reader, carries this convergence of activities one step closer to completion; but in so doing, it infringes upon the power of the writer, removing some of it and granting it to the reader.

One clear sign of such transference of authorial power appears in the reader's abilities to choose his or her way through the metatext, to annotate text written by others, and to create links between documents written by others. Hypertext does not permit the active reader to change the text produced by another person, but it does narrow the phenomenological distance that separates individual documents from one another in the worlds of print and manuscript. In reducing the autonomy of the text, hypertext reduces the autonomy of the author. In the words of Michael Heim, "as the authoritativeness of text diminishes, so too does the recognition of the private self of the creative author."[1] Granted, much of that so-called autonomy had been illusory and existed as little more than the difficulty that readers had in perceiving connections between documents. Nonetheless, hypertext — which I am here taking as the convergence of poststructuralist conceptions of textuality and electronic embodiments of it — does do away with certain aspects of the authoritativeness and autonomy of the text, and in so doing it does reconceive the figure and function of authorship.

William R. Paulson, who examines literature from the vantage point of information theory, arrives at much the same position when he argues that "to characterize texts as artificially and imperfectly autonomous is not to eliminate the role of the author but to deny the reader's or critic's submission to any instance of authority. This perspective leaves room neither for the authorial mastery of a communicative object nor for the authority of a textual coherence so complete that the reader's (infinite) task would be merely to receive its rich and multilayered meaning." Beginning from the position of information theory, Paulson finds that in "literary communication," as in all communication, "there is an irreducible element of noise," and therefore "the reader's task does not end with reception, for reception is inherently flawed. What literature solicits of the reader is not simply reception but the active, independent, autonomous construction of meaning."[2] Finding no reason to exile the author from the text, Paulson nonetheless ends up by assigning to the reader power that, in earlier views, had been the prerogative of the writer.

Hypertext and contemporary theory both reconceive the author in a second way. As we shall observe when we examine the notion of collaborative writing, both agree in configuring the author of the text *as a text*. As Barthes explains in his famous exposition of the idea, "this 'I' which approaches the text is already itself a plurality of other texts, of codes which are infinite" (*S/Z*, 10). Barthes's point, which should seem both familiar and unexceptional to anyone who has encountered Joyce's weaving of Gerty McDowell out of the texts of her class and culture, appears much clearer and more obvious from the vantage point of intertextuality. In this case, as in others at which we have already looked, contemporary theory proposes and hypertext disposes; or, to be less theologically aphoristic, hypertext embodies many of the ideas and attitudes proposed by Barthes, Derrida, Foucault, and others.

One of the most important of these ideas involves treating the self of author and reader not simply as (print) text but as a hypertext. For all these authors the self takes the form of a de-centered (or centerless) network of codes that, on another level, also serves as a node within another centerless network. Jean-François Lyotard, for example, rejects nineteenth-century Romantic paradigms of an islanded self in favor of a model of the self as a node in an information network: "A *self* does not amount to much," he assures us with fashionable nonchalance, "but no self is an island; each exists in a fabric of relations that is now more complex and mobile than ever before. Young or old, man or woman, rich or poor, a person is always located at 'nodal points' of specific communication circuits, however tiny these may be. Or better: one is always located at a post through which various kinds of messages pass."[3] Lyotard's analogy becomes even stronger if one realizes that by "post" he most likely means the modern European post office, which is a telecommunications center containing telephones and other networked devices.

Some theorists find the idea of participating in such a network to be demeaning and depressing, particularly since contemporary conceptions of textuality de-emphasize autonomy in favor of participation. Before succumbing to posthumanist depression, however, one should place Foucault's statements about "the author's disappearance" in the context of recent discussions of machine intelligence.[4] According to Heinz Pagels, machines capable of complex intellectual processing will "put an end to much discussion about the mind-body problem, because it will be very hard not to attribute a conscious mind to them without failing to do so for more human beings. Gradually the popular view will become that consciousness is simply 'what happens' when . . . electronic components are put together the right way."[5] Pagels's thoughts on the eventual electronic solution to the mind-body problem recall Foucault's discussion of "the singular relationship that holds between an author and a text [as] the manner in which a text apparently points to this figure who is outside and precedes it" ("Author," 115). This point of view makes apparent that literature generates precisely such appearance of a self, and that, moreover, we have long read a self "out" of texts as evidence that a unified self exists "behind" or "within" or "implicit in" it.

The problem for anyone who yearns to retain older conceptions of authorship or of the author function lies in the fact that radical changes in textuality produce radical changes in the author figure derived from that textuality. Lack of textual autonomy, like lack of textual centeredness, immediately reverberates through conceptions of authorship as well. Similarly, the unboundedness of the new textuality disperses the author as well. Foucault opens this side of the question when he raises what, in another context, might be a standard problem in a graduate course on the methodology of scholarship:

> If we wish to publish the complete works of Nietzsche, for example, where do we draw the line? Certainly, everything must be published, but can we agree on what "everything" means? We will, of course, include everything that Nietzsche himself published, along with the drafts of his works, his plans for aphorisms, his marginal notations and corrections. But what if, in a notebook filled with aphorisms, we find a reference, a reminder of an appointment, an address, or a laundry bill, should this be included in his works? Why not? . . . If some have found it convenient to bypass the individuality of the writer or his status as an author to concentrate on a work, they have failed to appreciate the equally problematic nature of the word "work" and the unity it designates. (118–19)

Within the context of Foucault's discussion of "the author's disappearance" (119), the illimitable plenitude of Nietzsche's oeuvre demonstrates that there's more than one way to kill an author. One can destroy (what we mean by) the author, which includes the notion of sole authorship, by removing the autonomy of text. One can also achieve the same end by de-centering text or by transforming text into a network. Finally, one can remove limits on textuality, permitting it to expand, until Nietzsche, the edifying philosopher, becomes equally the author of *The Gay Science* and laundry lists and other such trivia — as indeed he was. Such illimitable plenitude has truly "transformed" the author, or at least the older conception of him, into "a victim of his own writing" (117).

These fears about the death of the author, whether in complaint or celebration, derive from Claude Lévi-Strauss, whose mythological works demonstrated for a generation of critics that works of powerful imagination take form without an author. In *The Raw and the Cooked* (1969), for example, where he showed, "not how men think in myths, but how myths operate in men's minds without their being aware of the fact," he also suggests that "it would perhaps be better to go still further and, disregarding the thinking subject completely, proceed as if the thinking process were taking place in the myths, in the reflection upon themselves and their interrelation."[6] Lévi-Strauss's presentation of mythological thought as a complex system of transformations without a center turns it into a networked text — not surprising, since the network serves as one of the main paradigms of synchronous structure.[7] Edward Said claims that the "two principal forces that have eroded the authority of the human subject in contemporary reflection are, on the one hand, the host of problems that arise in defining the subject's authenticity and, on the other, the development of disciplines like linguistics and ethnology that dramatize the subject's anomalous and unprivileged, even untenable, position in thought" (*Beginnings*, 293). One may add to this observation that these disciplines' network paradigms also contribute importantly to this sense of the attenuated, depleted, eroding, or even vanishing subject.

Some authors, such as Said and Heim, derive the erosion of the thinking subject directly from electronic information technology. Said, for example, claims it is quite possible to argue "that the proliferation of information (and what is still more remarkable, a proliferation of the hardware for disseminating and preserving this information) has hopelessly diminished the role apparently played by the individual" (51).[8] Michael Heim, who believes loss of authorial power to be implicit in all electronic text, complains: "Fragments, reused material, the trails and intricate pathways of 'hypertext,' as Ted Nelson terms it, all these advance the disintegration of the centering voice of contemplative thought. The arbitrariness and availability of database searching decreases the felt sense of an authorial control over what is written" (*Electric Language*, 220). A data base search, in other words, permits the active reader to enter the author's text at any point and not at the point the author chose as the beginning. Of course, as long as we have had indices, scholarly readers have dipped into specialist publications before or (shame!) instead of reading them through from beginning to end. In fact, recent studies of the way specialists read periodicals in their areas of expertise confirm that the linear model of reading is often little more than a pious fiction for many expert readers.[9]

Although Heim here mentions hypertext in relation to the erosion of authorial prerogative, the chief problem, he argues elsewhere, lies in the way "digital writing turns the private solitude of reflective reading and writing into a public network where the personal symbolic framework needed for original authorship is threatened by linkage with the total textuality of human expressions" (215). Unlike most writers on hypertext, he finds participation in a network a matter for worry rather than celebration, but he describes the same world they do, though with a strange combination of prophecy and myopia. Heim, who sees this loss of authorial control in terms of a corollary loss of privacy, argues that "anyone writing on a fully equipped computer is, in a sense, directly linked with the totality of symbolic expressions — more so and more essentially so than in any previous writing element" (215). Pointing out that word processing redefines the related notions of publishing, making public, and privacy, Heim argues that anyone who writes with a word processor cannot escape the electronic network: "Digital writing, because it consists in electronic signals, puts one willy-nilly on a network where everything is constantly published. Privacy becomes an increasingly fragile notion. Word processing manifests a world in which the public itself and its publicity have become omnivorous; to make public has therefore a different meaning than ever before" (215).

The key phrase here, of course, is "in a sense," for, as a famous Princeton philosopher used to say when a student used that phrase, "Yes, yes, *in a sense* a cow and a pig are the same animal, but in what sense?" The answer must be in some bizarrely inefficient dystopic future sense — "future" because today few people writing with word processors participate very frequently in the lesser versions of such information networks that already exist, and "bizarrely inefficient" because one would have to assume that the billions and billions of words we would write all have equal ability to clutter the major resource that such networks will be. Nonetheless, although Heim may much overstate the case for universal loss of privacy, particularly in relation to de-centered networks, he has accurately presented both some implications of hypertext for writers and the reactions against them by the print author accustomed to the fiction of the autonomous text.

The third form of reconfiguration of self and author shared by theory and hypertext concerns the de-centered self, an obvious corollary to the network paradigm. As Said points out, major contemporary theorists reject "the human subject as grounding center for human knowledge. Derrida, Foucault, and Deleuze . . . have spoken of contemporary knowledge (*savoir*) as decentered; Deleuze's formulation is that knowledge, insofar as it is intelligible, is apprehensible in terms of *nomadic centers*, provisional structures that are never permanent, always straying from one set of information to another" (*Beginnings*, 376). These three contemporary thinkers advance a conceptualization of thought best understood, like their views of text, in an electronic, virtual, hypertextual environment.

Before mourning too readily for this vanished or much diminished self, we would do well to remind ourselves that, although Western thought long held such notions of the unitary self in a privileged position, texts from Homer to Freud have steadily argued the contrary position. Divine or demonic possession, inspiration, humors, moods, dreams, the unconscious — all these devices that serve to explain how human beings act better, worse, or just different from their usual behavior argue against the unitary conception of the self so central to moral, criminal, and copyright law. The editor of the Soncino edition of the Hebrew Bible reminds us that

Balaam's personality is an old enigma, which has baffled the skill of commentators. . . . He is represented in Scripture as at the same time heathen sorcerer, true Prophet, and the perverter who suggested a particularly abhorrent means of bringing about the ruin of Israel. Because of these fundamental contradictions in character, Bible Critics assume, that the Scriptural account of Balaam is a combination of two or three varying traditions belonging to different periods. . . . Such a view betrays a slight knowledge of the fearful complexity of the mind and soul of man. It is only in the realm of the Fable that men and women display, as it were in a single flash of light, some *one* aspect of human nature. It is otherwise in real life.[10]

Given such long-observed multiplicities of the self, we are forced to realize that notions of the unitary author or self cannot authenticate the unity of a text. The instance of Balaam also reminds us that we have access to him only in Scriptures and that it is the biblical text, after all, that figures the unwilling prophet as a fractured self.

In response to this and other problems that arise in changing conceptions of textuality, Said asks, "Wherein, then, lies the authority of writing?" He immediately recognizes, however, that "such questions make sense only if the writing in question is considered stable and documentary"; and we recall that hypertext removes some of the stability of writing.

. . . .

How I Am Writing This Book

As I sit here writing a work on hypertext and hypertextuality that will eventually result in an old-fashioned form, a book, I feel continually frustrated, because having gathered and typed in hundreds of passages from a range of critics and writers on computer hypertext, I long for a hypertextual mode, such as I use in my classroom. I long to produce a book, not by conventional argument, but by creating brief essays, almost abstracts, on the six or seven main points of convergence between these two attitudes toward textuality and then linking nested arrangements of the original texts. In some cases, a remark by Derrida deserves discussion in many separate contexts, but book technology demands that I use it only once. Its final placement will depend more on the requirements of argumentation than on any primary adequacy to truth. A hypertext version, such as that I have created on the Intermedia system, allows one to present Derrida's notions of an infinitely expandable, implicated, and linked text in a format that comes much closer to embodying its insights.

Let me tell you how I am writing — which is to say, composing or putting together — the book that you are now reading, after which I shall compare this form of composition to that practised within a hypertext environment. During my undergraduate years, I used to take preliminary preparatory notes, make outlines, and begin rough drafts directly on a typewriter. The same procedures continued when I shifted to a word-processing program on the university's mainframe computer, which I used by means of a terminal first across campus in the English department or in the computer center and then on one in my home that connected to the university by a telephone line. Increasingly, the virtuality and manipulatability of computer text processing changed my work habits. My usual manner of proceeding now entails taking reading notes, usually in the form of selected passages to which I append preliminary commentary, directly on the computer. I have long taken a few such notes, particularly in preparation for complex projects, but the movement first to a mainframe computer and then to an Apple Macintosh (and later a Macintosh II) made taking such notes both easier to carry out and potentially more valuable, since the ability to copy and paste electronic text encourages one to expend effort knowing that it need not be wasted by the later need to retype or recopy.

Two things about working with a word processor first attracted me to carrying out writing projects on a computer. First, there was the ease with which the writer can make changes and corrections, both the direct result of the virtuality of electronic text. Second, working with a word processor permits one to segment one's work, carrying out certain tasks, particularly less creative ones, as one's time, energy, and disposition permits. Thus, instead of having to complete one's writing before adding footnotes, or adding foot- or endnotes in the text of drafts before the last, one can take advantage of the automatic numbering (and renumbering) of notes to complete them ahead of time. Relying on this capacity of computing, I discovered early on that one can accomplish major projects in far less time than possible with typewriters and the inevitable errors of retyping.

The present work (which is to this point not a "work" or not yet one but still thus far a fragmentary set of separate documents or computer files in Microsoft Word) is taking form as a series of fragments that are imported and, when necessary, rearranged under the headings of a continually changing outline. Most of the first three chapters has been written in this manner, but those sections that discuss Vannevar Bush take advantage of the availability of digitized texts. When about to start the section discussing the memex, I mentioned to Paul Kahn, who is working on a book on Bush, that I wanted to borrow from him several of Bush's books in order to make photocopies on which I could then mark passages and prepare them for entry into my word processor. Paul replied, "Why would you want to do that? I have digitized copies of four of his most important articles and placed them on Intermedia and can easily export them from it into MS Word." True to his word, he made copies of Bush's essays for me, which he placed on a disk, after which, using the large two-page graphics monitor on which I work, I opened both the developing draft of the introduction and Bush's "As We May Think" and placed them side by side. Having decided which passages I wished to quote, I first copied and then pasted them as needed into the appropriate place in the text I was "writing." In some cases, I wrote the introductory passages, concluding discussion and transitions in the Bush document and then transferred these blocks to their new context; in others, I first copied the passages from Bush and only later worked them into my text.

This scenario began with my remarking upon the frustrations one who has written within a hypertext environment experiences when returning to the linear world of the printed book. Such frustrations derive from repeated recognitions that effective argument requires closing off connections and abandoning lines of investigation that hypertextuality would have made available. Here are two examples of what I mean.

Near the opening of this chapter, in the midst of discussing the importance of Lévi-Strauss to recent discussions of authorship, I made the following statement: "Lévi-Strauss's presentation of mythological thought as a complex system of transformations without a center turns it into a networked text — not surprising, since the network serves as one of the main paradigms of synchronous structure"; and to this text I appended a note, pointing out that in *The Scope of Anthropology* "Lévi-Strauss also employs this model for societies as a whole: 'Our society, a particular instance in a much vaster family of societies, depends, like all others, for its coherence and its very existence on a network — grown infinitely unstable and complicated among us — of ties between consanguineal families.' " At this point in the main text, I had originally planned to place Foucault's remark that "we can easily imagine a culture where discourse would circulate without any need for an author" ("Author," 138), and to this remark I had considered adding the observation that, yes, we can easily "imagine" such a culture, but we do not have to do so, since Lévi-Strauss's mythographic works have provided abundant examples of it. Although the diachronic relationship between these two influential thinkers seemed worthy of notice, I could not add the passage from Foucault and my comment because it disturbed my planned line of argument, which next required Said's relation of ethnology and linguistics to the erosion of "the authority of the human subject in contemporary reflection." Since Said's observation already produces a slight veer or change of direction in my discussion of the death of the author in contemporary thought, I did not want to veer off in yet another direction. I then considered putting this observation in note seven, but, again, it also seemed out of place there.

Had I written this chapter within a hypertext environment, the need to maintain a linear thrust would not have required this kind of choice. It would have required choices, but not this kind, and I could have linked two or more passages to this point in the main text, thereby creating multiple contexts both for my argument and for the quoted passage that served as my point of departure. I am not urging, of course, that in its print form this chapter has lost something of major importance because I could not easily append multiple connections without confusing the reader. (Had my abandoned remark seemed important enough to my overall argument, I could have managed to include it in several obvious ways, such as adding another paragraph or rewriting the main text to provide a point from which to hang another note.) No, I make this point to remind us that, as Derrida emphasizes, the linear habits of thought associated with print technology often force us to think in particular ways that require narrowness, decontextualization, and intellectual attenuation, if not downright impoverishment. Linear argument, in other words, forces one to cut off a quoted passage from other, apparently irrelevant contexts that in fact contribute to its meaning. The linearity of print also provides the passage with an illusory center whose force is intensified by such selection.

A second example points to another kind of exclusion associated with linear writing. During the course of composing these first three chapters, several passages, such as Barthes's description of the writerly text and Derrida's exposition of borders, boundaries, and *débordement*, forced themselves into the line of argument and hence deserved inclusion seven or eight times. One can repeat a quotation once, perhaps, but after that the fact of repetition rather than the passage itself most attracts notice. One can repeatedly refer to a particular passage, of course, by combining full quotation, selections, and skillful paraphrase, but in general the writer can concentrate on a quoted section of text in this manner only when it serves as the center, or one of the centers, of the argument. If I wished to write a chapter or an entire book about Derridean *débordement*, I could return repeatedly to it in different contexts, thereby revealing its richness of implication. But that is not the book I wish to write now, that is not the argument I wish to pursue here, and so I suppress that text and argument, which henceforth exist only *in potentia*. After careful consideration, I decide which of the many places in the text would most benefit from introduction of the quotation and then at the appropriate moment, I trundle it forward. As a result, I necessarily close off all but a few of its obvious points of connection.

As an experienced writer accustomed to making such choices, I realize that selection is one of the principles of effective argument. But why does one have to write texts in this way? If I were writing my Intermedia version of this text — and the versions would exist so differently that one has to place quotation marks around "version" and "text," and probably "my" as well — I would not have to choose to write a single text. I could, instead, produce one that contained a plurality of ways through it. For example, after preparing the reader for Derrida's discussion of *débordement*, I could then link my preparatory remarks either to the passage itself or to the entire text of "Living On," and I could provide temporary markings that would indicate the beginning and end of the passage I wished to emphasize. At the same time, my hypertext would link the same passage to other points in my argument. How would I go about creating such links?

To answer this question, let me return to my first and simpler example, which involved linking passages from Lévi-Strauss's *Scope of Anthropology* and Foucault's "What Is an Author?" to a remark about the anthropologist's use of the network model. Linking in Intermedia follows the now common cut-and-paste paradigm found in word processors, graphics editors, and spread sheets (figures 4 and 5). Using the mouse or other pointing device, one places the cursor immediately before the first letter of the first word in the passage one wishes to link. One then highlights the passage to be linked, either by holding down the mouse button and dragging the cursor across the entire passage, or if the passage is quite long, by clicking the cursor button on the last character in the passage while holding down the shift key. Either operation activates the passage in question, the sign of which is that the text appears highlighted — that is, it appears within a black rectangle, and the black type against a white background now appears in reverse video, white lettering against a black background. With the text highlighted, one moves the mouse until the point of the arrow-shaped cursor covers any part of the word "Intermedia" that appears in a horizontal list of words at top of the screen ("File," "Edit," "Intermedia," and so on). Holding down the mouse button, one draws the cursor down, thereby producing the Intermedia menu, which contains choices. Placing the pointer over "Start Link," one releases the mouse button, proceeds to the second text, and carries out the same operation until one opens the Intermedia menu, at which point one chooses "Complete Link."

The system then produces a panel containing places to type any desired labels for the linked passages; it automatically adds the title of

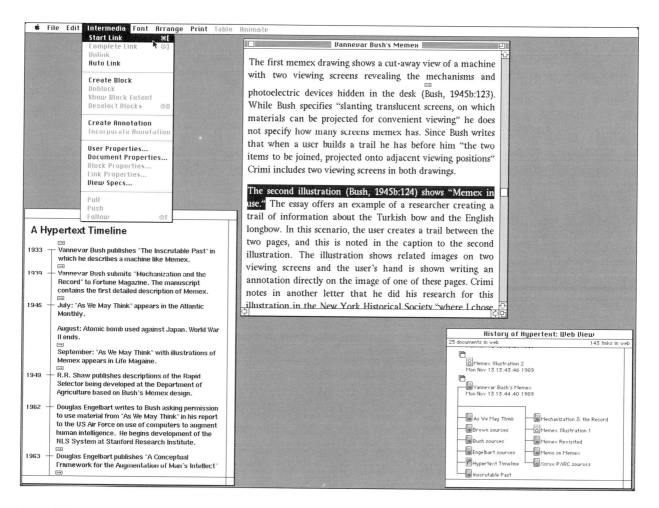

Figure 4. Creating a link: beginning. To create a new link, the user first selects a portion of the document as an anchor and chooses the "Start Link" command from the Intermedia menu. In this example, the reader-author has selected the sentence beginning "The second illustration. . . ." Link creation in Intermedia follows the standard copy-paste paradigm. Once the "Start Link" command is chosen, the selection, which will become one anchor for the bidirectional link, is saved in an invisible link board. One can perform any number of actions, including creating new documents or editing old ones, before completing the pending link. Using selections as anchors for links allows users to create fine-grained endpoints for their links. Anchors (or blocks) can range in size from an insertion point to the contents of an entire document. (Photograph copyright 1989 by Brown University. Used by permission.)

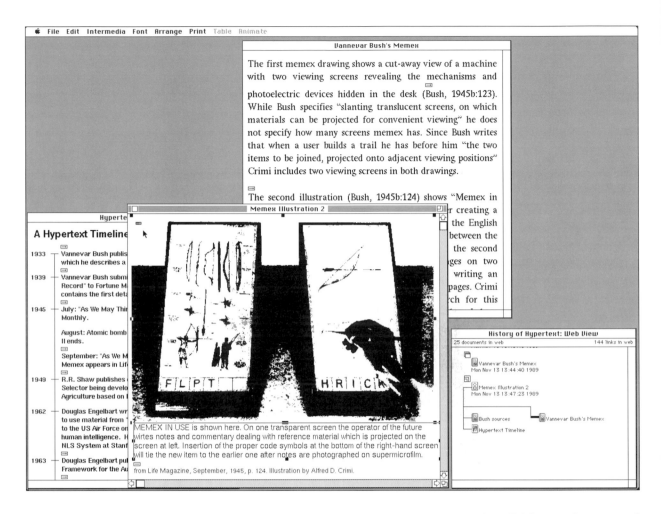

Figure 5. Completing a link. Choosing the "Complete Link" command from the Intermedia menu places link icons at the source and destination of the link. The Web View reflects the new connection. (Photograph copyright 1989 by Brown University. Used by permission.)

the entire text, and the writer can describe the linked passage within that text. For example, if I created a link between the hypermedia equivalent of my text for the previous section of this chapter and a passage in *The Scope of Anthropology,* Intermedia would automatically add the title of that text, "The Erosion of the Author," to which I would add a phrase, say, "Lévi-Strauss & myth as network." At the other end of the link, the system would furnish "Claude Lévi-Strauss, *The Scope of Anthropology,*" and I would add something like "Lévi-Strauss & society as network." When a reader activates the link marker in the main text, the new entry will appear as an option: "Claude Lévi-Strauss, *The Scope of Anthropology:* (Lévi-Strauss & society as network)," like the one shown in figure 6. Linking the second text, the passage from Foucault, follows the identical procedure with the single exception that one no longer has to provide a label for the lexia in the main text, since it already has one.

If instead of linking these two brief passages of quotation, documentation, and commentary, I created a more complex document set, focused upon Derridean *débordement,* one would follow the same procedure to create links. In addition, one would also create kinds of documents not found in printed text, some of which would be primarily visual or hieroglyphic. One, for example, might take the form of a concept map showing, among other things, uses of the term *débordement* in "Living On," other works by Derrida in which it appears, and its relation to a range of contexts and disciplines from cartography and histology to etymology and French military history. Current versions of Intermedia and other hypermedia systems permit one to link to interactive video, music, and animation as well as dictionaries, text, time lines, and static graphics. In the future these links will take more dynamic forms, and following them will animate some procedure, say, a search through a French thesaurus or a reader-determined tracking of *débordement* through various Indo-European languages. Other forms of linking will permit automatic data gathering, so that lists of relevant publications or current statements about *débordement* created after I had completed my document would automatically become available.[11]

My brief description of how I would go about producing this text were I writing it in Intermedia or a similar hypertext environment will probably strike most readers as simultaneously terrifying and bizarrely celebratory. One reason lies in the fact that a certain aspect of autho-

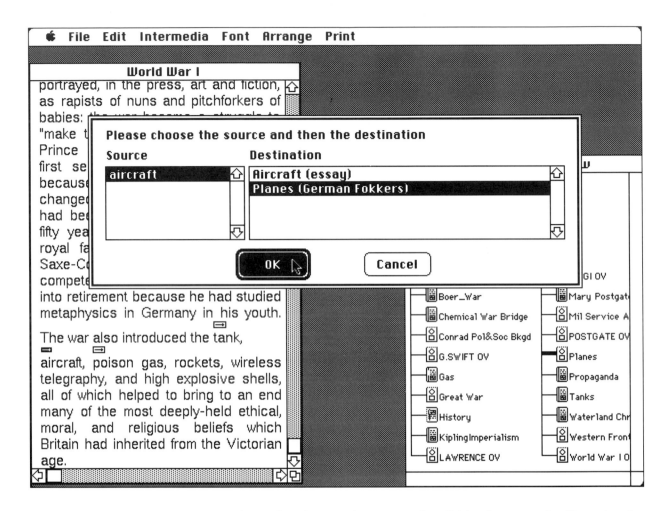

Figure 6. Link menu. To follow a link within the Intermedia environment, the user must select a link icon (an arrow enclosed in a rectangular box) and pick the "Follow" command from the Intermedia menu. Double clicking on the link icon is the same as selecting the "Follow" command. In this example the user has selected the link icon over the word *aircraft* in the current document, and this action produces two effects: (1) a menu appears that invites the reader to choose which link he or she would like to follow. In this case, the choice is between the "essay" anchor in the document entitled "Aircraft" or the "German Fokkers" anchor in the one entitled "Planes." The user selects the second choice. (2) When a link icon is selected in the current document, the corresponding link lines darken in the Web View. Readers navigate the materials by using either Web View or the link menu, which contains additional information about the destination point of the link within the entire document. (Photograph copyright 1989 by Brown University. Used by permission.)

rial control has vanished, or rather been ceded to the reader, another in that writing becomes different.

Electronic hypertext and contemporary discussions of critical theory, particularly those of the poststructuralists, display many points of convergence, but one point on which they differ is tone. Whereas most writings on theory, with the notable exception of Derrida, are models of scholarly solemnity, records of disillusionment and brave sacrifice of humanistic positions, writers on hypertext are downright celebratory. Whereas terms like *death*, *vanish*, *loss*, and expressions of depletion and impoverishment color critical theory, the vocabulary of freedom, energy, and empowerment marks writings on hypertextuality. One reason for these different tones may lie in the different intellectual traditions, national and disciplinary, from which they spring. A more important reason, I propose, is that critical theorists, as I have tried to show, continually confront the limitation — indeed, the exhaustion — of the culture of print. They write from an awareness of limitation and shortcoming, and from a moody nostalgia, often before the fact, at the losses their disillusionment has brought and will bring. Writers on hypertext, in contrast, glory in possibility, excited by the future of textuality, knowledge, and writing. Another way of putting this opposing tone and mood is that most writers on critical theory, however brilliantly they may theorize a much-desired new textuality, nonetheless write from within daily experience of the old and only of the old. Many writers on hypertext, on the other hand, have already had some experience, however merely proleptic and partial, of hypertext systems, and they therefore write from a different experiential vantage point. Most poststructuralists write from within the twilight of a wished-for coming day; most writers of hypertext write of many of the same things from within the dawn.

. . . . **Virtual Presence** Many features of hypermedia derive from its creating the virtual presence of all the authors who contribute to its materials. Computer scientists draw upon optics for an analogy when they speak of "virtual machines," created by an operating system that provides individual users sharing a system with the sense of working on their own individual machines. In the first chapter, when discussing electronic textuality, I pointed to another kind of "virtual" existence, the virtual text: all texts that one encounters on the computer screen are virtual, rather than real. In a similar manner, the reader experiences the virtual presence of other contributors.

Such virtual presence is of course a characteristic of all technology of cultural memory based on writing and symbol systems. Since we all manipulate cultural codes — particularly language but also mathematics and other symbols — in slightly different ways, each record of an utterance conveys a sense of the one who makes that utterance. Hypermedia differs from print technology, however, in several crucial ways that amplify this notion of virtual presence. Because the essential connectivity of hypermedia removes the physical isolation of individual texts characteristic of print technology, the presence of individual authors becomes both more available and more important. The characteristic flexibility of this reader-centered information technology means, quite simply, that writers have a much greater presence in the system, as potential contributors and collaborative participants but also as readers who choose their own paths through the materials.

■　■　■　■　■　■　■　■　The virtual presence of other texts and other authors contributes importantly to the radical

Collaborative Writing, reconception of authorship, authorial property, and collaboration associated with hypertext.

Collaborative Authorship Within a hypertext environment all writing becomes collaborative writing, doubly so. The first element of collaboration appears when one compares the roles of writer and reader, since the active reader necessarily collaborates with the author in producing a text by the choices he or she makes. The second aspect of collaboration appears when one compares the writer with other writers — that is, the author who is writing *now* with the virtual presence of all writers "on the system" who wrote *then* but whose writings are still present.

The word *collaboration*, which derives from the Latin for *working* plus that for *with* or *together*, conveys the suggestion, among others, of working side by side on the same endeavor. Most people's conceptions of collaborative work take the form of two or more scientists, songwriters, or the like continually conferring as they pursue a project in the same place at the same time. I have worked on an essay with a fellow scholar in this manner. One of us would a type a sentence, at which point the other would approve, qualify, or rewrite it, and then we would proceed to the next sentence. Far more common a form of collaboration, I suspect, is a second mode, described as "versioning,"[12] in which one worker produces a draft that another person then edits by modifying and adding. The first and the second forms of collaborative authorship tend to blur, but the distinguishing factor is that versioning takes place out of the presence of the other collaborator and at a later time.

Both of these models require considerable ability to work productively with other people, and evidence suggests that many people either do not have such ability or do not enjoy putting it into practice. In fact, according to those who have carried out experiments in collaborative work, a third form proves more common than the first two — the assembly-line or segmentation model of working together, according to which individual workers divide the overall task and work entirely independently. This last mode is the form that most people choose when they work on collaborative projects, ranging from programming to art exhibitions.

Networked hypertext systems like Intermedia offer a fourth model of collaborative work that combines aspects of the previous ones. By emphasizing the presence of other texts and their cooperative interaction, networked hypertext makes all additions to a system simultaneously a matter of versioning and of the assembly-line model. Once ensconced within a network of electronic links, a document no longer exists by itself. It always exists in relation to other documents in a way that a book or printed document never does and never can. From this crucial shift in the way texts exist in relation to others derive two principles that, in turn, produce this fourth form of collaboration: first, any document placed on any networked system that supports electronically linked materials potentially exists in collaboration with any and all other documents on that system; second, any document electronically linked to any other document collaborates with it.

According to the *American Heritage Dictionary of the English Language*, the verb *to collaborate* can mean either "to work together, especially in a joint intellectual effort" or "to cooperate treasonably, as with an enemy occupying one's country." The combination of labor, political power, and aggressiveness that appears in this dictionary definition well indicates some of the problems that arise when one discusses collaborative work. On the one hand, the notion of collaboration embraces notions of working together with others, of forming a community of action. This meaning recognizes, as it were, that we all exist within social groups, and it obviously places value on contributions to that group. On the other hand, collaboration also includes a deep suspicion of working with others, something aesthetically as well as emotionally engrained since the advent of romanticism, which exalts the idea of individual effort to such a degree that it often fails to recognize, or even suppresses, the fact that artists and writers work collaboratively with texts created by others.

Most of our intellectual endeavors involve collaboration, but we do not always recognize the fact for two reasons. The rules of our intellectual culture, particularly those that define intellectual property and authorship, do not encourage such recognitions; and furthermore, information technology from Gutenberg to the present — the technology of the book — systematically hinders full recognition of collaborative authorship.

Throughout this century the physical and biological sciences have increasingly conceived of scientific research, authorship, and publication as group endeavors. The conditions of scientific research, according to which many research projects require the cooperating services of a number of specialists in the same or (often) different fields, bear some resemblances to the medieval guild system in which apprentices, journeymen, and masters all worked on a single complex project. Nonetheless, "collaborations differ depending on whether the substance of the research involves a theoretical science, such as mathematics, or an empirical science, such as biology or psychology. The former are characterized by collaborations among equals, with little division of labor, whereas the latter are characterized by more explicit exchange of services, and more substantial division of labor."[13] The financing of scientific research, which supports the individual project, the institution at which it is carried out, and the costs of educating new members of the discipline all nurture such group endeavors and consequent conceptions of group authorship.[14]

In general, the scientific disciplines rely upon an inclusive conception of authorship: anyone who has made a major contribution to finding particular results, occasionally including specialized technicians and those who develop techniques necessary to carry out a course of research, can appear as authors of scientific papers, and similarly, those in whose laboratories a project is carried out may receive authorial credit if an individual project and the publication of its results depend intimately upon their general research. In the course of a graduate student's research for his dissertation, he or she may receive continual advice and evaluation. When the student's project bears fruit and appears in the form of one or more publications, the advisor's name often appears as co-author.

Not so in the humanities, where graduate student research is supported largely by teaching assistantships and not, as in the sciences, by research funding. Although an advisor of a student in English or art history often acts in ways closely paralleling the advisor of the student in physics, chemistry, or biology, explicit acknowledgments of cooperative work rarely appear. Even when a senior scholar provides the student with a fairly precise research project, continual guidance, and access to crucial materials that the senior scholar has discovered or assembled, the student does not include the advisor as co-author.

The marked differences between conceptions of authorship in the sciences and the humanities demonstrate the validity of Michel Foucault's observation that "the 'author-function' is tied to the legal and institutional systems that circumscribe, determine, and articulate the realm of discourses; it does not operate in a uniform manner in all discourses, at all times, and in any given culture it is not defined by the spontaneous attribution of a text to its creator, but through a series of precise and complex procedures; it does not refer, purely and simply, to an actual individual" ("Author," 131). One reason for the different conceptions of authorship and authorial property in the humanities and the sciences lies in the different conditions of funding and the different discipline-politics that result.

Another corollary reason is that the humanistic disciplines, which traditionally apply historical approaches to the areas they study, consider their own assumptions about authorship, authorial ownership, creativity, and originality to be eternal verities.[15] In particular, literary studies and literary institutions, such as departments of English, which still bathe themselves in the afterglow of Romanticism, uncritically inflate Romantic notions of creativity and originality to the point of absurdity. An example comes readily to hand from the preface of Lisa Ede and Andrea Lunsford's recent study of collaborative writing, the production of which they discovered to have involved "acts of subversion and of liberatory significance": "We began collaborating in spite of concerned warnings of friends and colleagues, including those of Edward P. J. Corbett, the person in whose honor we first wrote collaboratively. We knew that our collaboration represented a challenge to traditional research conventions in the humanities. Andrea's colleagues (at the University of British Columbia) said so when they declined to consider any of her coauthored or coedited works as part of a review for promotion."[16]

Ede and Lunsford, whose interest in their subject grew out of the "difference between our personal experience as coauthors and the responses of many of our friends and colleagues" (5), set the issue of collaborative writing within the contexts of actual practice in the worlds of business and academia, the history of theories of creative individualism and copyright in recent Western culture, contemporary critical theory, particularly that of Bakhtin, Barthes, and Foucault, and feminist analyses of many of these other contexts. They produce a wide range of evidence in convincingly arguing that "the pervasive commonsense assumption that writing is inherently and necessarily a solitary, individual act" (5) supports a traditional patriarchal construction of authorship and authority. After arguing against "univocal psychological theories of the self" (132) and associated notions of an isolated individualism, Ede and Lunsford call for a more Bakhtinian reconception of the self and for what they term a dialogic, rather than a hierarchical, mode of collaboration.

I shall return to their ideas when I discuss the role of hypertext in collaborative learning, but now I wish to point out that as scholars from McLuhan and Eisenstein to Ede and Lunsford have long argued, book technology and the attitudes it supports are the institutions most responsible for maintaining exaggerated notions of authorial individuality, uniqueness, and ownership that often drastically falsify the conception of original contributions in the humanities and convey distorted pictures of research. The sciences take a relatively expansive, inclusive view of authorship and consequently of text ownership.[17] The humanities take a far more restricted view that emphasizes individuality, separation, and uniqueness — often creating a vastly distorted view of the connection of a particular text to those that preceded it. Neither view possesses an obvious rightness. Each is obviously a social construction, and each has on occasion proved to distort actual conditions of intellectual work carried out in a particular field.

Whatever the political, economic, and other discipline-specific factors that maintain the conception of noncooperative authorship in the humanities, print technology has also contributed to the sense of a separate, unique text that is the product — and hence the prop- erty — of one person, the author. Hypertext changes all this, in large part because it does away with the isolation of the individual text that characterizes the book. As McLuhan and other students of the cultural influence of print technology have pointed out, modern con- ceptions of intellectual property derive both from the organization and financing of book production and from the uniformity and fixity of text that characterize the printed book. J. David Bolter explains that book technology itself created new conceptions of authorship and publication:

Because printing a book is a costly and laborious task, few readers have the opportunity to become published authors. An author is a person whose words are faithfully copied and sent around the literary world, whereas readers are merely the audience for those words. The distinction meant less in the age of manuscripts, when "publication" was less of an event and when the reader's own notes and glosses had the same status as the text itself. Any reader could decide to cross over and become an author: one simply sat down and wrote a treatise or put one's notes in a form for others to read. Once the treatise was written, there was no difference between it and the works of other "published" writers, except that the more famous works existed in more copies. (*Writing Space,* 148–49)

Printing a book requires a considerable expenditure of capital and labor, and the need to protect that investment contributes to notions of intellectual property. But these notions would not be possible in the first place without the physically separate, fixed text of the printed book. Just as the need to finance printing of books led to a search for the large audiences that in turn stimulated the ultimate triumph of the vernacular and fixed spelling, so, too, the fixed nature of the indi- vidual text made possible the idea that each author produces some- thing unique and identifiable as property.[18]

    The needs of the marketplace, at least as they are conceived by editors and publishing houses, reinforce all the worst effects of these conceptions of authorship in both academic and popular books. Alleen Pace Nilsen reports that Nancy Mitford and her husband wrote the best-selling *High Cost of Death* together, but only her name appears because the publisher urged that multiple authors would cut sales. In another case, to make a book more marketable a publisher replaced the chief editor of a major psychiatric textbook with the name of a prestigious contributor who had not edited the volume at all (cited by Ede and Lunsford, 3–4). I am sure all authors have examples of such distortion of authorial practice for what a publisher believes to be good business. I have mine: a number of years ago after an exercise in collaborative work and writing with three graduate students produced a publishable manuscript, we decided mutually upon the ordering of our names on the title page.[19] By the time the volume appeared, the three former graduate students all held teaching positions, and the book's appearance, one expects, might have helped them professionally. Unfortunately, the publisher insisted upon including only the first editor's name in all notices, advertisements, and catalogues. Such an action, of course, does not have so serious an effect as removing the editors' names from the title page, but it certainly discriminates unfairly between the first two editors, who did equal amounts of work, and it certainly conveys a strong message to beginning humanists about the culturally assigned value of cooperation and collaboration.

Even though print technology is not entirely or even largely responsible for current attitudes in the humanities toward authorship and collaboration, a shift to hypertext systems would change them by emphasizing elements of collaboration. As Tora K. Bikson and J. D. Eveland point out in relation to other, nonhumanities work, "the electronic environment is a rich context in which doing work and sharing work become virtually indistinguishable."[20] If we can make ourselves aware of the new possibilities created by these changes, we can at the very least take advantage of the characteristic qualities of this new form of information technology.

One relevant characteristic quality of networked hypertext systems is that they produce a sense of authorship, authorial property, and creativity that differs markedly from those associated with book technology. Hypertext changes our sense of authorship and creativity (or originality) by moving away from the constrictions of page-bound technology. In so doing, it promises to have an effect on cultural and intellectual disciplines as important as those produced by earlier shifts in the technology of cultural memory that followed the invention of writing and printing.[21]

■ ■ ■ ■ ■ ■ ■ Collaborative work on Intermedia takes many
forms, one of the most interesting of which illus-
Examples of Collaborative trates the principle that one almost inevitably
works collaboratively whenever creating docu-
Writing on Intermedia ments on a multiauthor hypertext system. One day
when I was linking materials to the overview (or
directory) file for Graham Swift's *Waterland*
(1983), I observed Nicole Yankelovich, project coordinator of the
Intermedia project at IRIS, working on materials for a course in arms
control and disarmament offered by Richard Smoke of Brown University's Center for Foreign Policy Development. Those materials,
which were created by someone from a discipline very different from
mine for a very different kind of course, filled a major gap in a project
I was working on. Although my co-authors and I had created materials about technology, including graphic and text documents on canals
and railroads, to attach to the science and technology section of the
Waterland overview, we did not have the expertise to create parallel
documents about nuclear technology and the antinuclear movement,
two subjects that play a significant part in Swift's novel. Creating a
brief introduction to the subject of *Waterland* and nuclear disarmament, I linked it first to the science and technology section in the
Waterland overview and then to the time line that the nuclear arms
course materials employ as a directory file. A brief document and
a few links enable students in the introductory survey of English literature to explore the materials created for a course in another discipline. Similarly, students from that course can now encounter
materials showing the effects on contemporary fiction of the concerns
covered in their political science course. Intermedia thus allows and
encourages collaborative work, and at the same time it encourages
interdisciplinary approaches by making materials created by specialists
in different disciplines work together — collaborate.

The important point here is that hypermedia linking automatically
produces collaboration. Looking at the way the arms control materials
joined to those supporting the four English courses, one encounters
a typical example of how the connectivity that characterizes hypertext
transforms independently produced documents into collaborative
ones and authors working alone into collaborative authors. When one
considers the arms control materials from the point of view of their
originator, they exist as part of a discrete body of materials. When

one considers them from the vantage point of a reader, their status changes: as soon as they appear within a hypertext environment, these and all other documents there exist as part of a larger system and in relation therefore to other materials on that system. By forming electronic pathways between blocks of texts, Intermedia links actualize the potential relations between them.

The Dickens Web, a sample Intermedia document set published by IRIS in 1990, exemplifies the kinds of collaborative authorship characteristic of hypertext. The web, which contains 245 documents and almost 680 links, takes the form of "a collection of materials about Charles Dickens, his novel *Great Expectations*, and many related subjects, such as Victorian history, public health issues, and religion." [22] Creating *The Dickens Web* involved dozens of "authors" and almost that many kinds of collaboration.

I created sixty-four text documents, three time lines, the original versions of ten graphic concept maps (more on this subject later), and provided captions, some elaborate enough to be brief essays, for thirty-odd reproductions of art works, mostly Victorian woodblock illustrations, and a few maps. David Cody, the most prolific of the four graduate or post-doctoral assistants on that part of the Intermedia project funded by the Annenberg/CPB Project, produced forty-four text documents, one or two time lines, and a similar number of concept maps; he also selected and first digitized many of the illustrations, all of which were later redigitized by Paul D. Kahn, the IRIS project coordinator, and Julie Launhardt, assistant project coordinator, both of whom also copyedited the verbal and graphic content of all the documents.

Working with his permission, I produced thirty documents from published and unpublished works by Anthony S. Wohl, professor of history, Vassar College, on the subjects of Victorian public health and race and class in Victorian Britain (figure 7). Since my work here consisted of little more than dividing Wohl's text into appropriate lexias, and since he then gave final approval to the resultant hypertext translations of his writing, the documents bear his name alone. Twenty documents created by undergraduates at Brown University were included after obtaining their written permission, and approximately the same number of documents take the form of brief one- or two-paragraph quotations by critics of Dickens; these quotations, which are often preceded by introductory remarks and followed by questions,

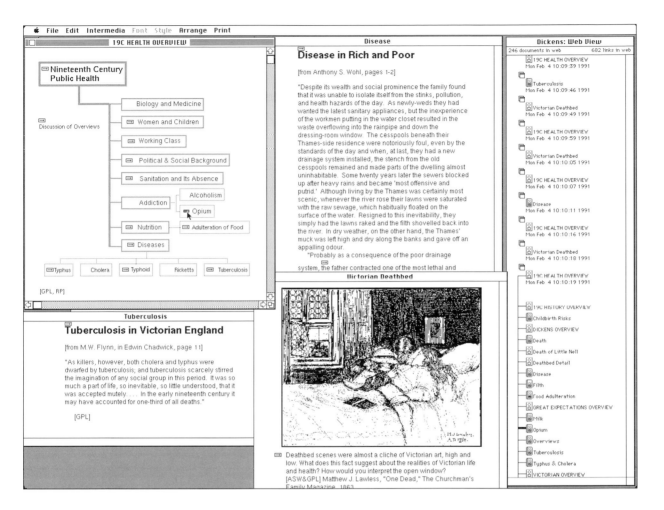

Figure 7. A sample of the materials on nineteenth-century public health from *The Dickens Web*. "Disease in Rich and Poor," an example of Anthony S. Wohl's many contributions, appears at the upper middle of the screen, surrounded by (1) 19C HEALTH OV, (2) the system-created Web View, (3) an example of a deathbed scene in Victorian art, and (4) a brief passage from a work by another author on Victorian public health.

act as hypertext versions of standard scholarly quotation and are quoted without specific permission under the fair use doctrine. Katherine B. Stockton, the sole graduate assistant during the third year of the project, created an additional fifteen text and graphic documents, to some of which materials have since been added others by additional graduate and undergraduate research assistants or students working on independent projects, who added another dozen or so lexias.

Five faculty members from several universities provided additional materials: Linda H. Peterson, associate professor of English, Yale University, contributed bibliographies on Victorian religion, art, and literature; and Joan D. Richardson, associate professor of history, Brown University, provided a bibliography for Victorian science. Peter Heywood, associate professor of biology, one of two original Intermedia teachers, allowed us to incorporate essays on Darwinism he had created for an upper-division course in plant cell biology; Walter L. Arnstein, professor of history, University of Illinois, contributed a bibliography of materials on religion in Victorian Britain; and Michel-André Bossy, professor of French and comparative literature, Brown University, kindly permitted the inclusion of his brief discussion of detective fiction.

Bossy's contribution exemplifies how complex decisions about authorship can be in a hypertext environment. Bossy's document, which he had developed as a handout for one of his courses in comparative literature, became part of the Intermedia materials after Barry J. Fishman, a student in that course, perceived the essay's connection to Dickens and to other authors he had read a year earlier in my course. Receiving permission from Professor Bossy, he placed it on the Intermedia system and made links so students in other courses could benefit from it. Now the question arises, who is "author" of this valuable summary? Bossy, obviously, because he summed up other experts "in his own words." But what about those critics on whom he drew? In print they would not appear worthy of inclusion as authors, but in hypertext the situation might change. Then, what about Fishman, who initially perceived the possible connection, gained permission from both Bossy and myself to include it, and then made the necessary links? To my mind, he obviously deserves to share some part of the hypertext document's authorship, as perhaps should those people who created the lexias to which it links.

An even more complex problem of authorship arises in relation to the many graphic overviews in *The Dickens Web*. After Nicole Yankelovich handed me a copy of James D. Novak and D. Bob Gowin's *Learning How to Learn*, which urges the use of concept mapping in support of its constructionist view of knowledge, I drew crude initial versions of graphic directories in which various phenomena, such as religion and philosophy, biography, and cultural context, surrounded an entity (Robert Browning, "My Last Duchess," or Victorianism) and were connected to it by lines radiating from it.[23] Since my then-twelve-year-old son had far more facility with the graphics program MacDraw than I did, he ended up creating computer versions of my concept map, which I then took to the development team at IRIS (where for a while it became known, only partly in jest, as "the Noah Landow paradigm"). Helen d'Andrade, the IRIS graphic designer, then produced elegant versions of these concept maps on the IBM equipment that first supported our hypermedia environment. Using her work as a template, David Cody modified it in creating the Dickens overview, and more than a year later, I created an additional one, for *Great Expectations*, and I added many more, including those for religion in England, public health, and Victorianism. When IRIS transferred ("ported") the Intermedia system to Apple Macintosh IIs, Shoshana M. Landow, an undergraduate summer research assistant, recreated all the overviews, making them smaller, clearer, and more efficient. Then, after IRIS decided to publish a small selection of these materials supporting humanities teaching in the form of *The Dickens Web*, Ronnie Peters of the Rhode Island School of Design undertook a major reconception of the graphic presentation of all materials included. He provided design principles, a graphics style sheet, and specific examples, but most of the overviews were actually designed by Paul D. Kahn.[24] Who, then, is the "author" of the Dickens, *Great Expectations*, and "Religion in England" overviews? Going over my preceding narrative of origins, I count at least ten individuals who partook of authorship in one important way or another — and I have not even mentioned those who linked these overviews to hundreds of other lexias. Some of those people who created links appear in the account above, but there was a host of others, the most important of whom were Suzanne Keene, now assistant professor, Yale University, and David Cody, assistant professor, University of Oklahoma, who created the first extensive linking on Intermedia.

In the published version, IRIS chose to append sets of initials to these overviews. The *Great Expectations* and "Religion in England" overviews, for example, list "GPL, RP" to indicate authorship, and the preceding account should indicate how misleading is such a limited attribution. "Dickens Literary Relations," which Kahn entirely reconceived following a design of his own, bears the initials "DC, SML, PDK," thus indicating its line of descent more than its direct parentage; and the graphic directory for "Victorian Bibliography," which replaces my standard, rather crude radiating design with a beautiful illustration of an ornate Victorian book, lists only "GPL," despite the fact that the conceit was Kahn's. The rationale seems to be that the person who first thought of the need for a particular document and mapped out its intellectual contents, in this case merely eight subject headings, receives credit. More important, part of the credit here arises in the generosity of colleagues, and part then in turn derives as a kind of reward for earlier, preparatory work.

As this account should make clear, "authorship" of individual texts in a hypermedia environment becomes even more problematic than in the world of print. The concept of "authorship" moves beyond quotation marks when one attempts to account for *The Dickens Web* as a whole: the title page of the user's manual fittingly reads only "IRIS Intermedia / The Dickens Web / User's and Installation Guide." The reverse, which makes required copyright announcements and prohibitions against unauthorized copying, credits the Henry W. and Albert A. Berg Collection of the New York Public Library for permission to publish Frederic W. Pailthorpe's illustrations for *Great Expectations*. The copyright page lists no authors. Instead, it states the following: "Developed by George P. Landow / Edited by Julie Launhardt and Paul Kahn / Graphic design by Ronnie Peters." This solution, which Launhardt and Kahn arrived at after consulting with others at IRIS, contains an important truth about writing within a hypertext environment. Hypertext has no authors in the conventional sense. Just as hypertext as an educational medium transforms the teacher from a leader into a kind of coach or companion, hypertext as a writing medium metamorphoses the author into an editor or developer. Hypermedia, like cinema and video or opera, is a team production.

Reconfiguring

Narrative

Hypertext and

the Aristotelian Conception

of Plot

Hypertext, which challenges narrative and all literary form based on linearity, calls into question ideas of plot and story current since Aristotle. Looking at the *Poetics* in the context of a discussion of hypertext suggests one of two things: either one simply cannot write hypertext fiction (and the *Poetics* show why that could be the case) or else Aristotelian definitions and descriptions of plot do not apply to stories read and written within a hypertext environment. At the beginning of this study, I proposed that hypertext permits a particularly effective means of testing literary and cultural theory. Here is a case in point. Although hypertext fiction is quite new, the examples of it that I have seen already call into question some of Aristotle's most basic points about plot and story.

In the seventh chapter of *Poetics*, Aristotle offers a definition of plot in which fixed sequence plays a central role:

Now a whole is that which has beginning, middle, and end. A beginning is that which is not itself necessarily after anything else, and which has naturally something else after it; an end is that which is naturally after something itself either as its necessary or usual consequent, and with nothing else after it; and a middle, that which is by nature after one thing and also has another after it.[1]

Furthermore, Aristotle concludes, "a well-constructed Plot, therefore, cannot either begin or end at any point one likes; beginning and end in it must be of the forms just described. Again: to be beautiful, a living creature, and every whole made up of parts, must not only present a certain order in its arrangement of parts, but also be of a certain definite magnitude" (1462). Hypertext therefore calls into question (1) fixed sequence, (2) definite beginning and ending, (3) a story's "certain definite magnitude," and (4) the conception of unity or wholeness associated with all these other concepts.

In hypertext fiction, therefore, one can expect individual forms, such as plot, characterization, and setting, to change, as will genres or literary kinds produced by congeries of these techniques. The novelty, the radical newness, of this subject appears in the fact that at the time of writing many, in fact almost all, the sources I cite in this chapter are unpublished, in the process of being published, or are published in nontraditional, electronic forms: these sources include unpublished notes on the subject of hypertext and fiction by a leading American novelist, chapters in forthcoming books, and pre-release versions of hypertext fictions.

Previous discussions of the effects of hypertext upon literary form either have sought to identify quasi hypertextuality in print texts and then suggest what hypertext fiction might be like or have deduced the rules of hypertextual narrative from first principles, particularly that involving the removal of linearity as a dominant principle of forms. The first approach to predicting the way hypertext might affect literary form has pointed to *Tristram Shandy*, *In Memoriam*, *Ulysses*, and *Finnegans Wake* and to recent French, American, and Latin American fiction, particularly that by Michel Butor, Marc Saporta, Robert Coover, and Jorge Luis Borges (Bolter, *Writing Space*, 132–39). Such texts might not require hypertext to be fully understood, but they reveal new principles of organization or new ways of being read to readers who have experienced hypertext. Hypertext, the argument goes, makes certain elements in these works stand out for the first time. The example of these very different texts suggests that those poems and novels that most resist one or more of the characteristics of literature associated with print form, particularly linear narrative, will be likely to have something in common with new fiction in a new medium.

This first approach therefore uses hypertext as a lens, or new agent of perception, to reveal something previously unnoticed or unnoticeable, and it then extrapolates the results of this inquiry to predict future developments. Because such an approach suggests that this new information technology has roots in prestigious canonical texts, it obviously has the political advantage of making it seem less threatening to students of literature and literary theory. At the same time, placing hypertext fiction within a legitimating narrative of descent from "great works" offers material for new critical readings of print texts and makes those canonical texts appear especially forward looking, since they can be seen to provide the gateway to a different and unexpected literary future. I find all these genealogical analyses attractive and even convincing, but I realize that if hypertext has the kind and degree of power that previous chapters have indicated, it *does* threaten literature and its institutions as we know them. One *should* feel threatened by hypertext, just as writers of romances and epics should have felt threatened by the novel and Venetian writers of Latin tragedy should have felt threatened by the *Divine Comedy* and its Italian text. Descendants, after all, offer continuity with the past, but only at the cost of replacing it.

The second and equally interesting approach to discussing hypertextual narrative involves deducing its qualities from the defining characteristics of hypertext — its non- or multilinearity, its multivocality, and its inevitable blending of media and modes, particularly its tendency to marry the visual and the verbal. Most who have speculated on the relation between hypertextuality and fiction concentrate, however, upon the effects it will have upon linear narrative. In order to comprehend the combined promise and peril with which hypertextuality confronts narrative, we should first recall that narratology generally urges that narration is intrinsically linear and also that such linearity plays a central role in all thought.[2] As Barbara Herrnstein Smith argues, "there are very few instances in which we can sustain the notion of a set and sequence of events altogether prior to and independent of the discourse through which they are narrated."[3]

Hayden White states only a particularly emphatic version of a common assumption when he asserts that "to raise the question of the nature of narrative is to invite reflection on the very nature of culture and, possibly, even on the nature of humanity itself. . . . Far from being one code among many that a culture may utilize for endowing experience with meaning, narrative is a metacode, a human universal on the basis of which transcultural messages about the nature of a shared reality can be transmitted."[4] What kind of a culture would have or could have hypertextual narration, which so emphasizes non- or multilinearity, and what happens to a culture that chooses such narration, when, as Jean-François Lyotard claims, in agreement with many other writers on the subject, "narration is the quintessential form of customary knowledge" (*Postmodern Condition*, 18)? Lyotard's own definition of postmodernism as "incredulity toward metanarratives" (xxiv) suggests one answer: any author and any culture that chooses hypertextual fiction will either already have rejected the solace and reassurance of linear narrative or will soon find their attachment to it loosening. Lyotard claims that "lamenting the 'loss of meaning' in postmodernity boils down to mourning the fact that knowledge is no longer principally narrative" (26), and for this loss of faith in narrative he offers several possible technological and political explanations, the most important of which is that science, which "has always been in conflict with narratives," uses other means "to legitimate the rules of its own game" (xiii).[5]

Even without raising such broader or more fundamental issues about the relation of narrative to culture, one realizes that hypertext opens major questions about story and plot by apparently doing away with linear organization. Conventional definitions and descriptions of plot suggest some of them. Aristotle long ago pointed out that successful plots require a "probable or necessary sequence of events" (*Poetics*, 1465). This observation occurs in the midst of his discussion of *peripeteia* (or in Bywater's translation, *peripety*); and in the immediately preceding discussion of episodic plots, which Aristotle considers "the worst," he explains that he calls "a Plot episodic when there is neither probability nor necessity in the sequence of its episodes" (1464).

One answer to Aristotle lies in the fact that removing a single "probable or necessary sequence of events" does not do away with all linearity. Linearity, however, now becomes a quality of the individual reader's experience within a single lexia and his or her experience of following a particular path, even if that path curves back upon itself or heads in strange directions. Robert Coover claims that with hypertext "the linearity of the reading experience" does not disappear entirely, "but narrative bytes no longer follow one another in an ineluctable page-turning chain. Hypertextual story space is now multidimensional and theoretically infinite, with an equally infinite set of possible network linkages, either programmed, fixed or variable, or random, or both."[6] Coover, inspired by the notion of the active hypertext reader, envisions some of the ways the reader can contribute to the story. At the most basic level of the hypertext encounter, "the reader may now choose the route in the labyrinth she or he wishes to take, following some particular character, for example, or an image, an action, and so on." Coover adds that readers can become reader-authors not only by choosing their paths through the text but also by reading more actively, by which he means they "may even interfere with the story, introduce new elements, new narrative strategies, open new paths, interact with characters, even with the author. Or authors." Although some authors and audiences might find themselves chilled by such destabilizing, potentially chaotic-seeming narrative worlds, Coover, a freer spirit, mentions "the allure of the blank spaces of these fabulous networks, these green-limned gardens of multiply forking paths, to narrative artists" who have the opportunity to "replace logic with character or metaphor, say, scholarship with collage and verbal wit, and turn the story loose in a space where whatever is possible is necessary."

Doing away with a fixed linear text, therefore, neither necessarily does away with all linearity nor removes formal coherence, though it may appear in new and unexpected forms. Bolter points out that

in this shifting electronic space, writers will need a new concept of structure. In place of a closed and unitary structure, they must learn to conceive of their text as a structure of possible structures. The writer must practice a kind of second-order writing, creating coherent lines for the reader to discover without closing off the possibilities prematurely or arbitrarily. This writing of the second order will be the special contribution of the electronic medium to the history of literature. (*Writing Space*, 144)

William Dickey, a poet who works with hypertext, similarly suggests that authors can pattern their hypertexts by creating links that offer several sets of distinct reading paths: "The poem may be designed in a pattern of nested squares, as a group of chained circles, as a braid of different visual and graphic themes, as a double helix. The poem may present a single main sequence from which word or image associations lead into subsequences and then return."[7] Hypertext systems that employ single directional as opposed to bidirectional linking make this kind of organization easier, of course, but fuller and freer forms of the medium also make such quasi-musical organization possible and even inevitable. The main requirement, as Paul Ricoeur suggests, becomes "this 'followability' of a story," and followability provides a principle that permits many options, many permutations.[8]

Another possible form of hypertextual literary organization involves parataxis, which is produced by repetition rather than sequence. Barbara Herrnstein Smith explains that in literary works that employ logical or temporal organization, "the dislocation or omission of any element will tend to make the sequence as a whole incomprehensible, or will radically change its effect. In paratactic structure, however (where the principle of generation does not cause any one element to 'follow' from another), thematic units can be added, omitted, or exchanged without destroying the coherence or effect of the poem's thematic structure." According to Smith, " 'variations on a theme' is one of the two most obvious forms that paratactic structure may take. The other one is the 'list.' " The main problem with which parataxis, like hypertext, confronts narrative is that any "generating principle that produces a paratactic structure cannot in itself determine a concluding point."[9]

Even if nonlinear hypertext fiction and poetry offer forms of organization that in some way parallel those of printed texts, a related, potentially crucial problem remains. Since some narratologists claim that morality ultimately depends upon the unity and coherence of a fixed linear text, one wonders if hypertext can convey morality in any significant form or if it is condemned to an essential triviality. White believes the unity of successful narrative to be a matter of ideology: "narrativity, certainly in factual storytelling and probably in fictional storytelling as well, is intimately related to, if not a function of, the impulse to moralize reality, that is, to identify it with the social system that is the source of any morality that we can imagine" ("Value of Narrativity," 14). Writing as a historian and historiographer, White argues that such ideological pressure appears with particular clarity in the "value attached to narrativity in the representation of real events," since that value discloses a desire to endow "real events" with a necessarily imaginary "coherence, integrity, fullness, and closure" possible only in fiction. The very "notion that sequences of real events possess the formal attributes of stories we tell about imaginary events," insists White, "could only have its origin in wishes, daydreams, reveries" (23). Does this signify or suggest that contemporary culture, at least its avante garde techno-logical phalanx, rejects such wishes, daydreams, and reveries? White's connection of plot and morality suggests several lines of inquiry. One could inquire if it is good or bad that linear narratives inevitably embody some morality or ideology, but first one should determine if rejecting linearity necessarily involves rejecting morality. After all, anyone taking seriously the fictional possibilities of hypertext wants to know if it will produce yet another form of postmodernist fiction that critics like John Gardner, Gerald Graff, and Charles Newman will attack as morally corrupt and corrupting.[10] If one wanted liberation from ideology, were such a goal possible, non-ideological storytelling might be fine. But before concluding that hypertext produced either ideology-free miracles or ideology-free horrors, one should look at the available evidence. In particular, one should examine prehypertext attempts to create nonlinear or multi-linear literary forms and evaluate the results. Not surprisingly, that is what I intend to do next.

A glance at previous experiments in avoiding the linearity of the printed text suggests that in the past authors have rejected linearity because it falsified their experience of things. Tennyson, for example, as we have already observed, created his poetry of fragments in an attempt to write with greater honesty and with greater truth about his own experience. Moreover, as several critics have pointed out, novelists at least since Laurence Sterne have sought to escape the potential confinements and falsifications of linear narrative.

One does not have to look back at the past for examples. In Robert Coover's review of *Dictionary of the Khazars*, a work by the Yugoslavian Milorad Pavic̀ that Coover describes as a hypertext novel, he asserts that "there is a tension in narrative, as in life, between the sensation of time as a linear experience, one thing fol-lowing sequentially (causally or not) upon another, and time as a patterning of interrelated experiences reflected upon as though it had a geography and could be mapped."[11] Nonlinear form, whether pleasing to readers or even practically possible, derives from attempts to be more truthful rather than from any amorality. Many contem-porary works of fiction explore this tension between linear and more spatial sensations of time that Coover describes. Graham Swift's *Waterland* (1983), for instance, questions all narrative based on sequence, and in this it agrees with other novels of its decade. Like

Penelope Lively's *Moon Tiger* (1987), another novel in the form of the autobiography of a historian, *Waterland* relates the events of a single life to the major currents of contemporary history.

Using much the same method for autobiography as for history, Swift's protagonist would agree with Lively's Claudia Hampton, whose deep suspicion of chronology and sequence explicitly derive from her experience of simultaneity. Ricoeur suggests that "the major tendency of modern theory of narrative — in historiography and the philosophy of history as well as in narratology — is to 'dechronologize' narrative," and these two novelists exemplify a successful "struggle against the linear representation of time" (*Time and Narrative*, 1:30). Thinking over the possibility of writing a history of the world, Lively's heroine rejects sequence and linear history as inauthentic and false to her experience:

The question is, shall it or shall it not be linear history? I've always thought a kaleidoscopic view might be an interesting heresy. Shake the tube and see what comes out. Chronology irritates me. There is no chronology inside my head. I am composed of a myriad Claudias who spin and mix and part like sparks of sunlight on water. The pack of cards I carry around is forever shuffled and re-shuffled; there is no sequence, everything happens at once.[12]

Like Proust's Marcel, she finds that a simple sensation brings the past back flush upon the present, making a mockery of separation and sequence. Returning to Cairo in her late sixties, Claudia finds it both changed and unchanged. "The place," she explains, "didn't look the same but it felt the same; sensations clutched and transformed me." She recounts that, standing near a modern concrete and plate-glass building, she picked a "handful of eucalyptus leaves from a branch, crushed them in my hand, smelt, and tears came to my eyes. Sixty-seven-year-old Claudia . . . crying not in grief but in wonder that nothing is ever lost, that everything can be retrieved, that a lifetime is not linear but instant." Her lesson for narratology is that "inside the head, everything happens at once" (68). Like Claudia, Swift's Tom Crick takes historical, autobiographical narratives whose essence is sequence and spreads them out or weaves them in a nonsequential way.

The difference between these quasi-hypertextual fictions and those in electronic form chiefly involves the greater freedom and power of the hypertext reader. Swift decides when Tom Crick's

narrative branches and Lively decides when Claudia Hampton's does,
but in Stuart Moulthrop's hypertext version of Borges's "Forking
Paths" and in Michael Joyce's *Afternoon*, the reader makes this decision. Important prehypertextual narrative has, however, also required
such reader decision. One of the most famous examples of an author's
ceding power to the reader is found in "The Babysitter," in which
Robert Coover, like an author of electronic hypertext, presents the
reader with multiple possibilities, really multiple endings, with two
effects.[13] First, the reader, who takes over some of the writer's role
and function, must choose which possibility, if any, to accept, and
second, by encountering that need to decide, readers realize both
that no true single narrative exists as the main or "right" one and that
reading traditional narrative has brainwashed them into expecting
and demanding a single right answer and a single correct story line.
Coover's story not only makes a fundamentally moral point about
the nature of fiction but also places more responsibility upon the
reader. One may say of Coover's text, in other words, what Bolter
says of Joyce's interactive hypertext, that "there is no single story of
which each reading is a version, because each reading determines
the story as it goes. We could say that there is no story at all; there
are only readings" (*Writing Space*, 124).

■ ■ ■ ■ ■ ■ ■ ■

Narrative Beginnings

and Endings

As we have already observed in chapter 2, the
problems that hypertext branching creates for narrativity appear with particular clarity in the matter
of beginning and ending stories. If, as Edward
Said claims, "a 'beginning' is designated in order
to indicate, clarify, or define a *later* time, place,
or action" (*Beginnings*, 5), how can hypertext fic-
tion begin or be said to begin? Furthermore, if as Said also convincingly argues, "when we point to the beginning of a novel . . . we mean
that from *that* beginning in principle follows *this* novel" (5), how can
we determine what novel follows from the beginnings each reader
chooses?

Thus far, most of the hypertext fictions I have read or heard
described, like many collections of educational materials, take an
essentially cautious approach to the problems of beginnings by offering the reader a lexia labeled something like "start here" that combines
the functions of title page, introduction, and opening paragraph (fig-

ure 8). They do so for several technological, rhetorical, and other reasons. Most authors writing with HyperCard, Guide, and Storyspace do not use these environments on networks that can distribute one's texts to other reading sites. To disseminate one's writings, the author must therefore copy it from one's own machine to a floppy disk and then give that disk to someone with another computer. This use of non-networked (or stand-alone) machines encourages writers to produce stories or poems that are both self-contained and small enough to fit on a single disk. In addition, since some of these early hypertextual environments do not give the reader the power to add links, authors in them necessarily tend to consider their works to be self-contained in a traditional manner. Another reason for using the "start here" approach appears in some writers' obvious reluctance to disorient readers upon their initial contact with a narrative, and some writers also believe that hypertextual fiction should necessarily change our experience of the middle but not the beginnings of narrative fiction.

In contrast, William Dickey, who has written hypertext poetry using Apple's HyperCard, finds it a good or useful quality of hypertext poetry that it "may begin with any one of its parts, stanzas, images, to which any other part of the poem may succeed. This system of organization requires that that part of the poem represented on any one card must be a sufficiently independent statement to be able to generate a sense of poetic meaning as it follows or is followed by any other statement the poem contains."[14] Dickey, who is writing about poetic rather than fictional structure, nonetheless offers organizational principles that apply to both.

Beginnings imply endings, and endings require some sort of formal and thematic closure. Ricoeur, using the image of "following" that is conventionally applied to narratives and that writers about hypertext also use to describe activating links, explains that "to follow a story is to move forward in the midst of contingencies and peripeteia under the guidance of an expectation that finds its fulfilment in the 'conclusion' of the story." This conclusion "gives the story an 'end point,' which, in turn, furnishes the point of view from which the story can be perceived as forming a whole." In other words, to understand a story requires first comprehending "how and why the successive episodes led to this conclusion, which, far from being foreseeable, must finally be acceptable, as congruent with the episodes brought together by the story" (*Time and Narrative*, 1:66–67).

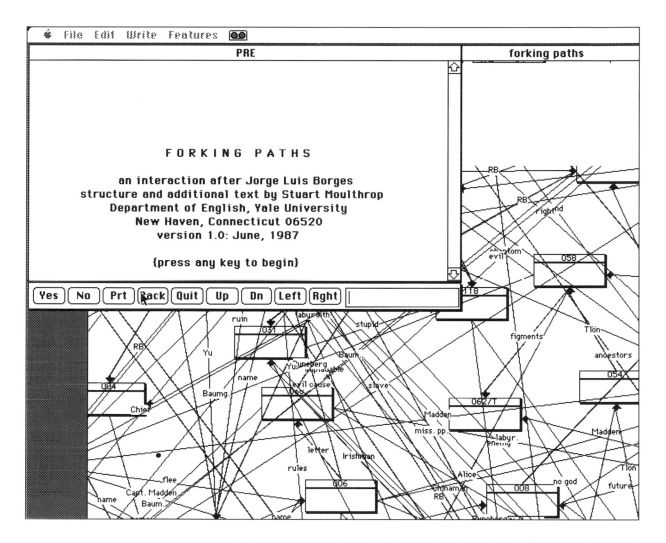

Figure 8. Entrance to a hypertextual fiction. The first text window of Stuart Moulthrop's electronic version of Borges's "Forking Paths" resembles the title page of a printed book. At the bottom of the text window appear two buttons ("Yes," "No") that permit the reader to respond to queries in the text and others ("Back," "Up," "Dn," "Left," and "Rght") that allow the reader to change directions in the work's hyperspace. Additional buttons provide a means of printing individual screens and of exiting the hypertext environment. A dialogue box at the right of the buttons offers yet another means of navigating hypertext fiction: entering one or more words prompts the system to open a lexia in which the word or phrase occurs. Storyspace's version of a global map appears beneath the text window.

In her classic study of how poems produce satisfying endings, Smith provides evidence that might prompt students of hypertext to conclude that it either creates fundamental problems in narrative and other kinds of literary texts or opens them to entirely new forms of textuality. She explains that since "a poem cannot continue indefinitely" (*Poetic Closure*, 33), it must employ devices that prepare the reader for ending rather than continuing. These devices produce in the reader "the sense of stable conclusiveness, finality, or 'clinch' . . . referred to here as *closure*. . . . Whether spatially or temporally perceived, a structure appears 'closed' when it is experienced as integral: coherent, complete, and stable" (*Poetic Closure*, 2) — qualities that produce a "sense of ultimate composure we apparently value in our experience of a work of art" and that we label "stability, resolution, or equilibrium" (34). Unlike texts in manuscript or print, those in hypertext apparently *can* continue indefinitely, perhaps infinitely, so one wonders if they can provide satisfying closure.[15] Or, to direct this inquiry in ways suggested by Smith's analysis of closure, one should ask what techniques might provide something analogous to that desirable "sense of stable conclusiveness, finality, or 'clinch.' "

Taking another clue from fiction created for print publication, one perceives that many prehypertext narratives provide instances of multiple closure and also a combination of closure with new beginnings. Both Charles Dickens's novels, written specifically for publication in periodicals at monthly intervals, and those by other nineteenth-century novelists intended for first publication in the conventional triple-decker form make use of partial closure followed by continuation. Furthermore, Trollope's Palliser series, Lawrence Durrell's *Alexandria Quartet*, Faulkner's works, and countless trilogies and tetralogies in both fantastic and realistic modes suggest that writers of fiction have long encountered problems very similar to those faced by writers of hypertext fiction and have developed an array of formal and thematic solutions to them. In fact, the tendency of many a twentieth-century work to leave its readers with little sense of closure — either because they do not learn of the "final" outcome of a particular narrative or because they leave the story before any outcome occurs — shows us that as readers and writers we have long learned to live (and read) with more open-endedness than discussions of narrative form might lead us to expect.

Michael Joyce's *Afternoon*:

The Reader's Experience

as Author

■ ■ ■ ■ ■ ■ ■ Michael Joyce, a hypertext author, is suspicious of closure. In Joyce's *Afternoon*, a hypertext fiction in 538 lexias, the section appropriately entitled "work in progress" advises readers: "Closure is, as in any fiction, a suspect quality, although here it is made manifest. When the story no longer progresses, or when it cycles, or when you tire of the paths, the experience of reading it ends." In other words, Joyce makes the responsibility for closure, for stopping, entirely the reader's. When the reader has had enough and decides to stop reading, why then the story is over. Joyce continues, however: "Even so, there are likely to be more opportunities than you think there are at first. A word which doesn't yield the first time you read a section may take you elsewhere if you choose it when you encounter the section again; and what sometimes seems a loop, like memory, heads off in another direction." Reading the highly allusive *Afternoon*, which has so many points of departure within each lexia as well as continually changing points of linkage, one sees what Joyce means.

The successive lexias one encounters seem to take form as chains of narrative, and despite the fact that one shifts setting and narrator, one's choices produce satisfying narrative sets. Moving from section to section, every so often one encounters puzzling changes of setting, narrator, subject, or chronology, but two things occur. After reading awhile one begins to construct narrative placements, so that one assigns particular sections to a provisionally suitable place — some lexias obviously have several alternate or rival forms of relation. Then, having assigned particular sections to particular sequences or reading paths, many, though not all, of which one can retrace at will, one reaches points at which one's initial cognitive dissonance or puzzlement disappears, and one seems satisfied. One has reached — or created — closure!

One might describe Joyce's hypertext fiction in the way Gérard Genette describes "what one calls Stendhal's *oeuvre*":

a fragmented, elliptical, repetitive, yet infinite, or at least indefinite, text, no part of which, however, may be separated from the whole. Whoever pulls a single thread must take the whole cloth, with its holes and lack of edges. To read Stendhal is to read the whole of Stendhal, but to read all of Stendhal is impossible, for the very good reason, among others, that the whole of Stendhal has not yet been published or deciphered, or discovered, or even written: I repeat, all the Stendhalian *text,* because the gaps, the interruptions of the text are not mere absences, a pure non-text: they are a lack, active and perceptible as lack, as non-writing, as non-written text.[16]

Genette, I suggest, describes the way a reader encounters the web of Joyce's hypertextual narrative. Even entering at a single point determined by the author, the reader chooses one path or another and calls up another lexia by a variety of means, and then repeats this process until he or she finds a hole or a gap. Perhaps at this point the reader turns back and takes another direction. One might just as well write something oneself or make present a remembered passage by another author in the manner that a book reader might begin a poem by Stevens, think of some parallel verses by Swinburne or a passage in a book by Helen Vendler or Harold Bloom, pull that volume off its shelf, find the passage, and then return to the poem by Stevens.

Whereas Genette's characterization of the Stendhalian *oeuvre* captures the reader's experience of the interconnectedness of *Afternoon* and other hypertext fictions, his description of temporality in Proust conveys the experience of encountering the disjunctions and jumps of hypertextual narrative. Citing George Poulet's observation that in *A la Recherche de temps perdu* time does not appear as Bergsonian duration but as a "succession of isolated moments," he points out that similarly "characters (and groups) do not evolve: one fine day, they find that they have changed, as if time confined itself to bringing forth a plurality that they contained *in potentia* from all eternity. Indeed, many of the characters assume the most contradictory roles *simultaneously*" (216). In other words, in *A la Recherche de temps perdu* readers find themselves taking leaps and jumping into a different time and different characters. In a hypertext narrative it is the author who provides multiple possibilities, by means of which the readers themselves construct temporal succession and choose characterization — though, to be sure, readers will take leaps, as we do in life, on the basis of inadequate or even completely inaccurate information.

So many different contexts cross and interweave that one must work to place the characters encountered in them. Joyce's world, which also inevitably includes the *other* Joyce, has many moving centers of interest, including marriage and erotic relationships, sexual politics, psychotherapy, advertising, film making and the history of cinema, computing, myth, and literature of all kinds. Reading habits one has learned from print play a role in how a reader organizes these materials. If one encounters a speaker's mention of his marriage and, in a later lexia, finds him at the scene of an automobile accident from which the bodies of injured people have already been removed, one might take the accident as an event in the recent present; the emotional charge it carries serves to organize other reported thoughts and events, inevitably turning some of them into flashbacks, others into exposition. Conversely, one could take that event as something in the past, a particularly significant moment, and then use it as a point of origin either that leads to other events or whose importance endows events it has not caused with a significance created by explanation or contrast or analogy. Our assistance in the storytelling or storymaking is not entirely or even particularly random, since Joyce provides many hooks that can catch at our thoughts, but we do become reader-authors and help tell the tale we read.

Nonetheless, as J. Hillis Miller points out, we cannot help ourselves: we must create meaning as we read. "A story is readable because it can be organized as a causal chain. . . . A causal sequence is always an implicit narrative organized around the assumption that what comes later is caused by what comes before, 'post hoc, propter hoc.' If any series of random and disconnected events is presented to me, I tend to see it as a causal chain. Or rather, if Kant and Kleist are right, I *must* see it as a causal chain."[17] Miller, who silently exchanges a linear model of explanation for one more appropriate to hypertextual narrative, later adds: "We cannot avoid imposing some set of connections, like a phantasmal spiderweb, over events that just happen as they happen" (139).

Miller's idea of reading printed text, which seems to owe a great deal to gestalt psychology's theories of constructionist perception, well describes the reader-author demanded by Joyce's *Afternoon* and other works of hypertext fiction.[18] According to Miller, reading is always "a kind of writing or rewriting that is an act of prosopopoeia, like Pygmalion giving life to the statue" (186).[19] This construction of an evanescent entity or wholeness always occurs in reading, but in reading hypertext it takes the additional form of constructing, however provisionally, one's own text out of fragments, out of separate lexias. It is a case, in other words, of Lévi-Strauss's *bricolage*, for every hypertext reader-author is inevitably a *bricoleur*.

Such *bricolage*, I suggest, provides a new kind of unity, one appropriate to hypertextuality. As long as one grants that plot is a phenomenon created by the reader-author with materials the lexias offers, rather than a phenomenon belonging solely to the text, then one can accept that reading *Afternoon* and other hypertext fictions produces an experience very similar to that provided by reading the unified plot described by narratologists from Aristotle to White and Ricoeur. White, for example, defines plot as "a structure of relationships by which the events contained in the account are endowed with a meaning by being identified as parts of an integrated whole" ("Value of Narrativity," 9). Ricoeur similarly defines plot, "on the most *formal* level, as an integrating dynamism that draws a unified and complete story from a variety of incidents, in other words, that transforms this variety into a unified and complete story. This formal definition opens a field of rule-governed transformations worthy of being called plots so long as we can discern temporal wholes bringing about a synthesis of the heterogeneous between circumstances, goals, means, interactions, and intended or unintended results" (*Time and Narrative*, 2:8). According to Ricoeur, the metaphorical imagination produces narrative by a process of what he terms "predicative assimilation," which " 'grasps together' and integrates into one whole and complete story multiple and scattered events, thereby schematizing the intelligible signification attached to the narrative taken as a whole" (1:x). To this observation I would add, with Miller, that as readers we find ourselves forced to fabricate a whole or, as he puts it, integrate "into one whole and complete story multiple and scattered events, separate parts."

In his chapter on Heinrich von Kleist in *Versions of Pygmalion*, Miller provides us with an unexpectedly related model for this kind of extemporized construction of meaning-on-the-run. He quotes Kleist's claim that Mirabeau was "unsure of what he was about to say" (104) when he began his famous speech that ended "by creating the new French nation and a new parliamentary assembly" (105). The speaker posits a "syntactically incomplete fragment, says Kleist, without any idea . . . of where the sentence is going to end, [and] the thought is gradually 'fabricated' "; and Kleist claims that the speaker's feelings and the general situation in some way produce his proposals. Disagreeing with him, Miller argues in the manner of Barthes that Mirabeau's revolutionary "thought is gradually fabricated not so much by the situation or by the speaker's feelings," as Kleist suggests, "but by his need to complete the grammar and syntax of the sentence he has blindly begun" (104). Structuralists and poststructuralists have long described thinking and writing in terms of this extemporized, in-process generation of meaning, the belief in which does so much to weaken traditional conceptions of self and author. Hypertext fiction forces us to extend this description of meaning-generation to the reader's construction of narrative. It forces us to recognize that the active author-reader fabricates text and meaning from "another's" text in the same way that each speaker constructs individual sentences and entire discourses from "another's" grammar, vocabulary, and syntax.

Vladimir Propp, following Veselovsky, long ago founded the "structuralist study of plot" and with it modern narratology by applying notions of linguistic combination to the study of folk tales.[20] Miller, who draws upon this tradition, reminds us that fabricated folk tales, spoken discourses, and interpretative readings of print narratives follow an essentially similar process that entails the immediate, in-process construction of meaning and text. Miller's observations allow us to understand that one must apply the same notions to the activities of the reader of hypertext fiction. In brief, hypertext demands that one apply this structuralist understanding of speaker and writer to the reader as well, since in hypertext the reader is a reader-author. From this theory of the reader and from the experience of reading hypertext narratives I draw the following, perhaps obvious but nonetheless important, conclusions: In a hypertext environment a lack of linearity does not destroy narrative. In fact, since readers always, but particularly in this environment, fabricate their own structures, sequences, and meanings, they have surprisingly little trouble reading a story or reading for a story. Obviously, some parts of the reading experience seem very different from reading a printed novel or a short story, and reading hypertext fiction provides some of the experience of a new orality that both McLuhan and Ong have predicted. Although the reader of hypertext fiction shares some experiences, one supposes, with the audience of listeners who heard oral poetry, this active reader-author inevitably has more in common with the bard, who constructed meaning and narrative from fragments provided by someone else, by another author or by many other authors.

Like Coover, who emphasizes the inevitable connection of death and narrative, Joyce seems to intertwine the two. In part it is a matter, as Brian McHale points out, of avante garde authors using highly charged subjects (sexuality, death) to retain readers' interest that might stray within puzzling and unfamiliar narrative modes. In part it is also a matter of endings: when the reader decides to stop reading *Afternoon*, he or she ends, kills, the story, because when the active reader, the reader-author, stops reading, the story stops, it dies, it reaches an ending. As part of that cessation, that willingness to stop creating and interpreting the story, certain acts or events in the story become deaths, because they make most sense that way; and by stopping reading, the reader prevents other alternatives from coming into being.

Perhaps this readerly responsibility is what Coover refers to when he proclaims that endings will and must occur even in infinitely expandable, changeable, combinable docuverses:

There is still movement, but in hyperspace it is that of endless expansion. "A" is, or may be, an infinite multiplicity of starting points, "B" a parenthetical "B" somewhere beyond the beyond, or within the within, yet clearly mapped, clearly routed, just somewhat less definite than, oh, say, dying. Which for all the networking maneuvers and funhouse mirrors cannot be entirely ignored. Sooner or later, whatever the game, the whistle is blown. Even in hyperspace, there is disconnection. One last windowless trajectory. ("Endings")

Hypertext fictions always end because readings always end, but they can end in fatigue or in a sense of satisfying closure. Writing of the printed text, Barbara Herrnstein Smith reminds us that "the end of the play or novel will not appear as an arbitrary cut-off if it leaves us at a point where, with respect to the themes of the work, we feel that we know all there is or all there is to know" (*Poetic Closure*, 120). If individual lexias provide readers with experiences of formal and thematic closure, they can be expected to provide the satisfactions that Smith describes as requisite to the sense of an ending.

Enthusiastic as he is about the possibilities of writing in this electronic medium, Coover describes a number of "major problems facing future creators of hypertextual fictions," among which one of the most important is that " 'narrative' . . . runs the risk of being so distended and slackly driven as to lose its force of attraction, giving way to a kind of static low-charged lyricism, that dreamy, gravityless, lost-in-space feeling of the early sci-fi films." In addition to encountering the possibly "reductive nature of interactive fiction," hypertext authors also have to fear "the loss of vision in a text trod upon by anonymous others. . . ."

> On-line talent wars will occur: [there will be a] need to keep the lines clean and open. . . . Above all, perhaps, the author's freedom to take a story anywhere at any time and in as many directions as he or she wishes . . . becomes the obligation to do so: in the end it can be paralyzing. . . . One will feel the need, even while using these vast networks and principles of randomness and expansive story lines, to struggle against them, just as one now struggles against the linear constraints of the printed book. ("Endings")

Even within the vastness of hyperspace, the author, like the reader-author, will find limits, and from them construct occasions to struggle.

Reconfiguring

Literary Education

· · · · · · ·

Threats and Promises

Like many other observers of the relations between information technology and education, Jean-François Lyotard perceives that "the miniaturization and commercialization of machines is already changing the way in which learning is acquired, classified, made available, and exploited. It is reasonable to suppose that the proliferation of information-processing machines is having, and will continue to have, as much of an effect on the circulation of learning as did advancements in human circulation (transportation systems) and later, in the circulation of sounds and visual images (the media)" (*Postmodern Condition*, 4). One chief effect of electronic hypertext lies in the way it challenges now conventional assumptions about teachers, learners, and the institutions they inhabit. It changes the roles of teacher and student in much the same way it changes those of writer and reader. Its emphasis upon the active, empowered reader, which fundamentally calls into question general assumptions about reading, writing, and texts, similarly calls into question our assumptions about the literary education and its institutions that so depend upon these texts. Gary Marchionini, who created evaluation procedures for Project Perseus, reminds us that "each time a new technology is applied to teaching and learning, questions about fundamental principles and methods arise."[1] Hypertext, by holding out the possibility of newly empowered, self-directed students, demands that we confront an entire range of questions about our conceptions of literary education.

As a means of examining this enormous range of issues, I propose first to examine the educational message in hypertext conceived as an educational medium, after which I shall discuss some of the specific effects of hypertext upon instructors, students, and literary education. Having examined these more general issues, I shall look at instances of collaborative work, thereby returning to matters broached in the third chapter. Finally, after considering the effect of hypertext on canon and curriculum, I shall consider what chance hypertext has to fulfill its educational potential.

Hypertext systems promise — or threaten — to have major effects on literary education, and the nature of hypertext's potential effect on human thought appears in descriptions of it from its earliest days. Writing of Bush, Englebart, Nelson, and other pioneers of hypertext, John L. Leggett and members of his team at the Hypermedia Lab at the University of Texas point out that "the revolutionary content of their ideas was, and continues to be, the extent to which these systems engage the user as an active participant in interactions with information."[2] Students making use of hypertext systems participate actively in two related ways: they act as reader-authors both by choosing individual paths through linked primary and secondary texts and by adding texts and links to the docuverse.[3] The ways in which hypertext produces an active student make writers on the medium, like David H. Jonassen and R. Scott Grabinger, urge that "hypermedia learning systems will place more responsibility on the learner for accessing, sequencing and deriving meaning from the information." Unlike users of "most information systems, hypermedia users *must* be mentally active while interacting with the information."[4]

From this emphasis upon the active reader follows a conception of an active, constructivist learner and an assumption that, in the words of Philippe C. Duchastel, "hypermedia systems should be viewed not principally as teaching tools, but rather as learning tools."[5] As Terry Mayes, Mike Kibby, and Tony Anderson from the Edinburgh Centre for the Study of Human-Computer Interaction urge, systems of computer-assisted learning "based on hypertext are rightly called *learning systems*, rather than *teaching systems*. Nevertheless, they do embody a theory of, or at least an approach to, instruction. They provide an environment in which *exploratory* or *discovery* learning may flourish. By requiring learners to move towards nonlineal thinking, they may also stimulate processes of integration and contextualization in a way not achievable by linear presentation techniques."[6] Mays and his collaborators therefore claim:

> At the heart of understanding interactive learning systems is the question of how deliberate, explicit learning differs from implicit, incidental learning. Explicit learning involves the conscious evaluation of hypotheses and the application of rules. Implicit learning is more mysterious: it seems almost like a process of osmosis and becomes increasingly important as tasks or material to be mastered becomes more complex. Much of the learning that occurs with computer systems seems implicit. (228)

Rand J. Spiro, working with different teams of collaborators, has developed one of the most convincing paradigms yet offered for educational hypertext and the kind of learning it attempts to support. Drawing upon Ludwig Wittgenstein's *Philosophical Investigations*, Spiro and his collaborators propose that the best way to approach complex educational problems — what he terms "ill-structured knowledge domains" — is to approach them as if they were unknown landscapes: "The best way to [come to] understand a given landscape is to explore it from many directions, to traverse it first this way and then that (preferably with a guide to highlight significant features). Our instructional system for presenting complexly ill-structured 'topical landscape' is analogous to physical landscape exploration, with different routes of traversing study-sites (cases) that are each analyzed from a number of thematic perspectives."[7] Concerned with developing efficient methods of nurturing the diagnostic skills of medical students, Spiro's team of researchers involve themselves in knowledge domains that present problems similar to those found in the humanistic disciplines. Like individual literary texts, patients offer the physician ambiguous complexes of signs whose interpretation demands the ability to handle diachronic and synchronic approaches. Young medical doctors, who must learn how to "take a history," confront symptoms that often point to multiple possibilities. They must therefore learn how to relate particular symptoms to a variety of different conditions and diseases. Since patients may suffer from a combination of several conditions at once, say, asthma, gall bladder trouble, and high blood pressure, physicians have to learn how to connect a single symptom to more than one explanatory system.

Spiro's explanation of his exploration-of-landscape paradigm provides an excellent description of educational hypertext:

The notion of "criss-crossing" from case to case in many directions, with many thematic dimensions serving as routes of traversal, is central to our theory. The treatment of an irregular and complex topic *cannot be forced in any single direction* without curtailing the potential for transfer. If the topic can be applied in many different ways, none of which follow in rule-bound manner from the others, then limiting oneself in acquisition to, say, a single point of view or a single system of classification, will produce a relatively *closed* system instead of one that is open to context-dependent variability. By criss-crossing the complex topical landscape, the twin goals of highlighting multifacetedness and establishing multiple connections are attained. Also, awareness of variability and irregularity is heightened, alternative routes of traversal of the topic's complexities are illustrated, multiple entry routes for later information retrieval are established, and the general skill of working around that particular landscape (domain-dependent processing skill) is developed. *Information that will need to be used in a lot of different ways needs to be taught in lots of different ways.* (187–88; emphasis in original)

In such complex domains, "single (or even small numbers of) connecting threads" do not run "continuously through large numbers of successive cases." Instead, they are joined by " 'woven' interconnectedness. In this view, strength of connection derives from the partial overlapping of many different strands of connectedness across cases rather than from any single strand running through large numbers of the cases" (193).

▪ ▪ ▪ ▪ ▪ ▪ ▪ Educational hypertext redefines the role of instructors by transferring some of their power and authority to students. This technology has the potential to make the teacher more a coach than a lecturer, and more an older, more experienced

Reconfiguring the Instructor

partner in a collaboration than an authenticated leader. Needless to say, not all my colleagues respond to such possibilities with cries of glee and hymns of joy.

Before some of my readers pack their bags for the trip to Utopia and others decide that educational computing is just as dangerous as they thought all along, I must point out that hypertext systems have a great deal to offer instructors in all kinds of institutions of higher education. To begin with, a hypermedia corpus of multidisciplinary materials provides a far more efficient means of developing, preserving, and obtaining access to course materials than has existed before. One of the greatest problems in course development lies in the fact that it takes such a long time and that the materials developed, however pioneering or brilliant, rarely transfer to another teacher's course, because they rarely match that other teacher's needs exactly. Similarly, teachers often expend time and energy developing materials potentially useful in more than one course that they teach but do not use the materials because the time necessary for adaptation is lacking. These two problems, which all teachers face, derive from the classic, fundamental problem with hierarchical data structures that was Vannevar Bush's point of departure when he proposed the memex. A hypertext corpus, which is a descendent of the memex, allows a more efficient means of preserving the products of past endeavors because it requires so much less effort to select and reorganize them. It also encourages integrating all one's teaching, so that one's efforts function synergistically. A hypermedia corpus preserves and makes easily available one's past efforts as well as those of others.

Hypertext also obviously provides us with a far more convenient and efficient means than has previously existed of teaching courses in a single discipline that need the support of other disciplines. As I discovered in my encounter with the nuclear arms materials, which I discussed in chapter 3, this educational technology permits teachers to teach in the virtual presence of other teachers and other subsections of their own discipline or other closely related disciplines. Thus, someone teaching a plant-cell biology course can draw upon the materials created by courses in very closely related fields, such as animal-cell biology, as well as slightly more distant ones, such as chemistry and biochemistry. Similarly, someone teaching an English course that concentrates on literary technique in the nineteenth-century novel can nonetheless draw upon relevant materials in political, social, urban, technological, and religious history. All of us try to allude to such aspects of context, but the limitations of time and the need to cover the central concerns of the course often leave students with a decontextualized, distorted view.

Inevitably, hypertext gives us a far more efficient means than has previously existed of teaching interdisciplinary courses, of doing, that is, what almost by definition "shouldn't be done." (When most departmental and university administrators are not applying for funding from external agencies, they use the term *interdisciplinary* to mean little more than "that which should not be done" or "that for which there is no money." After all, putting together biology and chemistry to study the chemistry of organisms is not interdisciplinary; it is the subject of a separate discipline called biochemistry.) Interdisciplinary teaching no longer has its earlier glamor for several reasons. First, some have found that the need to deal with several disciplines has meant that some or all end up being treated superficially or only from the point of view of another discipline. Second, such teaching requires faculty and administration to make often extraordinarily heavy commitments, particularly when such courses involve teams of two or more instructors. Then, when members of the original team take a leave or cover an essential course for their department, the interdisciplinary course comes to a halt. In contrast to previous educational technology, hypertext offers instructors the continual virtual presence of teachers from other disciplines.

All the qualities of connectivity, preservation, and accessibility that make hypertext an enormously valuable teaching resource make it equally valuable as a scholarly tool. The medium's integrative quality, when combined with its ease of use, offers a means of efficiently integrating one's scholarly work and work-in-progress with one's teaching. In particular, one can link portions of data upon which one is working, whether they take the form of primary texts, statistics, chemical analyses, or visual materials, and integrate these into courses. Such methods, which we have already tested in undergraduate and graduate courses at Brown, allow faculty to explore their own primary interests while showing students how a particular discipline arrives at the materials, the "truths of the discipline," it presents to students as worthy of their knowledge. Materials on anti-Catholicism and anti-Irish prejudice in Victorian Britain created by Anthony S. Wohl, like some of my recently published work on Graham Swift and sections of this book, represent such integration of the instructor's scholarship and teaching. Such use of one's own work for teaching, which one can use to emphasize the more problematic aspects of a field, accustoms students to the notion that for the researcher and theorist many key problems and ideas remain in flux.

Hypermedia linking, which integrates scholarship and teaching and one discipline with others, also permits the faculty member to introduce beginners to the way advanced students in a field think and work while it gives beginners access to materials at a variety of levels of difficulty. Such materials, which the instructor can easily make available to all or only to advanced students, again permit a more efficient means than do textbooks of introducing students to the actual work of a discipline, which is often characterized by competing schools of thought. Because hypertext interlinks and interweaves a variety of materials at differing levels of difficulty and expertise, it encourages both exploration and self-paced instruction. The presence of such materials permits faculty members to accommodate the slower as well as the faster, or more committed, learners in the same class.

■ ■ ■ ■ ■ ■ ■ ■

Reconfiguring the Student

For students hypertext promises new, increasingly reader-centered encounters with text. In the first place, experiencing a text as part of a network of navigable relations provides a means of gaining quick and easy access to a far wider range of background and contextual materials than has ever been possible with conventional educational technology. Students in schools with adequate libraries have always had the materials available, but availability and accessibility are not the same thing. Until students know how to formulate questions, particularly about the relation of primary materials to other phenomena, they are unlikely to perceive a need to investigate context, much less know how to go about using library resources to do so.

Even more important than having a means of acquiring factual material is having a means of learning what to do with such material when one has it in hand. Critical thinking relies upon relating many things to one another. Since the essence of hypertext lies in its making connections, it provides an efficient means of accustoming students to making connections among materials they encounter. A major component of critical thinking consists in the habit of seeking the way various causes impinge upon a single phenomenon or event and then evaluating their relative importance, and hypertext encourages this habit.

Hypertext also offers a means for a novice reader to learn the habit of nonsequential reading necessary for both student anthologies and scholarly apparatuses. Hypertext, which has been defined as text designed to be read nonsequentially or in a nonlinear mode, efficiently models the kind of text characteristic of scholarly and scientific writing. These forms of writing require readers to leave the main text and venture out to consider footnotes, evidence of statistics and other authorities, and the like. Our experience at Brown University suggests that using hypertext teaches students to read in this advanced manner. This effect upon reading, which first appears in students' better use of anthologies and standard textbooks, exemplifies the way that hypertext and appropriate materials used together can quickly get students up to speed.

In addition, a corpus of hypertext documents intrinsically joins materials students encounter in separate parts of a single course and in other courses and disciplines. Hypertext, in other words, provides a means of integrating the subject materials of a single course with other courses. Students, particularly novice students, continually encounter problems created by necessary academic specialization and separation of single disciplines into individual courses. In the course of arguing for the historic contextualization of literary works, Brook Thomas describes this all too familiar problem:

The notion of a piece of literature as an organic, autonomous whole that combats the fragmentation of the modern world can easily lead to teaching practices that contribute to the fragmentation our students experience in their lives; a fragmentation confirmed in their educational experience. At the same time sophomores take a general studies literature course, they might also take economics, biology, math, and accounting. There is nothing, not even the literature course, that connects the knowledge they gain from these different courses. . . . Furthermore, because each work students read in a literature course is an organic whole that stands on its own, there is really no reason why they should relate one work to another taught in the same course. As they read one work, then another, then another, each separate and unique, each reading can too easily contribute to their sense of education as a set of fragmented, unrelated experiences in which wholeness and unity are to be found only in temporary, self-enclosed moments.[8]

Experience of teaching with hypertext demonstrates that its intrinsic capacity to join varying materials creates a learning environment in which materials supporting separate courses exist in closer relationship to one another than is possible with conventional educational technology. As students read through materials for one English course, they encounter those supporting others and thereby perceive relationships among courses and disciplines.

Hypertext also offers a means of experiencing the way a subject expert makes connections and formulates inquiries. One of the great strengths of hypertext lies in its capacity to use linking to model the kinds of connections that experts in a particular field make. By exploring such links, students benefit from the experience of experts in a field without being confined by them, as students would be in a work-book or book approach.

Hypertext thus provides novices with means of quickly and easily learning the culture of a discipline. From the fact that hypertext materials provide the student with a means of experiencing the way an expert works in an individual discipline it follows that such a body of electronically linked material also provides the student with an efficient means of learning the vocabulary, strategies, and other aspects of a discipline that constitute its particular culture.

The capacity of hypertext to inculcate the novice with the culture of a specific discipline and subject suggests that this new information medium has an almost totalitarian capacity to model encounters with texts. The intrinsically antihierarchical nature of hypertext, however, undercuts such possibilities and makes it a means of efficiently adapting the materials to individual needs. A body of hypertext materials functions as a customized electronic library that makes available materials as they are needed and not, as lectures and other forms of scheduled presentation of necessity must often do, just when the schedule permits.

The infinitely adaptable nature of hypertext also provides students a way of working up to their abilities by providing access to sophisticated, advanced materials. Considered as an educational medium, hypertext also permits the student to encounter a range of materials that vary in terms of difficulty, because authors no longer have to pitch their materials to single levels of expertise and difficulty. Students, even novice students, who wish to explore individual topics in more depth therefore have the opportunity of following their curiosity and inclination as far as they wish. At the same time, more advanced students always have available more basic materials for easy review when necessary.

The reader-centered, reader-controlled characteristics of hypertext also mean that it offers student-readers means of shaping and hence controlling major portions of what they read. Since readers shape what they read according to their own needs, they explore at their own rate and according to their own interests. In addition, the ease of using hypertext means that any student can contribute documents and links to the system. Students can thus experience the way contributions in various fields are made.

Finally, hypertext produces an additional form of discussion and a new means of contributing to class discussions that assist many students. Jolene Galegher and Robert Kraut, like most students of cooperative work, point out that "one of the failures of group discussion is the social influence that inhibits the quantity of original ideas that the members would have generated had they been working in isolation." In this context, hypermedia exemplifies those "permissive technologies" that "allow current practices to be extended into new realms in which they had previously been impracticable."[9] This feature of hypertext doubly permits students to contribute to the activity of a class: they can contribute materials in writing if they find group discussions difficult, and other students can cite and discuss their hypertext contributions. By giving an additional means of expression to those people shy or hesitant about speaking up in a group, hypertext, electronic conferencing, and other similar media shift the balance of exchange from speaking to writing, thus addressing Derrida's calls to avoid phonocentricism in that eccentric, unexpected, very literal manner that, as we have seen before, characterizes such hypertext instantiations of theory.

Nontraditional Students

The combination of the reader's control and the virtual presence of a large number of authors makes an efficient means of learning at a distance. The very qualities that make hypertext an efficient means of supporting interdisciplinary learning also permit students to work without having to be in residence at a geographical or spatial site. In other words, the adaptable virtual presence of hypermedia contributors serves both the distant, unconventional learner and the college student in a more conventional setting. For those interested in the efficient and just distribution of costly educational resources, hypertext offers students at one institution a way to share the resources of another. Hypermedia provides an efficient means for students anywhere potentially to benefit from materials created at any participating institution.

The very strengths of hypertext that make it work so well in conventional educational settings also make it the perfect means of informing, assisting, and inspiring the unconventional student. Because it enables students to choose their own reading paths with far more freedom than do such quasi-hypertext systems as those based on HyperCard, hypertext provides the individualistic learner with the perfect means for exploration and enrichment of particular areas of study. By permitting one to move from relatively familiar areas to less familiar ones, a hypertext corpus encourages the autodidact, the continuing education student, and the student with little access to instructors to get into the habit of making precisely those kinds of connections that constitute such an important part of the liberally educated mind that is so necessary in government and business. At the same time, the manner in which hypertext places the geographically distant learner in the virtual presence of many instructors both disperses, in a particularly effective manner, the resources they have created and allows the individual access to some of the major benefits of an institutional affiliation with little cost to either party in time and money.

■ ■ ■ ■ ■ ■ ■ Two of the most exciting and objectively verifiable effects of using educational hypertext systems

Reconfiguring involve the way they change the limiting effects of time. The modularization that John G. Blair has

the Time of Learning described as characteristic of American (as opposed to European) higher education appears in the concepts of credit hours, implicitly equivalent courses, and transcripts.[10] It also appears, one may add, in the precise, necessarily rigid scheduling of the syllabus for the individual course, which embodies what Joseph E. McGrath describes as a naively atomistic Newtonian conception of time:

Two of the assumptions of the Newtonian conception of time, which dominates our culture and organizations within it, are (a) an atomistic assumption that time is infinitely divisible, and (b) a homogeneity assumption that all the "atoms" of time are homogeneous, that any one moment is indistinguishable from and interchangeable with any other. But these assumptions do not hold in our experience. . . . Ten 1-minute work periods, scattered throughout the day, are not of equivalent productivity value to one 10-minute period of work from 9:15 to 9:25 a.m. Nor is the day before Christmas equivalent to February 17th for most retailers. A piece of time derives its epochal meaning, and its temporal value, partly in terms of what activities can (or must) be done in it.[11]

The division — segregation, really — of individual weeks into isolated units to which we have all become accustomed has the unfortunate effect of habituating students to consider in isolation the texts and topics encountered during these units. The unfortunate effects of pre-

cise scheduling, which coverage requires, became apparent to me
only after teaching with hypertext. Here, as in other cases, one of the
chief values of teaching with a hypertext system has proved to be
light it unexpectedly has cast on otherwise unexamined conventional
assumptions about education.

Here are several examples reported by the ethnographical team
that devoted three years to studying the effects of using hypermedia in
teaching.[12] The first example comes from the experience of Peter
Heywood, associate professor of biology, who used an Intermedia
component in his upper-class course in plant-cell biology. The term
paper for his course, which is intended to be a means of introducing
students both to the literature of the field and to the way it is written,
requires that students include all materials on their particular topic
that have seen publication up to the week before papers are handed in.
This demanding assignment had required that Heywood devote a
great deal of time to assisting individual students with their papers and
their bibliographies, and one of the chief attractions of the Intermedia
component to him lay in its potential to make such information more
accessible. Using hypermedia produced a completely unexpected
effect that greatly surprised Heywood. In the previous seventeen years
that he had taught this course, he had observed that many term
papers came in after the deadline, some long after, and that virtually
all papers concerned topics covered in the first three weeks of the
course. The first year that students used the Intermedia component,
all thirty-four papers came in on time. Moreover, their topics were
equally distributed throughout the fourteen weeks of the semester.
Heywood explains this dramatic improvement in student performance
as a result of the way hypertext linking permits students to perceive
connections among materials covered at different times during the
semester. Although all other components of the course remained the
same, the capabilities of hypermedia permitted students to follow
links to topics covered later in the course and thereby encounter
attractive problems for independent work. For example, while reading
Intermedia materials about the cell membrane in the first weeks of
the course, students could follow links that brought them to related
materials not covered until week eight, when the course examined
genetics, or until the last weeks of the course, when it concerned eco-
logical questions or matters of bioengineering. Many who enrolled
in this upper-division course had already taken advanced courses

in genetics, biochemistry, or similarly related subjects. From the very beginning of the semester, linking permitted these students to integrate materials encountered in this course with those previously encountered in other courses.

Educational hypertext in this way serves as what McGrath describes as one of those "technological tools . . . designed in part to ease the constraints of the time/activity match in relation to communication in groups. For example, certain forms of computer conference arrangements permit so-called asynchronous communication among group members" ("Time Matters," 39). As the example from Heywood's course shows, hypertext systems also support this "asynchronous communication" between students and chronologically ordered modular components of the course.

The way that hypertext thus frees learners from constraints of scheduling without destroying the structure and coherence of a course appears in more impressionistic observations reported by members of both biology and English courses. One of Heywood's students described working with hypertext as providing something like the experience of studying for a final examination every week, by which, he explained, he meant that each week, as students encountered a new topic, they discovered they were rearranging and reintegrating the materials they had previously learned, an experience that previously they had encountered only during preparations for major examinations. English students similarly contrasted their integrative experience of course readings with those of acquaintances in sections of the survey course that did not use Intermedia. The English students, for example, expressed surprise that whereas they placed each new poem or novel within the context of those read previously as a matter of course — considering, say, the relation of *Great Expectations* to "Tintern Abbey" and "The Vanity of Human Wishes" as well as to *Pride and Prejudice* and *Gulliver's Travels* — their friends in other sections assumed that, once a week was over, one should set aside the reading for that week until the final exam. In fact, students in other sections apparently expressed surprise that my students wanted to make all these connections.

A second form of asynchronous communication involves the creation by hypertext of a course memory that reaches beyond a single semester. Galegher and Kraut propose that "technologies that allow users to observe each others' contributions (such as computer conferences and hypermedia systems) may provide a system for sustaining group memory independent of the presence of specific individuals in an organization" (*Intellectual Teamwork*, 15). The contributions of individual student (and faculty) reader-authors, which automatically turn Intermedia into a fully collaborative learning environment, remain on the system for future students to read, quote, and argue against. Students in the survey course at the present time already encounter essays, comments, concept maps, and imitations in poetry and prose by at least nine groups of students from earlier years.[13] Coming upon materials created by other students, some of whom one may know or whose name one recognizes, serves to convince students that they are in a very different, more active kind of learning situation. As we shall also observe when we return to this subject in discussing the political implications of such educational media, this technology of memory produces effects quite unusual in a university setting.

■ ■ ■ ■ ■ ■ ■

Reconfiguring Assignments and Methods of Evaluation

To take advantage of hypertext's potential educational effects, instructors must decide what role it will play and must consciously teach with it. Therefore, students unacquainted with this new information medium must use it from the beginning of the course. At the same time, one must make clear to students both the goals of the course and the role of the hypertext system in meeting them. Peter Whalley correctly points out that "the most successful uses of hypertext will involve learners and lead them to adopt the most appropriate learning strategy for their task. They must . . . allow the learner to develop higher level skills, rather than simply become the passive recipients of a slick new technology."[14] Instructors therefore must create assignments that emphasize precisely those qualities and features of hypertext that furnish the greatest educational advantages. I have elsewhere described in detail such an initial assignment and will summarize it below before providing the example of a more complex exercise.[15]

Whether it is true or not that readers retain less of the information they encounter while reading text on a screen than while reading a printed page, electronically linked text and printed text have different advantages. Instructors using hypertext should therefore prepare an initial assignment that provides the student with experience of its advantages — the advantages of connectivity. Obviously, instructors wishing to introduce students to the capacity hypertext gives them to choose their own reading paths and hence construct their own document must employ assignments that encourage students to do so.

The first Intermedia assignment in all my courses instructs students to follow links from the same location or link marker and then report what they encounter. Similarly, since I employ a corpus of linked documents to accustom students to discovering or constructing contexts for individual blocks of text or data, my assignments require multiple answers to the same question or multiple parts to the same answer. If one wishes to accustom students to the fact that complex phenomena involve complex causation, one must arrange assignments in such a way as to make students summon different kinds of information to explain the phenomena they encounter. Since my courses have increasingly taken advantage of Intermedia's capacity to promote collaborative learning, my assignments, from the beginning of the course, require students to comment upon the materials and links they find, to suggest new ones, and to add materials.

Instructors employing educational hypertext must also rethink examinations and other forms of evaluation. If hypertext's greatest educational strength as well as its most characteristic feature is its connectivity, then tests and other evaluative exercises must measure the results of using that connectivity to develop the ability to make connections. Independent of educational use of hypertext, dissatisfaction with American secondary school students' ability to think critically has recently led to a new willingness to try evaluative methods that emphasize conceptual skills — chiefly making connections — rather than those that stress simple data acquisition.[16]

Taking advantage of the full potential of hypertext obviously forces instructors to rethink the goals and methods of education. If one wishes to develop student skills in critical thinking, then one might have to make one's goal elegance of approach rather than quantitative answers. Particularly when dealing with beginning students, instructors will have to recognize that several correct answers may exist for a single problem and that such multiplicity of answers does not indicate that the assigned problem is subjective or that any answer will do. If, for example, one asks students to provide a context in contemporary philosophy or religion for a literary technique or historical event, one can expect to receive a range of correct solutions.

Several of the courses that I teach with hypertext employ the following exercise, which may take the form of either an in-class exercise or a take-home exam that students have a week or more to complete. The exercise consists of a series of passages from the assigned readings that students have to identify and then relate to a single work in brief essays; in the past, these exercises have used Wordsworth's "Tintern Abbey," *Great Expectations*, and Austen's *Pride and Prejudice* as the central texts. The instructions for the exercise asking students to relate passages to "Tintern Abbey" direct them thus:

Begin each essay by identifying the full name, exact title, and date of the passage, after which you should explain at least three ways in which the passage relates (whatever you take that term to mean) to the poem. One of these connections should concern theme, a second should concern technique, and a third some aspect of the religious, philosophical, historical, or scientific context. . . . Not all the relations you discover or create will turn out to be obvious ones, such as matters of influence or analogous ideas and techniques. Some may take the form of contrasts or oppositions that tell us something interesting about the authors, literary forms, or times in which these works appeared.

To emphasize that demonstrating skill at formulating possible explanations and hypothesizing significant relations counts as much as factual knowledge alone, the directions explain that some subjects, "particularly matters of context, may require you to use materials in *Context32* on Intermedia to formulate an hypothesis. In many cases *Context32* provides the materials to create an answer but not answers themselves."

Using this exercise in six iterations of the survey course as well as in two other courses has convinced me that it provides a useful and accurate means of evaluation that has several additional beneficial effects. Although the exercise does not directly ask for specific factual information other than titles, authors, and dates, students soon recognize that without such additional information they cannot effectively demonstrate connections between or among texts. In comparing a passage from Pope's "Essay on Man" with "Tintern Abbey," for example, they soon realize that only specific examples and specific comments on those examples produce effective discussion. Gary Marchionini points out that "hypermedia is an enabling technology rather than a directive one, offering high levels of user control. Learners can construct their own knowledge by browsing hyperdocuments according to the associations in their own *cognitive structures*. As with access, however, control requires responsibility and decision making."[17] By making students choose which literary techniques, themes, or aspects of context they wish to relate, the exercise emphasizes the major role of student choice.

This assignment itself proves an effective educational tool, because while attempting to carry it out many students realize that they have difficulty handling matters of context, which at the outset they often confuse with the theme or main idea of a passage. Discussions of context require one to posit a connection between one phenomenon, say, the imagery in a poem, and some other, often more general, phenomenon, such as conceptions of the human mind, gender roles, or religious belief contemporaneous with the imagery under discussion. Perceiving possible connections and then arguing for their validity is a high-level intellectual skill. Since students are permitted and in fact encouraged to redo these exercises as many times as they wish, these exercises simultaneously furnish students the opportunity to make conceptual breakthroughs and teachers the opportunity to encourage and then measure them.

Two additional advantages of this exercise for the courses in which it appears involve writing. Since both the survey and the more advanced courses are intended to be intensive writing courses, the opportunity for students to do a large amount of writing (and rewriting) supports one of the goals of these courses, although obviously that might prove a hindrance in other kinds of courses, particularly those with large enrollments. Second, the several short essays that the structure of the assignment requires seem to accomplish more than did a single long essay. At the same time that students find writing many short essays easier than constructing a single much longer one, they cover far more material than they could with a more conventional assignment and they cover different approaches, each demanding the kind of materials generally available only in a hypermedia corpus.

Another advantage of this exercise, which I find well suited to courses with hypertext supplements, lies in the fact that, particularly in its take-home version, it demonstrates the usefulness of the hypertext system at the same time that it draws on the skills encouraged by using it. The hypertext materials show students possible connections they might wish to make and furnish information so they may make their own connections. Our hypermedia corpus also permits them to range back and forth throughout the course, thereby effecting their own syntheses of the materials.

A final utility of this exercise lies in the fact that by encouraging students to take a more active, collaborative approach to learning, it thereby creates more materials for students to read. This past year approximately one third of the students in my survey wrote their answers to these exercises directly on Intermedia, and the writers of the most successful ones later linked them to relevant documents. Of the remaining students, almost all wrote their essays with Intermedia-compatible word-processing programs, such as Microsoft Word, producing documents that can be placed directly onto Intermedia; integrating these new student materials into the docuverse is easy and efficient and hence requires little support.

■ ■ ■ ■ ■ ■ ■

Examples of Collaborative

Learning from Intermedia

In the early days of developing and using Intermedia the reader's shaping of the text and choice of link paths provided the only form of student collaborative work. Those of us who created the first version of the survey's hypertext component, four graduate or postdoctoral students and I, worked collaboratively, of course, but only in ways characteristic of traditional group projects. Each person wrote documents on a set of authors and topics and gathered relevant graphic materials. Acting in the manner of the editor of an encyclopedia or anthology, I then coordinated the materials and made them conform to a uniform style. Once we reached the stage of putting documents onto Intermedia, some of the contributors modified materials created by others and linked them to their own creations. At this point, the Intermedia materials were still the collaborative product of the five original contributors alone.

Ever since students in the survey began using the hypertext component, however, they have become collaborators, and their collaboration has proved increasingly important. The first assignment in each course that uses Intermedia is intended to acquaint the student with the nature of the system and the materials it contains. After instructing students to open an overview file and follow various links, the assignment asks them to record what they encounter and then asks for suggestions of additional links or materials. Another part of the assignment asks the students to choose a passage from the week's reading and append it to one of the maps or other graphic documents. From the first, somewhat to our surprise, these assignments had the happy effect of convincing a substantial portion of the class that they had control over the material and could contribute to it. Students in English 32 therefore offered proofreading corrections, suggestions for links, and requests for additional materials throughout the semester. In fact, after students expressed the view that discussions of technical devices, such as imagery and narration, worked best with specific proof-texts, we created new materials for later readings. In addition to the clearly demonstrated general acceptance by students of participation and collaboration in shaping the materials on Intermedia, several students took the initiative and, after receiving permission (and passwords), began to make their own links as well as obvious corrections (for example, moving links that had been labeled mistakenly or correcting typographical errors).

During the following semester of Intermedia's first year, it supported English 61, an upper-class seminar in Victorian poetry. The fourteen students enrolled in this course used it to work in a more intensively collaborative manner than had the students in English 32. They created documents, and some entered them onto the system themselves and also made links. Observing students from an upper-class course reading and benefiting from materials created by those in another class convinced me that I should attempt an even more elaborate experiment in collaborative hypertext with graduate students, some of whom had begun to use Intermedia to prepare for their qualifying examinations. Therefore, the following term, when our hypertext materials again supported the teaching of the survey, I also used it for my graduate seminar in Victorian literature, whose six members contributed to the *In Memoriam* project described below.

On Intermedia the student makes four kinds of contributions to the hypertext materials, each of which, as we shall see, involves collaborative work: (1) reading, in which the reader plays a more important role in shaping the reading path than does the reader of a book; (2) creating links among documents present on the system; (3) creating text documents and linking them to others; and (4) creating graphic documents and linking them to others. Contributors to the system have produced graphics documents by adding digitized images, such as maps or reproductions of pictures, and by creating concept maps accompanied by varying amounts of text. Students have both created entirely new concept maps in the form of overview or literary relations

documents and used earlier ones as templates, making minor modifications and changing the texts.

The way hypertext changes both our notions of collaborative work
and our experience of it is apparent in student contributions. The
most basic kind of contribution to Intermedia, and the most fundamental, is the addition of a link, something students are encouraged to
do by an assignment due a few days after each course begins. As I
described above, introductory exercises require them to explore the
Intermedia materials by following links and then suggesting other
possible ones. Students have to link a text from the first week's reading, in Graham Swift's *Waterland*, to one of several maps intended
to illuminate that novel.

The next most complex form of contribution to Intermedia
involves creating a document, either text or graphic, and then linking
it to existing documents on Intermedia. Emma Leheny thus collaborated with the system and its many other authors when she added
the following document, entitled "What Do Maps of Railroads and
Canals Tell Us about the Novel?", to the materials on *Waterland* and
then linked it to a file that contains both a picture of Chirk Aqueduct
and a map of the waterway system in 1789:

The Cricks of the Fens are occupied with business related to the river. The picture of the
aqueduct [reproduced on Intermedia] . . . is reminiscent of the opposing forces of human
power and nature in *Waterland*. The aqueduct is the result of a massive human effort to
control the course of water. Similarly, Henry Crick [the narrator's father] is the lock-keeper of
the river, the lock being a seemingly absurd human attempt to control the river. For the
most part, the people of the Fens do seem in control, but nature overpowers them when the
river overflows, drowns them, and destroys their crops. An important theme in the novel
is that the water, like all nature, has power over people. As Tom Crick tells his students,
"When you work with water, you have to know and respect it. When you labour to subdue it,
you have to understand that one day it may rise up and turn all your labours to nothing."

Because the student has here created her own text, which includes a
quotation from the work in question, rather than simply linking
something in *Context32* to another text, this form of collaboration
represents a more complex contribution than that chosen by some
students, who simply appended a passage without comment. (In practice, however, they proved similar: since a portion but not the entire
text of *Waterland* appears in Intermedia, one may have to add a passage

to which one wishes to make a link, just as one has to write one's own text and then link it to pre-existing documents. In a more complete hypertext corpus, such as that exemplified by the *In Memoriam* project, one simply links blocks of texts from complete works to one another, connecting, say, the description of Miss Havisham in Dickens's *Great Expectations* to one of a similar character in Swift's *Waterland*.)

Two things about these student contributions demand comment. First, presented by means of print technology, as they are here, they at first seem separate, discrete documents created as student exercises that do not collaborate with anything else. But on a hypertext system they are experienced differently, because they link to other documents, which qualify and supplement them. Second, these student documents mingle with ones created by faculty members. They therefore represent a radical departure from current modes of learning and scholarship. We encourage our students to think independently, and some of us even prompt them to challenge our pet theories and interpretations. Occasionally, in our books and articles we thank students for having helped us formulate these theories in the pressure of discussion or for having uncovered some interesting bit of evidence; but we do not publish their comments in our books. Hypertext, however, enables student-faculty collaboration by including a large number of links and documents created by students. Whereas few students can contribute general essays or much in the way of original scholarly research, all can contribute links and many can produce valuable graphic and text documents that supplement faculty-created ones. These documents, as we shall observe, can add materials not included previously, qualify existing approaches, and even simply contradict existing presentations of individual topics.

These kinds of contributions appear in the graphic concept maps that students in several courses have created. Laura M. Henrickson, a member of my graduate seminar on Victorian poetry, produced, for example, a graphic document entitled "Tennyson's 'Lady of Shalott': Literary Relations." This graphic image of the poem's intertextuality takes the form of a modified wheel-diagram in which the poem's title appears in a rectangle at the center; this rectangle is surrounded by seven others, each of which indicates a work in some way related to Tennyson's poem. One box includes the text "Malory's *Morte d'Arthur:* compare Elaine, the Maid of Astolat, to the Lady of Shalott," and another suggests a far older source: "Sappho's fragment 102: especially for the weaving. Tennyson marked this fragment in his copy of *Poetae Lyrici Graeci*." Other rectangles suggest a fourteenth-century Italian analogue, Spenser's *Faerie Queene*, poems by Shelley, and nineteenth-century collections of fairy stories. The center of the diagram also contains the words "for another view" and an accompanying link marker that permits access to other documents, which include a concept map, created earlier by a student in my undergraduate seminar, that offers a quite different approach to the poem.

In what ways, then, does this document exemplify collaborative work? First, it adds something new to *Context32*'s Tennyson materials. Second, it links to various documents on one particular poem, "The Lady of Shalott," thereby working together with them. Third, one of those documents to which it links, another concept map, was created by a student in an undergraduate course, and Henrickson's document therefore exists related to one produced by an undergraduate student. It is worthwhile emphasizing this point, because just as we do not ordinarily produce work together with our students, so, too, graduate and undergraduate students rarely collaborate. I have observed graduate students reading documents written by freshmen and freshmen reading ones created by advanced graduate students. I have also observed students at widely differing places in their academic careers creating links to documents produced by those at different academic levels. Hypertext, in other words, allows collaboration not only among those of equivalent academic rank or status but also among those of widely different rank or status.

The *In Memoriam* Project

The *In Memoriam* project, which employs all the forms of collaborative work described thus far, takes advantage of the capacities of hypermedia to do things virtually impossible with book technology. In particular, the dual capacity of hypertext to record relations between text blocks and to allow readers quickly to navigate these links offers enormous possibilities to the humanistic disciplines. As an experiment in collaboration to determine precisely how one goes about creating, maintaining, and using hypertext to study the internal and external connections implicit in a major literary work, the members of a graduate seminar and I placed a particularly complex poem on the hypertext system and then linked to it (1) variant readings from manuscripts,

(2) published critical commentary, as well as (3) commentary by members of the seminar, and (4) passages from works by other authors. Tennyson's *In Memoriam*, a radically experimental mid-Victorian poem, perfectly suits this experiment, in part because it attempts to create new versions of traditional major poetic forms from 133 separate sections, each a poem that can stand on its own. It makes extensive use of echoing, allusion, and repetition, all of which are perfectly suited to hypertext linking.

The *In Memoriam* project made use of documents created as an exercise for the undergraduate seminar in Victorian poetry that directed students to take a single section of the work and "show either by an essay of no more than two pages (typed) or by a one-page diagram its connections or relations to other sections of the poem." Kristen Langdon's "Relations of *In Memoriam* 60 to Other Sections," which relies on a wheel diagram in which blocks of text are connected by spokes to a center, reinvents the Intermedia concept map by making a more concrete use of it. Langdon demonstrates how Tennyson enriches his straightforward, simple diction by linking individual phrases, such as "dark house," "some poor girl," and "sphere," to other sections of the poem. This author's decision to link partial blocks of text to a complete one and avoid generalizing statements or summaries distinguished her approach from most previous material on the system. Her solution to the assignment, which was paralleled by those of several other students, manages to convey on one page or screen information that would take many more words in an essay format.

The six members of the graduate seminar added links and documents to the body of materials already on line.[18] In addition to the 133 sections of the poem, these included several dozen files on the poet and his other poems as well as relevant materials on Victorian religion, science, history, and art. Students from the undergraduate seminar created approximately a dozen graphic or text documents and linked them to individual sections of *In Memoriam*. I had already created an overview file (see figure 1) for the poem itself, basing it on the one for Tennyson; and to this student consultants, room monitors, and I linked individual sections and a few of the relevant motifs.

Between January and April 1988 the members of the graduate seminar added more than a hundred documents, each student commenting specifically on one or more sections of the poem or on one another's work. The first assignment for the project required them to create five documents to append to individual sections of the poem. Each week members of the seminar read the contributions of others, added more documents, and then made links. The final assignment directly involving the *In Memoriam* project required each student to put on line the texts of poems by another poet, Christina Rossetti, that had obvious relevance to individual sections of Tennyson's work. Members of the class had earlier added texts from works by writers other than Tennyson, and this assignment was intended to explore hypertext presentation of interauthor relations in specific terms.

Working independently and yet together, the members of the seminar created a presentation of a major nineteenth-century literary work that makes obvious many of its internal and external relations. Equally interesting, graduate students in English have worked collaboratively in a manner rare in their discipline, and since their work has taken the form of contributions to Intermedia, those who follow them will have access to what they have created.

One can argue, of course, that all writing inevitably follows this form of collaboration, however much book-bound technology hides or obscures it. Such is precisely the argument made by Roland Barthes and other structuralists who continually emphasize that each speaker or writer manipulates a complex semiotic system containing layers of linguistic, semantic, rhetorical, and cultural codes with which one always collaborates. Unlike book technology, however, hypertext does not hide such collaborative relationship. Even if all texts (however defined) always exist in some relation to one another, before the advent of hypertext technology, such interrelations could exist only within the individual minds that perceived these relations or within other texts that asserted the existence of such relations. The texts themselves, whether art objects, laws, or books, existed in physical separation from one another.

Networked hypermedia systems, in contrast, record and reproduce the relations among texts, one effect of which is that they permit the novice to experience the reading and thinking patterns of the expert. Another result of such linking appears in the fact that all texts on a hypertext system potentially support, comment upon, and collaborate with one another. Once placed within a hypertext environment, a document no longer exists alone. It always exists in relation to other documents in a way that a book or printed document never does and never can. From this follow two corollaries. First, any document placed on a networked system that supports electronically linked materials potentially exists in collaboration with any and all other documents on that system. Second, any document electronically linked to any other document collaborates with it.

To create a document or a link in hypertext is to collaborate with all those who have used it previously and will use it in future. The essential connectivity of Intermedia encourages and demands collaboration. By making each document in the docuverse exist as part of a larger structure, Intermedia places each document in what one can term the "virtual presence" of all previously created documents and their creators. This electronically created virtual presence transforms documents created in an assembly-line mode into ones that could have been produced by several people working at the same time. In addition, by permitting individual documents to contribute to this electronically related overarching structure, hypertext also makes each contribution a matter of versioning. In so doing, it provides a model of scholarly work in the humanities that better records what actually takes place in such disciplines than does traditional book technology.

The behavior of the twenty students in the survey course during the second semester of the 1989–1990 academic year provided an indication of the way students can work collaboratively with the documents already present on the system. On receiving one of the assignments, a student in the course asked how I wanted members of the class to indicate indebtedess, and I responded that they should avoid footnotes and simply use parenthetical in-text citations. Since several students either missed class or later told me that they (correctly) believed citing one's sources was not required, the following figures represent a particularly conservative picture of the way students make use of lexias created by other students. Ten students, or fifty percent of the class, cited an average of 4.3 documents on Intermedia, and of these students, six, or thirty percent, cited work by students in earlier classes an average of 3.3 times each. In comparison eight, or forty percent, cited the Norton *Anthology of English Literature* or the Oxford *Companion to English Literature*, which is not on the reading list, an average of 5.4 times each. One student cited Intermedia documents 6 times, none of which had student authors, and she cited the introductions and other critical materials in the Norton anthology a dozen times. Another cited 4 documents by faculty and graduate student developers, InterLex (an electronic version of the Houghton Mifflin

American Heritage Dictionary) once, students' documents twice, and the Norton anthology 8 times. In contrast, seven students, thirty-five percent, mentioned no outside sources, though in at least two of these cases the use of large numbers of Intermedia documents was clear. Since I observed most of the students working on the Intermedia system various times during the semester, these citations demonstrate to me not the use of the system per se but the fact that, in the role of authors, the students wished to connect their texts with those of other students. Whether or not they agreed with the student authors they cited, they inserted their own work into an existing network of textual relations.[19]

The Soyinka Web and *Context34*

The latest and perhaps most interesting example of collaborative writing on Intermedia involves the Soyinka web — a set of more than seventy, mostly student-created, documents — and its offspring, *Context34*, which is six times as large. As an experiment, I taught the second half of the 1989–1990 survey course during the autumn semester, in order to align it with Brown University's Curricular Advising Program, in which freshmen enroll in a course taught by their advisor. Students were apparently not notified of the existence of the course, and the enrollment was that of a seminar — an even dozen. With a class this small, I decided to try an experiment in the collaborative production of a hypertext corpus on a single author, Wole Soyinka, a contemporary Nigerian poet, about whom Intermedia provided little material. After putting onto Intermedia several maps of Nigeria, the standard graphic overview for an author, a detailed list of works, and a chronology based upon James Gibbs's *Critical Perspectives on Wole Soyinka* (1980), I asked students to write at least two brief Intermedia essays, one on any poem from *The Shuttle in the Crypt*, Soyinka's prison poems, and a second on any aspect of the writer's context — political, historical, literary, religious, artistic, or whatever. It was late in the semester and the class had already done a great deal of writing in this intensive reading course, so I did not have high hopes for the quality of work they would produce on short notice when many were already preparing for term papers and final examinations in other courses.

To my surprise, the class produced twenty-one documents of high enough quality to remain on the system for use by later students. In addition to interpretations of individual poems, their documents included discussions of Nigeria under British colonial rule, a bibliography of materials on Yoruban religion, "Soyinka and the Biafran War," "The Yoruba Oba or King," "Negritude," and "Soyinka's Use of Jungian Archtypes." Students interested in the relation of Soyinka's poems to his other works added essays on a novel, *The Interpreters*, and an introduction to his drama; those who wanted to set him in the context of others' writings produced "Wole Soyinka and Dylan Thomas: Time and Mystery" and a comparison of Soyinka's "Ulysses" to Joyce's novel. I realized that this class had created the basis for a body of materials on the poet and the African context.

Adding a concept map for Soyinka's literary relations based on the lexias the students had already created, I gave the same assignment when I repeated the course the following semester, the only difference being that this time I requested students not to write about something already covered unless they disagreed with the previous contribution. Those twenty students, who contributed an additional forty documents to the Soyinka web, seemed to have been inspired by the materials they encountered there, for they wrote a wide range of essays that clearly integrate this Nigerian poet into the canon of English literature while providing a foundation for future work by other students.[20] In general, these documents created by beginning students who have used Intermedia for a semester match or surpass in usefulness (and often in quality) those produced by graduate developers who had not yet used hypertext. Of course, the present hypermedia corpus cannot rival what specialists in African literature, history, and culture might create were they given a year or so, but how many institutions have available such a flexible, growing resource now?

The success of this ongoing experiment has recently led me to expand the Soyinka web into *Context34*, a set of more than five hundred largely student-created documents that support the teaching of a new course on recent postcolonial fiction and autobiography in English. Work done by students in English 32 and other courses provided, I realized, the basis for a rich hypertext corpus. After creating graphic overviews for the thirteen authors read in the course (see figure 2, *lower left corner*) and for relevant topics, such as Nigeria (figure 9) and women in India, Pakistan, and Bangladesh (figure 10), I proceeded to edit and then link a range of student documents to

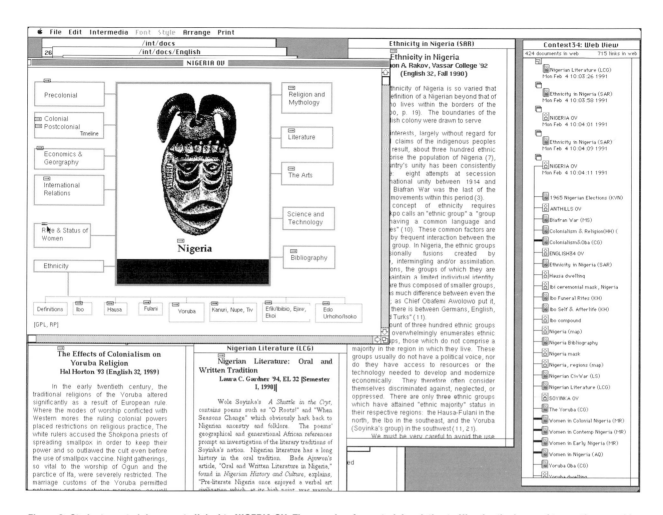

Figure 9. Student-created documents linked to NIGERIA OV. The overview for materials relating to Nigeria, the home of two authors read in the course on postcolonial fiction, resembles those for individual literary works. Tribal and ethnic groupings, however, occupy the positions filled by literary techniques in the directory for novels. Beneath the overview appear "The Effects of Colonialism on Yoruban Religion," by Hal Horton '93, and "Nigerian Literature: Oral and Written Tradition," by Laura C. Gardner '94; and at the right appears "Ethnicity in Nigeria," by Simon A. Rakov '92, from Vassar College. The reader has activated the link marker for "Role and Status of Women," thereby darkening lines attached to five icons in the Web View at right.

Figure 10. Student-created documents linked to SOUTH ASIAN WOMEN OV. At screen left appears "Women in India, Pakistan, and Bangladesh," which has link icons labeled "Women's Lives," "Women Authors," and "Bibliography." Beneath this overview appears "Changing Images of Women in South Asian Fiction," by Shoshana M. Landow '91 (Princeton University); and at the right appear "Contemporary Nonfiction and Sara Suleri's *Meatless Days*," by Yishane Lee '91 (the text currently active), "Undercutting Authorial Control in Suleri's *Meatless Days*," by Rachel Solotaroff '93, and my brief selection from Desai's *In Custody* with appended reading questions entitled "Sarla's Aspirations." The Web View at right shows the documents linked to Lee's essay.

these overviews and to one another. The sheer practicality of a hyper-text system like Intermedia for teachers appears in the fact that I managed to create *Context34* between the end of the first semester and the beginning of the second.

■ ■ ■ ■ ■ ■ ■

Reconceiving Canon and Curriculum

The same factors — connectivity, virtual presence, and shifting of the balance between writer and reader — that prompt major, perhaps radical, shifts in teaching, learning, and the organization of both activities inevitably have the potential to affect the related notions of canon and curriculum. For a work to enter the literary canon — or, more properly, to be entered into the canon — gains it certain obvious privileges. That the passive grammatical construction more accurately describes the manner in which a book or painting receives that not-so-mysterious stamp of cultural approval reminds us that those in positions of power decide what enters this select inner circle. The gatekeepers of the fortress of high culture include influential critics, museum directors and their boards of trustees, and a far more lowly combine of scholars and teachers. One of the chief institutions of the literary canon is the middlebrow anthology, that hanger-on of high culture that in the Victorian period took the form of pop anthologies with titles like *Golden Treasury* and today exists principally in the form of major college anthologies. In America, to be in the Norton or the Oxford anthology is to have achieved, not greatness, but what is more important, certainly — status. And that is why, of course, it matters that so few women have managed to gain entrance to such anthologies.

The notion of a literary canon descends from that of the biblical one, in which, as Gerald L. Bruns explains, canonization functions as "a category of power":

What is important is not only the formation, collection, and fixing of the sacred texts, but also their application to particular situations. A text, after all, is canonical, not in virtue of being final and correct and part of an official library, but because it becomes *binding* upon a group of people. The whole point of canonization is to underwrite the authority of a text, not merely with respect to its origin as against competitors in the field . . . but with respect to the present and future in which it will reign or govern as a binding text. . . . From a hermeneutic standpoint . . . the theme of canonization is *power*.[21]

One sees the kind of privileges and power belonging to canonization in the conception that something is a work of art; the classification of a work as art enters it into a form of the canon. Such categorization means that the work receives certain values, meanings, and modes of being perceived. A work of art, as some modern aestheticians have pointed out, is functionally what someone somewhere takes to be a work of art. Saying it's so makes it so. If one says the found object is a work of art, then it is; and having become such (however temporarily), it gains a certain status, the most important factor of which is simply that it is looked at in a certain way: taken as a work of art, it is contemplated aesthetically, regarded as the occasion for aesthetic pleasure or, possibly, for aesthetic outrage. It enters, one might say, the canon of art; and the contemporary existence in the Western world of galleries permits it to inhabit, for a time, a physical space that is taken by the acculturated to signify, "I am a work of art. I'm not (simply) an object for holding open a door. Look at me carefully." If that object is sold, bartered, or given *as a work of art* to one who recognizes the game or accedes in the demand to play his role in it, then it brings with it the capacity to generate that special space around it that signals it to be an object of special notice and a special way of noticing.

In precisely the same way, calling something a work of literature invokes a congeries of social, political, economic, and educational practices. If one states that a particular text is a work of literature, then for one it is, and one reads it and relates it to other texts in certain definite ways. As Terry Eagleton correctly observes, "anything can be literature, and anything which is regarded as unalterably and unquestionably literature — Shakespeare, for example — can cease to be literature. Any belief that the study of literature is the study of a stable, well-definable entity, as entomology is the study of insects, can be abandoned as a chimera. . . . Literature, in the sense of a set of works of assured and unalterable value, distinguished by certain shared inherent properties, does not exist" (*Literary Theory*, 10–11). The concept of literature (or literariness) therefore provides the fundamental and most extended form of canonization, and classifying a text as a work of literature is a matter of social and political practice. I first became aware of the implications of this fact several decades ago when I was reading the sermons of the evangelical Anglican, Henry Melvill, in an attempt to understand Victorian hermeneutic practice.

Upon encountering works by a man who was the favorite preacher of John Ruskin, Robert Browning, W. E. Gladstone, and many of their contemporaries, I realized that his sermons shared literary qualities found in writings by Ruskin, Carlyle, Arnold, and Newman. At first Melvill interested me solely as an influence upon Ruskin and as a means of charting the sage's changing religious beliefs. In several studies, I drew upon his extraordinarily popular sermons as extraliterary sources or as indications of standard Victorian interpretative practice.[22] If I were to write my study of Ruskin now, two decades later, I would treat Melvill's sermons also as works of literature, in part because contemporaries did so and in part because classifying them as literature would foreground certain intertextual relations that might otherwise remain invisible. At the time, however, I never considered discussing Melvill's sermons as literary texts rather than as historical sources; and when I mentioned to colleagues that his works seemed in some ways superior to Newman's, none of us considered the implications of that remark for a concept of literature. Remarks by colleagues, even those who specialized in Victorian literature, made clear that paying close attention to such texts was in some way eccentric and betokened a capacity to endure reading large amounts of necessarily boring "background material." When I taught a course in Anglo-American nonfiction some fifteen years after first discovering Melvill, I assigned one of his sermons, "The Death of Moses," for students to read in the company of works by Thomas Carlyle and Henry David Thoreau. Reading Melvill's sermon for an official course given under the auspices of the Department of English, they assumed that it was a work of literature and treated it as such. Considering "The Death of Moses," which has probably never before appeared in an English course, as a work of "real" literature, my students, it became clear, assumed that Melvill's writing possessed a certain canonical status.

The varieties of status that belonging to the canon confers — social, political, economic, aesthetic — cannot easily be extricated one from the other. Belonging to the canon is a guarantee of quality, and that guarantee of high aesthetic quality serves as a promise, a contract, that announces to the viewer, "Here is something to be enjoyed as an aesthetic object. Complex, difficult, privileged, the object before you has been winnowed by the sensitive few and the not-so-sensitive many, and it will re*pay* your attention. You will receive a frisson; at least you're supposed to, and if you don't, well, perhaps there's something wrong with your apparatus." Such an announcement of status by the poem, painting, building, sonata, or dance that has appeared ensconced within a canon serves, as I have indicated, a powerful separating purpose: it immediately stands forth as different, better, to be valued, loved, enjoyed. It is the wheat winnowed from the chaff, the rare survivor, and has all the privileges of such survival.

Anyone who has studied literature in a secondary school or university in the Western world knows what that means. It means that the works in the canon get read, read by neophyte students and expert teachers. It also means that to read these privileged works is a privilege and a sign of privilege. It is also a sign that one has been canonized oneself—beautified by the experience of being introduced to beauty, admitted to the ranks of those of the inner circle, who are acquainted with the canon and can judge what belongs and what does not. Becoming acquainted with the canon, with those works at the center, allows (indeed forces) one to move to the center or, if not absolutely to the center, at least much closer to it than one had been before.

This canon, it turns out, appears far more limited to the neophyte reader than to the instructor, for few of the former read beyond the reading list of the course, few know that one *can* read beyond, believing that what lies beyond is by definition dull, darkened, dreary. One can look at this power, this territoriality of the canonized work in two ways. Gaining entrance clearly allows a work to be enjoyed; failing to do so thrusts it into the limbo of the unnoticed, unread, unenjoyed, unexisting. Canonization, in other words, permits the member of the canon to enter the gaze and to exist. Like the painting accepted as a painting and not, say, a mere decorative object or even paint spill, it receives a conceptual frame; and although one can remark upon the obvious fact that frames confine and separate, it is precisely such appearance within the frame that guarantees its aesthetic contemplation, its capacity to make the viewer respect it.

The very narrowness of the frame and the very confinement within such a small gallery of framed objects produces yet another effect, for the framed object, the member of the canon, gains an intensification not only by its segregation but also because, residing in comparative isolation, it gains splendor. Canonization both permits a work to be seen and, since there are so relatively few objects thus privileged, intensifies the gaze; potentially distracting objects are removed from the spectator's view, and those that are left benefit from receiving exclusive attention (or bear the burden of it).

Within academia, however, to come under this gaze, works must be teachable. They must conform to whichever currently fashionable pedagogy allows the teacher to discuss this painting or that poem. In narrating the formation of the modernist canon, Hugh Kenner explains that "when Pound was working in his normal way, by lapidary *statement*, New Critics could find nothing whatever to say about him. Since 'Being-able-to-say-about' is a pedagogic criterion, he was largely absent from a canon pedagogues were defining. So was Williams, and wholly. What can Wit, Tension, Irony enable you to say about The Red Wheelbarrow?"[23] Very little, one answers, and the same is true for the poetry of Swinburne, which has many similarities to that of Stevens but which remains unteachable for many trained in New Criticism. In painting, the situation is much the same: critics of purely formalist training and persuasion *have nothing to say* about the complex semiotics of Pre-Raphaelite painting. To them it doesn't really seem to be art.

Thematic as well as formal filters render individual texts teachable. As Sandra M. Gilbert and Susan Gubar, Ellen Moers, Elaine Showalter, and many others have repeatedly demonstrated, people who for one reason or another do not find interesting a particular topic — say, the works, fates, and subjectivities of women — do not see them and have little to say about them. They remove them from view. If belonging to the canon brings a text to notice, thrusts it into view, falling out of the circle of light or being absent or exiled from it keeps a text out of view. The work is in effect excommunicated. For, as in the Church's excommunication, one is not permitted to partake of the divine refreshing acts of communion with the divinity, one is divorced from sacramental life, from participation in the eternal, and one is also kept from communicating with others. One is exiled from community. Likewise, one of the most savage results of not belonging to the canon is that these works do not communicate with one another. A work outside the canon is forgotten, unnoticed, and if a canonical author is under discussion, any links between the uncanonical work and the canonical tend not to be noticed.

I write *tend* because under certain conditions, and with certain gazes, they can be at the other end of the connections. But within the currently dominant information technology, that of print, such connections and such linkages to the canonical require almost heroic and certainly specialized efforts. The average intelligent educated reader, in other words, is not expected to be able to make such connections with the noncanonical work. For him or her they do not exist. The connections are made among specialized works and by those readers — professionalized by the profession of scholarship — whose job it is to explore what is the reader's equivalent of the darkest Africa of the nineteenth- and early-twentieth-century imagination — the darkest stacks of the library where reside the unimportant, unnoticed books, those one is supposed not to know, not even to have seen. The situation, not so strangely, resembles that of the unknown dark continent, which certainly was not dark nor unknown to itself or to its inhabitants but only to Europeans, who labeled it so because to them, from their vantage point, it was out of view and perception. They did so for obviously political — indeed, obviously colonialist — reasons, and one may inquire if this segregation, this placement at a distance accurately figures the political economy of works canonized and uncanonized.

Like the colonial power, say, France, Germany, or England, the canonical work acts as a center — the center of the perceptual field, the center of values, the center of interest, the center, in short, of a web of meaningful interrelations. The noncanonical works act as colonies or as countries that are unknown and out of sight and mind. That is why feminists object to the omission or excision of works by female authors from the canon, for by not appearing within the canon works by women do not . . . appear. One solution to this more or less systematic dis-appearance of women's works is to expand the canon.

A second approach to the decanonization of works is the creation of an alternate tradition, an alternate canon. Toril Moi points to the major problems implicit in the idea of a feminist canon of great works (though she does not point to the possibility of reading without a canon) when she argues that all ideas of a canon derive from the humanist belief that literature is "an excellent instrument of education" and that the student becomes a better person by reading great works. "The great author is great because he (occasionally even she) has managed to convey an authentic vision of life." Furthermore, argues Moi — and thus incriminates all canons, and all bodies of special works with the same brush — "the literary canon of 'great literature' ensures that it is this 'representative experience' (one selected by male bourgeois critics) that is transmitted to future generations, rather than those deviant, unrepresentative experiences discoverable in much female, ethnic and working-class writing. Anglo-American feminist criticism has waged war on this self-sufficient canonization of middle-class male values. But they have rarely challenged the very notion of such a canon." [24] Arguing that Showalter aims to create a "separate canon of women's writing, not to abolish all canons," she points out that "a new canon would not be intrinsically less oppressive than the old" (78).

Unfortunately, one cannot proclaim the end of canons or do away with them, since they cannot be ended by proclamation. "To teach, to prescribe a curriculum, to assign one book for a class as opposed to another," Reed Way Dasenbrock points out, "is ineluctably to call certain texts central, to create a canon, to create a hierarchy." [25] Rather, we must learn to live with them, appreciate them, benefit from them, but, above all, remain suspicious of them. Grandiose announcements that one is doing away with The Canon fall into two categories: announcements, doomed to failure, that one is no longer going to speak in prose, and censorship that in totalitarian fashion tells others what they cannot read. Doing away with the canon leaves one not with freedom but with hundreds of thousands of undiscriminated and hence unnoticeable works, works we cannot see or notice or read. Better to recognize a canon, or numerous versions of one, and argue against it, revise it, and add to it.

Having thus far paraphrased — but I hope not parodied — now-popular notions of the positive and negative effects of a literary canon, I have to express some reservations. I have little doubt that a canon focuses attention, provides status, and screens noncanonical works from the attention of most people. That seems fairly clear. But I do not believe the one canon about which I know very much, that for English and American literature, has ever been terribly rigid. The entire notion of world literature, great touchstones, and studying English academically has a comparatively brief history. Victorian literature, that area of literature to which I devote most of my attention, certainly shows astonishing changes of reputations. When I first encountered the Victorians in undergraduate courses some thirty years ago, Tennyson, Browning, and Arnold claimed positions as the only major poets of the age, and Hopkins, when he was considered, appeared as a proto-modernist. In the following decades, Swinburne and the Pre-Raphaelites, particularly Christina Rossetti and her brother Dante Gabriel Rossetti, have seemed more important, as has Elizabeth Barrett Browning, who had a major reputation during her own lifetime. Arnold, meanwhile, has faded rather badly. Looking at older anthologies, one realizes that some of the poets whose reputations have of late taken such a turn for the better had fairly strong reputations in the 1930s and forties but disappeared into a shade cast by modernism and the New Criticism.

Such evidence, which reminds us how ideological and critical fashions influence what we read as students and what we have our students read now, suggests, perhaps surprisingly, that the literary canon, such as it is, changes with astonishing speed. Viewing it over a scholarly or critical career, only the historically myopic could claim that the academic canon long resists the pressures of contemporary interests. No matter how rigid and restrictive it may be at any one moment, it has shown itself characterized by impermanence, even transience, and by openness to current academic fashion. Viewed over a university "generation," a far shorter span of time, the lag seems intolerably long. What good does it do an individual student to know that students will be able to study, say, a particular Nigerian writer a few years after *they* graduate?

Nonetheless, the canon, particularly that most important part of it represented by what educational institutions offer students in secondary school and college courses, takes a certain amount of time to respond. One factor in such resistance to change derives from interest and conviction, though as we have seen, such conviction can change surprisingly quickly in the right circumstances — right for change, not necessarily right according to any other standard. Another factor, which every teacher encounters, derives from book technology, in particular from the need to capitalize a fixed number of copies of a particular work. Revising, making additions, taking into account new works requires substantial expenditure of time and money; and the need to sell as many copies as possible to cover publication costs means that one must pitch any particular text book, anthology, or edition toward the largest possible number of potential purchasers.

As Richard Ohmann has so chillingly demonstrated in his study of American fiction from 1960 to 1975, the constraints of the marketplace have even more direct control of more recent fiction, both bestsellers and those few books that make their way into the college curriculum. The combination of monopoly capitalism and a central-ized cultural establishment, entrenched in a very few New York–based periodicals, has meant that for a contemporary novel to "lodge itself in our culture as precanonical — as 'literature,' " however briefly, it has to be "selected, in turn, by an agent, an editor, a publicity department, a review editor (especially the one at the Sunday *New York Times*), the New York metropolitan book buyers whose patronage [is] neces-sary to commercial success, critics writing for gatekeeper intellectual journals, academic critics, and college teachers."[26] Once published, "the single most important boost" for a novel is a "prominent review in the Sunday *New York Times*," which, Ohmann's statistics suggest, heavily favors the largest advertisers, particularly Random House (380).[27]

Historians of print technology have long argued that the cost of book technology necessitates standardization, and although education benefits in many ways from such standardization, it is also inevitably harmed by it as well. Most of the great books courses, which had so much to offer within all their limitations, require some fixed text or set of texts.

Although hypertext can hardly provide a universal panacea for the ills of American education, it does allow one to individualize any corpus of materials by allowing reader and writer to connect them to other contexts. In fact, the connectivity, virtual presence, and shift-ing of the balance between writer and reader that permit interdiscipli-nary team teaching do away with this kind of time lag at the same time that they permit one to preserve the best parts of book technol-ogy and its associated culture. Let me give an example of what I mean. Suppose, as is the case, that I am teaching a survey course in English literature and I wish to include works by women. A few years ago, if one turned to the Oxford or Norton anthologies, one received the impression that someone had quite consciously excluded the presence of women from them — and therefore from most beginning under-graduates' sense of literature. One could of course complain, and in fact many did complain. After a number of years, say, seven or eight, a few suitable texts began to appear in these anthologies, and Norton also took the route of publishing an anthology of women's literature in English. This new presence of women is certainly better than the former nonpresence of women, but it takes and is taking a long time. What is worse, many of the texts that appear at last in these anthologies may well not be those one would have chosen.

Let us consider a second problem I have encountered introducing new materials into my teaching, one less likely to find redress anywhere as quickly as has the first. I refer to the difficulty of introducing into English literature courses authors of non-English ethnic backgrounds who write in English. This problem, which precisely typifies the difficulties of redefining the canon and the curriculum alike, arises because a good many of Britain's major authors during the past century have not been English.[28] In Britain, where the inhabitants distinguish quite carefully among English, Welsh, Scots, and Irish, the major figures since the rise of modernism have not necessarily been English: Conrad was Polish; James, American; Thomas, Welsh; and Joyce and Yeats, Irish. Generally, anthologies work in these figures without placing too much emphasis on their non-Englishness, which shows a nice capacity to accommodate the realities of literary production. Of course, such accommodation has taken a rather long time to materialize.

Today the situation has become far more complex, and in Great Britain's postcolonial era, if one wishes to suggest the nature of writing in English — which is how I define English literature — one must include both writers of Commonwealth and ex-Commonwealth countries and also those with a wide range of ethnic origins who live in the United Kingdom and write in English. Surveying leading novelists writing in English in Britain, one comes upon important English men and women, of course, like Graham Swift, Jane Gardam, and Penelope Lively; but such a survey almost immediately brings up the matter of national origins. After all, among the novelists who have won prestigious prizes of late one must include Salman Rushdie (India and Pakistan), Kazuo Ishiguro (Japan), and Timothy Mo (Hong Kong); and if one includes novels in English written by authors occasionally resident in Britain one must include the works of Chinua Achebe and Nobel Prize winner Wole Soyinka (Nigeria), and of Anita Desai (India). And then there are all the Canadian, Australian, not to mention American, novelists who play important roles on the contemporary scene. The contemporary English novel, in other words, is and is not particularly English. It is English in that it is written in English, published in England, and widely read in England and the rest of

Britain; it is non-English insofar as its authors do not have English ethnic origins or even live in England.

The canon, such as it is, has rather easily accommodated itself to such facts, and while the academic world churns away attacking or defending the supposedly fearsome restrictions of the canon and the virtual impossibility of changing it, contemporary writers, their publishers, and readers have made much of the discussion moot, if not downright comical. The problem faced by the teacher of literature, then, is how in the case of contemporary English literature to accommodate the curriculum to a changing canon. Of course, one can include entire novels in a course on fiction, but that means that the new does not enter the curriculum very far. In practice, the academic version of expanding the canon of contemporary literature will almost certainly take the form of including Afro-American literature, which now appears most often in separate courses and is experienced as essentially unconnected to the central, main, defining works.

Hypertext offers one solution to this problem. In my section of the standard survey course, which is a prerequisite for majoring in English at Brown University, I include works by Derek Walcott (Jamaica) and Wole Soyinka and plan in future years to add fiction by Mo or Achebe. How can hypertext aid in conveying to students the ongoing redefinition, or rather self-redefinition, of English literature? First of all, since Soyinka writes poems alluding to *Ulysses* and *Gulliver's Travels*, one can easily create electronic links from materials on Joyce and Swift to Soyinka, thus effortlessly integrating the poems of this Nigerian author into the literary world of these Irish writers.

Since hypertext linking also encourages students to violate the rigid structure of the standard week-by-week curriculum, it allows them to encounter examples of Soyinka's work or questions about its relation to earlier writers in the course of reading those writers earlier in the curricular schedule. By allowing students to range throughout the semester, hypertext permits them to see various kinds of connections, not only historical ones of positive and negative influence but equally interesting ones involving analogy. In so doing, this kind of educational technology effortlessly inserts new work within the total context.

Such contextualization, which is a major strength of hypermedia, has an additional advantage for the educator. One of the great difficulties of introducing someone like Soyinka into an English literature course, particularly one that emphasizes contextualization, involves the time and energy — not to mention additional training required — to add the necessary contextual information. Our hypertext component, for example, already contains materials on British and continental history, religion, politics, technology, philosophy, and the like. Although Soyinka writes in English, received his undergraduate degree from Leeds, and wrote some of his work in England, he combines English and African contexts, and therefore to create for him a context analogous to that which one has created for Jonathan Swift and Robert Browning, one has to provide materials on colonial and postcolonial African history, politics, economics, geography, and religion. Since Soyinka combines English literary forms with Yoruban myth, one must provide information about that body of thought and encourage students to link it to Western and non-Western religions.

Such an enterprise, which encourages student participation, draws upon all the capacities of hypertext for team teaching, interdisciplinary approaches, and collaborative work and also inevitably redefines the educational process, particularly the process by which teaching materials, so called, develop. In particular, because hypertext corpora are inevitably open-ended, they are inevitably incomplete. They resist closure, which is one way of stating that they never die; and they also resist appearing to be authoritative: they can provide information beyond a student's or teacher's wildest expectations, yes, but they can never make that body of information appear to be the last and final word.

What Chance Has Hypertext in Education?

My experience of teaching with Intermedia since 1986 convinces me that even the comparatively limited systems and bodies of literary materials thus far available demonstrate that hypertext and hypermedia have enormous potential to improve teaching and learning. Skeptical as I first was when I became involved with the Intermedia experiment, I discovered two years later that the hypertext component of my courses allowed me to accomplish far more with them than ever before possible.

Nonetheless, I do not expect to see dramatic changes in educational practice for some time to come, in large part because of the

combination of technological conservatism and general lack of concern with pedagogy that characterize the faculty at most institutions of
higher learning, particularly at those that have pretensions to prestige.
An attendee at the 1988 Sloan-sponsored conference on educational
hypermedia at Dartmouth made this comment on the technological
conservatism of university and college educators: "It took *only* twenty-
five years for the overhead projector to make it from the bowling
alley to the classroom. I'm optimistic about academic computing; I've
begun to see computers in bowling alleys."

The Politics of Hypertext: Who Controls the Text?

Answered Prayers; or,

The Politics of Resistance

• • • • • • • After a lecture I had delivered at an Ivy League campus on the role of hypertext in literary education, a distinguished historical scholar worried aloud in conversation with me that the medium might serve primarily to indoctrinate students into poststructuralism and Marxist theory. After another talk, at a large state university in the Deep South, a younger academic, concerned with critical theory and the teaching of writing, argued (on the basis of my use of Intermedia in a historical survey) that hypertext would necessarily enforce historical approaches and prevent the theorizing of literature. Such responses have proved typical of a sizable minority of those to whom I and others who work with this new medium have introduced educational and other applications of hypertext. Many with whom I have spoken have shown interest and enthusiasm, of course, and some of those concerned with critical theory as a major professional interest have responded with valuable suggestions and advice, even while remaining guardedly skeptical. For a sizable minority, however, hypertext represents the unknown, and one is not surprised to find that they project their fears upon it, as people do on any unknown Other.

Not all observers find themselves troubled by the entrance of this latest educational technology into the portals of academe. Jean-François Lyotard, for example, argues that "it is only in the context of the grand narratives of legitimation — the life of the spirit and/or the emancipation of humanity — that the partial replacement of teachers by machines may seem inadequate or even intolerable" (*Postmodern Condition*, 51).[1] Since he has abandoned these "grand narratives," he does not resist technology that might threaten them. The historical record reveals, however, that university teachers have fiercely resisted all educational technology and associated educational practice at least since the late Middle Ages. Those who feel threatened by hypertext and associated technologies might do well to remember that, after the introduction of spacing between words made reading to oneself possible, in "fourteenth-century universities, private silent reading [was] forbidden in the classroom."[2] One can easily imagine the objections to the new technology and its associated practice, since those objections have not changed very much in the last seven centuries: "Students, if left to their own devices, will construe the texts incorrectly. Everyone knows that permitting them such control over their own education before they are ready for it is not good for them. They don't yet know enough to make such decisions. And besides, what is to become of us if they use this insidious technology by themselves? What are we to *do?*" Similarly, when books appeared, many faculty members feared these dangerous new teaching machines, which clearly ceded much of the instructor's knowledge and power to the student. The mass production and wide distribution made possible by printing, which threatened to swamp ancient authority in a flood of modern mediocrity, also permitted people to teach themselves outside institutional control. Therefore, well into the eighteenth century, undergraduates in European universities had access to the library only a few hours per week.

Hypertext systems, just like printed books, dramatically change the roles of student, teacher, assignment, evaluation, reading list, as well as relations among individual instructors, courses, departments, and disciplines. No wonder so many faculty find so many "reasons" not to look at hypertext. Perhaps scariest of all for the teacher, hypertext answers teachers' sincere prayers for active, independent-minded students who take more responsibility for their education and are not afraid to challenge and disagree. The problem with answered prayers is that one may get that for which one asked, and then . . . What more terrifying for professors of English, who have for decades called for creativity, independent mindedness, and *all those other good things*, to receive them from their students! Complaining, hoping, even struggling heroically, perhaps, to awaken their students, they have nonetheless accommodated themselves to present-day education and its institutions, which include the rituals of lecture, class discussions, examinations through which they themselves have passed and which (they are the evidence) have some good effects on some students.

■ ■ ■ ■ ■ ■ ■

The Marginalization

of Technology

and the Mystification

of Literature

Discussions of the politics of hypertext have to mention its power, at least at the present time, to make many critical theorists, particularly Marxists, very uncomfortable. Alvin Kernan wryly observes, "That the primary modes of production affect consciousness and shape the superstructure of culture is, not since Marx, exactly news, but . . . both Whiggish theories of progress and Marxist historical dialectic have failed to satisfy the desire to understand the technologically generated changes or to provide much real help in deciding what might be useful and meaningful responses to such radical change."[3] Anyone who encounters the statements of Fredric Jameson and other critical theorists about the essential or basic lack of importance of technology, particularly information technology, to ideology and thought in general recognizes that these authors conspicuously marginalize technology. As Terry Eagleton's fine discussions of general and literary modes of production demonstrate, contemporary Marxist theory has drawn upon the kind of materials Kernan, McLuhan, and other students of information technology have made available.[4] For this reason, when other Marxists, like Jameson, claim that examining the effects of technology on culture inevitably produces technological determinism, one should suspect that such a claim derives more from widespread humanist technophobia than from anything in Marxist thought itself. Jameson's statements about technological determinism bear directly upon the reception of ideas of hypertext within those portions of the academic world for which it has most to offer but which, history suggests, seem most likely to resist its empowerment. This rejection of a powerful analytical tool lying ready to hand appears particularly odd given that, as Michael Ryan observes, "technology—form-giving labor—is, according to Marx, the 'nature' of human activity, thereby putting into question the distinction between nature and culture, at least as it pertains to human life."[5]

In *Marxism and Form*, Jameson reveals both the pattern and the reason for this apparently illogical resistance to work that could easily support his own. There he argues that,

however materialistic such an approach to history may seem, nothing is farther from Marxism than the stress on invention and technique as the primary cause of historical change. Indeed, it seems to me that such theories (of the kind which regard the steam engine as the cause of the Industrial Revolution, and which have recently been rehearsed yet again, in streamlined modernistic form, in the works of Marshall McLuhan) function as a substitute for Marxist historiography in the way they offer a feeling of concreteness comparable to economic subject matter, at the same time that they dispense with any consideration of the human factors of classes and of the social organization of production. (74)

One must admire Jameson's forthrightness here in admitting that his parodied theories of McLuhan and other students of the relations of technology and human culture potentially "function as a substitute for Marxist historiography," but the evidence I have presented in previous pages makes clear that Eisenstein, McArthur, Chartier, Kernan, and many other recent students of information technology often focus precisely on "the human factors of classes and of the social organization of production." In fact, these historians of information technology and associated reading practices offer abundant material that has potential to support Marxist analyses.

Jameson attacks McLuhan again a decade later in *The Political Unconscious*. There he holds that an old-fashioned naive conception of causality, which he "assumed to have been outmoded by the indeterminacy principle of modern physics," appears in what he calls "that technological determinism of which MacLuhanism [*sic*] remains the most interesting contemporary expression, but of which certain more properly Marxist studies like Walter Benjamin's ambiguous *Baudelaire* are also variants" (25). In response to the fact that Marxism itself includes "models which have so often been denounced as mechanical or mechanistic," Jameson gingerly accepts such models, though his phrasing suggests extraordinary reluctance: "I would want to argue that the category of mechanical effectivity retains a purely local validity in cultural analysis where it can be shown that billiard-ball causality remains one of the (nonsynchronous) laws of our particular fallen social reality. It does little good, in other words, to banish 'extrinsic' categories from our thinking, when the latter continue to have a hold on the objective realities about which we plan to think." He then offers as an example the "unquestionable causal relationship" between changes in "the 'inner form' of the novel itself" (25) and the late-nineteenth-century shift from triple-decker to single-volume format. I find this entire passage very confusing, in part because in it Jameson seems to end by accepting what he had begun by denying — or at least he accepts what those like McLuhan have stated rather than what he apparently assumes them to have argued. His willingness to accept that "mechanical effectivity retains a purely local validity in cultural analysis" seems to do no more than describe what Eisenstein, Chartier, and others do. The tentativeness of his acceptance also creates problems. I do not understand why Jameson writes, "I would want to argue," as if the matter were as yet only a distant possibility, when the end of this sentence and those that follow show that he definitely makes that argument. Finally, I find troubling the conspicuous muddle of his apparently generous admission that "it does little good . . . to banish 'extrinsic' categories from our thinking, when they continue to have a hold on the objective realities about which we plan to think." Such extrinsic categories might turn out to match "the objective realities about which we plan to think," or again, these objective realities might turn out to support the hypothesis contained in extrinsic categories, but it only mystifies things to describe categories as having "a hold on . . . objective realities."

Such prose from Jameson, who often writes with clarity about particularly difficult matters, suggests that this mystification and muddle derives from his need to exclude technology and its history from Marxist analyses. We have seen how hard Jameson works to exclude technological factors from consideration, and we have also observed that they not only offer no threat to Jamesonian Marxism but even have potential to support it (Eisenstein, *Printing Press*, 406).[6] Jameson's exclusions, I suggest, therefore have little to do with Marxism. Instead, they exemplify the humanist's common technophobia, which derives from that "venerable tradition of proud ignorance of matters material, mechanical, or commercial" that Eisenstein observes in students of literature and history (706).

Such resistance to the history of technology does not appear only in Marxists, though in them, as I have suggested, the exclusion strikes one as particularly odd. While reading Annette Lavers's biography of Roland Barthes, I encountered another typical instance of the humanist's curious, if characteristic, reticence to grant any importance to technology, however defined, as if so doing would remove status and power: "The contemporary expansion of linguistics into cybernetics, computers, and machine translation," she tells us, "probably played its part in Barthes's evolution on this subject; but the true reason is no doubt to be found in the metaphysical change in outlook which resulted in his new literary doctrine" (*Roland Barthes*, 138). After pointing to Barthes's obvious intellectual participation in some of the leading currents of his own culture (or strands that weave his own cultural context), she next takes back what she has granted. Although her first clause announces that computing and associated technologies "probably" played a part in "Barthes's evolution on this subject," she immediately takes back that "probably" by stating unequivocally that "the true reason" — the other factors were apparently false reasons, now properly marginalized — "without a doubt" lies in Barthes's "metaphysical change." One might have expected to encounter a phrase like "the most important reason," but Lavers instead suddenly changes direction and brings up matters of truth and falsity and of doubt and certainty.

Two things about Lavers's discomfort deserve mention: First, when confronted with the possibility that technology may play a contributing role in some aspect of culture, Lavers, like Jameson and so many other humanists, resorts to devices of mystification, which suggests that such matters intrude in some crucial way upon matters of power and status. Second, her mystification consists of reducing complexity to simplicity, multivocality to univocality. Her original statement proposes that several possible contributing factors shaped Barthes's "evolution," but once we traverse the semicolon, the possibilities, or rather probabilities, that she herself has just proposed instantly vanish into error, and a "metaphysical change in outline" in all its vagueness becomes the sole causation.

One wonders why critical theorists thus marginalize technology, which, like poetry and political action, is a production of society and individual imagination. Since marginalization results from one group's placement of itself at a center, one must next ask which group places itself at the center of power and understanding, and the answer must be one that feels itself threatened by the importance of technology. Ryan asks, "What is the operation of exclusion in a philosophy that permits one group, or value, or idea to be kept out so that another can be safeguarded internally and turned into a norm?" (*Marxism and Deconstruction*, 3). One such operation that I have frequently encountered after talks on educational hypertext takes the form of a statement something like "I am a Luddite" or "What you say is very interesting, but I can't use (or teach with) computers, because I'm a Luddite." (Can you imagine the following? "I can't use lead pencils — ballpoint pens — typewriters — printed books — photocopies — library catalogues because I'm a Luddite.") All the self-proclaimed Luddites in academe turn out to oppose only the newest machines, not machines in general and certainly not machines that obviate human drudgery. Such proclamations of Ludditism come permeated by irony, since literary scholars as a group entirely depend on the technologies of writing and printing. The first of these technologies, writing, began as the hieratic possession of the politically powerful, and the second provides one of the first instances of production-line interchangeable parts used in heavily capitalized production. Scholars and theorists today can hardly be Luddites, though they can be suspicious of the latest form of information technology, one whose advent threatens, or which they believe threatens, their power and position. In fact, the self-presentation of knowledge workers as machine-breakers defending their chance to survive in conditions of soul-destroying labor in bare, subsistence conditions tell us a lot about the resistance. Such mystification simultaneously romanticizes the humanists' resistance while presenting their anxieties in a grotesquely inappropriate way. In other words, the self-presentation of the modern literary scholar or critical theorist as Luddite romanticizes an unwillingness to perceive actual conditions of their own production.

Perhaps my favorite anecdote and possibly one that makes a particularly significant contribution to our understanding of resistance is this: after a lecture on hypertext and critical theory at one institution, a young European-trained faculty member who identified his specialty as critical theory candidly admitted, "I've never felt old-fashioned before." As the latest of the newfound, new-fangled developments, hypertext and computing in general have the (apparent) power to make those who position themselves as the advocates of the new appear to themselves and others as old-fashioned.

■ ■ ■ ■ ■ ■ ■ ■   The discussions of hypertext in the previous chapters all raise political questions — questions of

The Politics of   power, status, and institutional change. All these
changes have political contexts and political impli-

Particular Technologies   cations. Considerations of hypertext, like all considerations of critical theory and literature, have to
take into account what Fredric Jameson terms
the basic "recognition that there is nothing that is not social and historical — indeed, that everything is 'in the last analysis' political"
(*Political Unconscious*, 20). A fully implemented embodiment of a networked hypertext system such as I have described obviously creates
empowered readers, ones who have more power relative both to the
texts they read and to the authors of these texts. The reader-author
as student similarly has more power relative to the teacher and the
institution. This pattern of relative empowerment, which we must
examine with more care and some skepticism, appears to support the
notion that the logic of information technologies, which tend toward
increasing dissemination of knowledge, implies increasing democratization and decentralization of power.

Technology always empowers someone. It empowers those who
possess it, those who make use of it, and those who have access to
it. From the very beginnings of hypertext (which I locate in Vannevar
Bush's proposals for the memex), its advocates have stressed that it
grants new power to people. Writers on hypertext almost always
continue to associate it with individual freedom and empowerment.
"After all," claim the authors of a study concerning what one can learn
about learning from the medium, "the essence of hypertext is that
users are entirely free to follow links wherever they please."[7] Although
Bush chiefly considered the memex's ability to assist the researcher
or knowledge worker in coping with large amounts of information, he
still conceived the issue in terms of ways to empower individual
thinkers in relation to systems of information and decision. The
inventors of computer hypertext have explicitly discussed it in terms
of empowerment of a more general class of reader-authors. Douglas
Englebart, for example, who invented the first actual working hypertext environment, called his system Augment; and Ted Nelson, who
sees Xanadu as the embodiment of the sixties New Left thought, calls
on us to "imagine a new accessibility and excitement that can unseat
the video narcosis that now sits on our land like a fog. Imagine a new

libertarian literature with alternative explanations so that anyone can choose the pathway or approach that best suits him or her; with ideas accessible and interesting to everyone, so that a new richness and freedom can come to the human experience; imagine a rebirth of literacy" (*Literary Machines*, 1/4).[8]

Like other technologies, those centering on information serve as artificial, human-made means of amplifying some physical or mental capacity. Lyotard describes computing and other forms of information technology in terms usually assigned to wooden legs and artificial arms: "Technical devices originated as prosthetic aids for the human organs or as physiological systems whose function it is to receive data or condition the context. They follow a principle, and it is the principle of optimal performance: maximizing output (the information or modifications obtained) and minimizing input (the energy expended in the process)" (*Postmodern Condition*, 44). According to the *American Heritage Dictionary*, the term *prosthesis* has the two closely related meanings of an "artificial replacement of a limb, tooth, or other part of the body" and "an artificial device used in such replacement." Interestingly, *prosthesis* has an early association with language and information, since it derives from the late Latin word meaning "addition of a letter or syllable," which in turn comes from the Greek for "attachment" or "addition, from *prostithenai*, to put, add: *pros-*, in addition + *tithenai*, to place, to put." Whereas its late Latin form implies little more than an addition following the rules of linguistic combination, its modern application suggests a supplement required by some catastrophic occurrence that reduced the individual requiring the prosthesis to a condition of severe need, as in the case of a person who has lost a limb in war, in an automobile accident, or from bone cancer or, conversely, of a person suffering as a result of a "birth defect." In each case the individual using the prosthesis requires an artificial supplement to restore some capacity or power.

Lyotard's not uncommon use of this term to describe all technology suggests a powerful complex of emotional and political justifications for technology and its promises of empowerment. Transferring the term *prosthesis* from the field of rehabilitation (itself an intriguing term) gathers a fascinating, appalling congeries of emotion and need that accurately conveys the attitudes contemporary academics and intellectuals in the humanities hold toward technology. Resentment of the device one needs, resentment at one's own need and guilt, and a

Romantic dislike of the artificiality of the device that answers one's needs mark most humanists' attitudes toward technology, and these same factors appear in the traditional view of the single most important technology we possess — writing. These attitudes result, as Derrida has shown, in a millennia-long elevation of speech above writing, its supposedly unnatural supplement.

Walter J. Ong, who reminds us that writing is technology, exemplifies the comparatively rare scholar who considers its artificiality as something in its favor: "To say writing is artificial is not to condemn it but to praise it. Like other artificial creations and indeed more than any other, it is utterly invaluable and indeed essential for the realization of fuller, interior, human potentials. . . . Alienation from a natural milieu can be good for us and indeed is in many ways essential for full human life. To live and to understand fully, we need not only proximity but also distance" (*Orality and Literacy*, 82). Like McLuhan, Ong claims that "technologies are not mere exterior aids but also interior transformations of consciousness" (82), and he therefore holds that writing created human nature, thought, and culture as we know them. Writing empowers people by enabling them to do things otherwise impossible — permitting them not just to send letters to distant places or to create records that preserve some information from the ravages of time but to think in ways otherwise impossible.

Abstractly sequential, classificatory, explanatory examination of phenomena or of stated truths is impossible without writing and reading. . . . In the total absence of any writing, there is nothing outside the thinker, no text, to enable him or her to produce the same line of thought again or even to verify whether he or she has done so. . . . In an oral culture, to think through something in non-formulaic, non-patterned, non-mnemonic terms, even if it were possible, would be a waste of time, for such thought, once worked through, could never be recovered with any effectiveness, as it could be with the aid of writing. It would not be abiding knowledge but simply a passing thought. (8–9, 34–35)

Technology always empowers someone, some group in society, and it does so at a certain cost. The question must always be, therefore, what group or groups does it empower? Lynn White shows in *Medieval Technology and Social Change* that the introduction from the Far East of three inventions provided the technological basis of feudalism: the horse collar and the metal plow produced far higher yields than had scratch plowing on small patches of land, and these two new devices produced food surpluses that encouraged landowners to amass large tracts of land. The stirrup, which seems to have come from India, permitted a heavily armored warrior to fight from horseback; specifically it permitted him to swing a heavy sword or battle axe, or to attack with a lance, without falling off his mount. The economic power created by people employing the horse collar and the metal plow provided wealth to pay for the expensive weaponry, which in turn defended the farmers. According to White, these forms of farming and military technology provided crucial, though not necessarily defining, components of feudalism.[9] Whom did this technology empower? Those who ultimately became knights and landowners in an increasingly hierarchical society obviously obtained more power, as did the church, which benefited from increasing surplus wealth. Those who made and sold the technology also obtained a degree of status, power, and wealth. What about the farm worker? Those freemen in a tribal society who lost their land and became serfs obviously lost power. But were any serfs better off, either safer or better fed, than they had been before feudalism, as apologists for the Middle Ages used to argue? I do not know how one could answer such questions, though one component of an answer is certain: even if one had far more detailed evidence about living conditions of the poor than we do, no answer would come forth garbed in neutrality, because one cannot even begin to consider one's answer without first deciding what kind of weight to assign to matters such as the relative value of nutrition, safety, health, power, and status both in our own and in an alien culture. Another thing is clear as well: the introduction of new technology into a culture cuts at least two ways.

Like other forms of technology, those involving information have shown a double-edged effect, though in the long run — sometimes the run has been very long indeed — the result has always been to democratize information and power. Writing and reading, which first belonged to a tiny elite, appears in the ancient Middle East as an arcane skill that supports the power of the state by recording taxes, property, and similar information. Writing, which can thus conserve or preserve, has other political effects, Ong tells us, and "shortly after it first appeared, it served to freeze legal codes in early Sumeria" (*Orality and Literacy*, 41). Only careful examination of the historical evidence can suggest which groups within society gained and which lost from such recording. In a particular society within a particular battle of forces, only nobility or nobility and priesthood could have gained, whereas in other situations the common person could have benefited from stability and clear laws.

Another political implication inheres in the fact that a "chirographic (writing) culture and even more a typographic (print) culture can distance and in a way denature even the human, itemizing such things as the names of leaders and political divisions in an abstract, neutral list entirely devoid of a human action context. An oral culture has no vehicle so neutral as a list" (42). The introduction of writing into a culture effects many changes, and all of them involve questions of power and status. When it first appeared in the ancient world, writing made its possessors unique. Furthermore, if writing changes the way people think as radically as McLuhan, Ong, and others have claimed, then writing drove a sharp wedge between the literate and the illiterate, encouraged a sharp division between these two groups that would rapidly become classes or castes, and greatly increased the power and prestige of the lettered. In the millennia that it took for writing to diffuse through large proportions of entire societies, however, writing shifted the balance from the state to the individual, from the nobility to the polis.

Writing, like other technologies, possesses a logic, but it can produce different, even contrary, effects in different social, political, and economic contexts. Marshall McLuhan points to its multiple, often opposing effects when he remarks that "if rigorous centralism is a main feature of literacy and print, no less so is the eager assertion of individual rights" (*Gutenberg Galaxy*, 220). Historians have long recognized the contradictory roles played by print in the Reformation and in the savage religious wars that followed. "In view of the carnage which ensued," Eisenstein observes, "it is difficult to imagine how anyone could regard the more efficient duplication of religious texts as an unmixed blessing. Heralded on all sides as a 'peaceful art,' Gutenberg's invention probably contributed more to destroying Christian concord and inflaming religious warfare than any of the so-called arts of war ever did" (*Printing Press*, 319).[10] One reason for these conflicts, Eisenstein suggests, lies in the fact that when fixed in print — put down, that is, *in black and white*, "positions once taken were more difficult to reverse. Battles of books prolonged polarization, and pamphlet wars quickened the process" (326).

I contend that the history of information technology from writing to hypertext reveals an increasing democratization or dissemination of power. Writing begins this process, for by exteriorizing memory it converts knowledge from the possession of one to the possession of more than one. As Ryan correctly argues, "writing can belong to anyone; it puts an end to the ownership or self-identical property that speech signaled" (*Marxism and Deconstruction*, 29). The democratic thrust of information technologies derives from their diffusing information and the power that such diffusion can produce.[11]

Such empowerment has always marked applications of new information technology to education. As Eisenstein points out, for example, Renaissance treatises, such as those for music, radically reconfigured the cultural construction of learning by freeing the reader from a subordinate relation to a particular person: "The chance to master new skills without undergoing a formal apprenticeship or schooling also encouraged a new sense of independence on the part of many who became self-taught. Even though the new so-called 'silent instructors' did no more than duplicate lessons already being taught in classrooms and shops, they did cut the bonds of subordination which kept pupils and apprentices under the tutelage of a given master" (*Printing Press*, 244). Eisenstein cites Newton as an example of someone who used books obtained at "local book fairs and libraries" to teach himself mathematics with little or no outside help (245). First with writing, then with print, and now with hypertext one observes increasing synergy produced when readers widely separated in space and time build upon one another's ideas.

Tom McArthur's history of reference materials provides another reminder that all developments and inflections of such technology serve the interests of particular classes or groups. The early-seventeenth-century "compilers of the hard-word dictionaries" did not in the manner of modern lexicographers set out to record usage. Instead, they achieved great commercial success by "transferring the word-store of Latin wholesale into their own language. . . . They sought (in the spirit of both the Renaissance and Reformation) to broaden the base of the educated Elect. Their works were for the nonscholarly, for the wives of the gentry and the bourgeoisie, for merchants and artisans and other aspirants to elegance, education and power" (*Worlds of Reference*, 87). These dictionaries served, in other words, to diffuse status and power, and the members of the middle classes who created them for other members of their classes self-consciously followed identifiable political aims.

The dictionary created by the French Academy, McArthur reminds us, also embodied a lexicographical program that had clear and immediate political implications. Claude Favre de Vaugelas, the amateur grammarian who directed the work of the Academy, sought "to regulate the French language in terms of aristocratic good taste," as a means of making French the "social, cultural, and scientific successor to Latin" (94). This dictionary is one of the most obvious instances of the way print technology sponsors nationalism, the vernacular, and relative democratization. It standardizes the language in ways that empower particular classes and geographical areas, inevitably at the expense of others. Nonetheless, it also permits the eventual homogenization of language and a corollary, if long-in-coming, possibility of democratization.

By the end of the eighteenth century, Kernan argues, print technology had produced many social and political changes that altered the face of the literary world. "An older system of polite or courtly letters — primarily oral, aristocratic, amateur, authoritarian, court-centered — was swept away at this time and gradually replaced by a new print-based, market-centered, democratic literary system" (*Printing Technology*, 4). Furthermore, by changing the standard literary roles of scholar, teacher, and writer, print "noticeably increased the importance and the number of critics, editors, bibliographers, and literary historians" at the same time that it increasingly freed writers from patronage and state censorship. Print simultaneously transformed the audience from a few readers of manuscripts to a larger number "who bought books to read in the privacy of their homes." Copyright law, which dates from this period, also redefined the role of the author by making "the writer the owner of his own writing" (4–5).

Like earlier technologies of information and cultural memory, electronic computing has obvious political implications. As Gregory Ulmer argued during a recent conference on electronic literacy, artificial intelligence projects, which use computers either to model the human mind or to make decisions that people would make, necessarily embody a particular ideology and a particular conception of humanity.[12] What, then, are the political implications of hypertext and hypertext systems?

■ ■ ■ ■ ■ ■ ■ ■ I propose to begin examining that question by looking at the political implications of events

Hypertext and described in a scenario that opened an article on the use of hypertext in literary education that I

the Politics of Reading published several years ago. It is 8:00 P.M., and, after having helped put the children to bed, Professor Jones settles into her favorite chair and reaches for her copy of Milton's *Paradise Lost* to prepare for tomorrow's class. A scholar who specializes in the poetry of Milton's time, she returns to the poem as one turns to meet an old friend. Reading the poem's opening pages, she once again encounters allusions to the Old Testament, and because she knows how seventeenth-century Christians commonly read these passages, she perceives connections both to a passage in Genesis and to its radical Christian transformations. Furthermore, her previous acquaintance with Milton allows her to recall other passages later in *Paradise Lost* that refer to this and related parts of the Bible. At the same time, she recognizes that the poem's opening lines pay homage to Homer, Vergil, Dante, and Spenser and simultaneously issue them a challenge.

Meanwhile John H. Smith, one of the most conscientious students in Professor Jones's survey of English literature, begins to prepare for class. What kind of a poem, what kind of text, does he encounter? Whereas Professor Jones experiences the great seventeenth-century epic situated within a field of relations and connections, her student encounters a far barer, less connected, reduced poem, most of whose allusions go unrecognized and almost all of whose challenges pass by unperceived. An unusually mature student, he pauses in his reading to check the footnotes for the meaning of unfamiliar words and allusions, a few of which he finds explained. Suppose one could find a way to allow Smith to experience some of the connections obvious to Professor Jones. Suppose he could touch the opening lines of *Paradise Lost,* for instance, and the relevant passages from Homer, Vergil, and the Bible would appear, or that he could touch another line and immediately encounter a list of other mentions of the same idea or image later in the poem or elsewhere in Milton's writings — or, for that matter, interpretations and critical judgments made since the poem's first publication — and that he could then call up any or all of them.[13]

This scenario originally ended with my remark that hypertext

allows students to do "all these things." Now I would like to ask what
such a scenario implies about the political relations that obtain
between teachers and students, readers and authors. These issues,
which writers on hypertext have long discussed, also arose in questions
I encountered when delivering invited talks on my experiences in
teaching with hypertext. One of the administrators at my own university, for example, asked a question I at first thought rather curious
but have since encountered frequently enough to realize is quite typical for those first encountering the medium. After I had shown some
of the ways that Intermedia enabled students to follow far more
connections than ever before possible between texts and context, she
asked if I was not worried because hypertext limited the students
too much, because it restricted them only to what was available on the
system. My first response then as now was to remark that as long as
I used print technology and the limited resources of a very poor
university library, no administrator or member of the faculty ever
worried that I found myself unable to suggest more than a very limited
number of connections, say, five or six, in a normal class discussion;
now that I can suggest six or ten times that number, thus permitting
students a far richer, less controlled experience of text, helpful educators suddenly begin to worry that I am "limiting" students by allowing
them access to some potentially totalitarian system.

One part of the reason for this reaction to educational hypertext
lies in a healthy skepticism. Another appears in the way we often
judge new approaches to pedagogy as simultaneously ineffective, even
educationally useless, and yet overpoweringly and dangerously influential. Nonetheless, the skeptical administrator raised important questions, for she is correct that the information available limits the
freedom of students and general readers alike. At this early, still experimental stage in the development of hypertext, one must pay great
attention to ensuring a multiplicity of viewpoints and kinds of information. For this reason I emphasize creating multiple overviews and
sets of links for various document sets, and I also believe that one
must produce educational materials collaboratively whenever possible;
as I have suggested, such collaboration is very easy to carry out
between individual instructors in the same department as well as
between those in different disciplines and different institutions.

Several key features of hypertext systems intrinsically promote a
new kind of academic freedom and empowerment. Reader-controlled

texts permit students to choose their own way. The political and educational necessity for this feature provides one reason why hypertext systems must always contain both bidirectional links and efficient navigational devices; otherwise developers can destroy the educational value of hypertext with instructional systems that alienate and disorient readers by forcing them down a predetermined path as if they were rats in a maze. A second feature of hypertext that has crucial political implications appears in the sheer quantity of information the reader encounters, since that quantity simultaneously protects readers against constraint and requires them to read actively, to make choices. A third liberating and empowering quality of hypertext appears in the fact that the reader also writes and links, for this power, which removes much of the gap in conventional status relations between reader and author, permits readers to read actively in an even more powerful way — by annotating documents, arguing with them, leaving their own traces. As long as any reader has the power to enter the system and leave his or her mark, neither the tyranny of the center nor that of the majority can impose itself. The very open-endedness of the text also promotes empowering the reader.

The Political Vision of Hypertext; or, The Message in the Medium

Does hypertext as medium have a political message? Does it have a particular bias? As the capacity of hypertext systems to be infinitely re-centerable suggests, they have the corollary characteristic of being antihierarchical and democratic in several different ways. To start, as the authors of "Reading and Writing the Electronic Book" point out, in such systems, "ideally, authors and readers should have the same set of integrated tools that allow them to browse through other material during the document preparation process and to add annotations and original links as they progress through an information web. In effect, the boundary between author and reader should largely disappear" (Yankelovich, Meyrowitz, and van Dam, 21). One sign of the disappearance of boundaries between author and reader consists in its being the reader, not the author, who largely determines how the reader moves through the system, for the reader can determine the order and principle of investigation. Hypertext has the potential, thus far only

partially realized, to be a democratic or multicentered system in yet
another way: as readers contribute their comments and individual
documents, the sharp division between author and reader that characterizes page-bound text begins to blur and threatens to vanish, with
several interesting implications: first, by contributing to the system,
users accept some responsibility for materials anyone can read; and
second, students thus establish a community of learning, demonstrating to themselves that a large part of any investigation rests on the
work of others.

Writing about electronic information technology in general rather
than about hypertext in particular, McLuhan proposed: "The 'simultaneous field' of electric information structures, today reconstitutes
the conditions and need for dialogue and participations, rather than
specialism and private initiative in all levels of social experience"
(*Gutenberg Galaxy*, 141). McLuhan's point that electronic media privilege collaborative, cooperative practice, which receives particular
support from hypertext, suggests that such media embody and possibly
support a particular political system or construction of relations of
power and status. J. Hillis Miller similarly argues that "one important
aspect of these new technologies of expression and research is political. These technologies are inherently democratic and transnational.
They will help create new and hitherto unimagined forms of democracy, political involvement, obligation, and power" ("Literary Theory,"
20). Writing in the spring of 1989, Miller commented: "Far from
being necessarily the instruments of thought control, as Orwell in
1984 foresaw, the new regime of telecommunications seems to be
inherently democratic. It has helped bring down dictator after dictator
in the past few months" (21).

Michael Ryan, who is also not writing about hypertext, nonetheless
offers more specific clues to its political implications and effects.
Beginning from the assumption that "there is a necessary relationship
between conceptual apparatuses and political institutions" (*Marxism
and Deconstruction*, 8), he argues that Derridean deconstruction implies

that absolute truth, defined as the adequacy of language to conscious intention, without any
unconscious remains or side effects, is not a justifiable norm of political theory and practice
[and should] . . . be abandoned in favor of multiple, situationally defined, complexly mediated,
differentiated strategies. In other words, the "decentering" of the metaphysical assumption

implies a decentering of the political project. . . . What is at stake, then, is a politics of multiple centers and plural strategies, less geared toward the restoration of a supposedly ideal situation held to be intact and good than to the micrological fine-tuning of questions of institutional power, work and reward distribution, sexual political dynamics, resource allocation, domination, and a broad range of problems whose solutions would be situationally and participationally defined. . . . Deconstruction comes closest to theorizing (and discursively practicing) this decentered plurality, but the nature of the object described defuses any potential centering privilege this theoretical insight might bestow. (114–116)

The political vision Ryan offers, which he terms "critical marxism," resembles that implied by hypertextuality, Bakhtinian multivocality, and the dialogic mode of collaborative endeavor proposed by Lisa Ede and Andrea Lunsford. Like Bakhtin, whose emphasis upon multivocality and critical practice responds to Stalinism, Ryan's amalgam of Marxism and Derridean deconstruction responds to the threat of a totalitarian Marxist-Leninism by dissolving its conceptual foundations, which include a rigid linearity.[14] Ryan defines his critical Marxism specifically in contrast to Russian communism. The economic theory of critical Marxism, for example, which rejects "the model of authoritarian central state communism," instead advances "models of socialism which are dehierarchized, egalitarian, and democratic. Whereas the Soviet model privileges productive forces (technology, heavy industry, and the like) over productive relations, thus permitting the preservation of capitalist work relations, critical marxists demand a complete transformation of the form of work and of all social power relations, in 'private' as much as in the 'public' sphere. They see capital and patriarchy as equally important adversaries" (xiii–xiv).

Ryan defines critical Marxist politics and political organization by means of an equally sharp contrast to the Soviet model:

Critical marxists depart from the leninist tradition in that they call for political organizational forms that are not exclusive, elitist, hierarchical, or disciplinarian. The postrevolutionary "arrangement of things," to use Marx's phrase, should include the political advances made by the bourgeoisie (such as democracy and civil rights), just as a socialist economy must necessarily presuppose the technological and economic advances that capitalism produces. . . . Rather than to anarchism as some might contend, this critique leads, I shall argue, to a radical socialism that is more akin to the participatory and egalitarian models of self-government and self-management proposed by democratic socialists, socialist feminists, and autonomists than to the hierarchical and party-elitist, central state, leninist variety that exists in the East. (xiv, 7)

Ryan draws upon major points of deconstruction, particularly
upon Derrida's meditations on textuality that theorize hypertextuality,
to construct a defence against communist totalitarianism. Like de-
centeredness and plurality, the theorized "inconclusivity," "indeterminacy," and "undecidability" of deconstruction keep the iron doors
of the Leninist tradition from slamming shut on Ryan's appealing
political vision. Critical Marxism, according to Ryan, is a politics of
continuing process that will never lead either to utopian stasis or
dystopian tyranny. The openness of deconstruction offers the caution
that removing the metaphysical roots of ideology "can never be completed, either *at one go* or *once and for all*. The work involved is constant and repetitive, like, as Gayatri Spivak put it, keeping a house
clean" (117). Ryan uses the word *caution*, to be sure, but in doing so
he simultaneously reassures himself and us that critical Marxism will
not — cannot — repeat the horrors of Stalinism.

I have my doubts, I admit, that Ryan offers an authentically Marxist
political vision. Attractive as I find the goals his critical Marxism
embraces, I suspect that he tries to eat his cake and still have it. He
clearly wages a war on two fronts, trying to attack both Marxist-
Leninism and capitalism. He tries to convince the leftist audience,
from which he clearly assumes most of his readers will come, and
works hard to win converts from orthodox Marxism to his decentralized quasi-Marxism. To achieve this end, he relies primarily on two
strategies. He tries to establish his credentials as an authentic radical
by relating his personal history of political belief, and he attacks
Western capitalist democracies, and only them, when both they and
Marxist countries provide abundant targets for his criticism. For
example, his mentioning "the poisoning of the world by transnationals" (43) appears rather unnecessarily biased, particularly now that
Eastern bloc countries, such as East Germany, freely admit they have
created some of the world's most toxically polluted environments
and ask for assistance. I emphasize Ryan's one-sidedness not to create
a balance by claiming, "See, the Commies do it, too!" Rather, if one
attempts to construct a politico-economic system that combines the
best of East and West, of capitalism and Marxism, as Ryan proposes to
do, one must clearly locate the sources of major problems, such as
ravaging the environment. Attacking only the "transnationals," however justly, for destroying the environment while classical Marxist
regimes bear equal responsibility will not help one perceive that the

problems derive from a certain kind of industrial technology rather than from economic systems.

Whatever rhetorical and other difficulties Ryan stumbles over in his advocacy of critical Marxism, he manages to offer the vision of a truly de-centered, or multiply centered, politics that seems the political equivalent of Richard Rorty's edifying philosophy whose purpose is "to keep the conversation going rather than to find objective truth. . . . The danger which edifying discourse tries to avert is that some given vocabulary, some way in which people might come to think of themselves, will deceive them into thinking that from now on all discourse could be, or should be, normal discourse. The resulting freezing-over of culture would be, in the eyes of edifying philosophers, the dehumanization of human beings" (*Philosophy*, 377).[15] Like Bakhtin, Derrida, and Rorty, Ryan presents his views as an explicit reaction against totalitarian centrism. He and Bakhtin have the example of Marxist-Leninism, particularly during the Stalin years, whereas Derrida and Rorty react against Plato and his heirs in a manner reminiscent of Karl Popper in *The Open Society and Its Enemies*.[16] Hypertext is the technological embodiment of such a reaction and such a politics.

Gregory Ulmer comments that "the use of communications technology is a concretization of certain metaphysical assumptions, consequently that it is by changing these assumptions (for example, our notion of identity) that we will transform our communicational activities" (*Applied Grammatology*, 147). We may add that the use of communications technology is also a concretization of certain political assumptions. In particular, hypertext embodies Ryan's assumptions of the necessity for nonhierarchical, multicentered, open-ended forms of politics and government.

Having drawn upon Ryan's proposals for a critical Marxism to delineate the political implications of this information technology, I would now like to use Ellen Rooney's *Seductive Reasoning* to raise a fundamental question about open-endedness, ideology, and hypertext: Does hypertext, in a manner analogous to critical pluralism in literary theory, appropriate threatening political positions? Does it, in particular, enforce dialogue (on its own terms) and thereby exclude extremist positions? Rooney's attack on critical pluralism centers on the charge that in purporting to include all positions, it in fact excludes its most powerful opponents under the guise of sweet reasonableness. "The pluralist's invitation to critics and theorists of all

kinds to join him in 'dialogue,'" she explains, "is a seductive gesture
that constitutes every interpreter — *no matter what her conscious critical
affiliation* — as an effect of the desire to persuade. . . . Pluralistic forms
of discourse first imagine a universal community in which every
individual (reader) is a potential convert, vulnerable to persuasion,
and then require that . . . every critic must address a general or universal audience."[17] After examining Rooney's explanation of the ways
pluralism appropriates opposition, I propose to raise the question
whether hypertext systems do the same.

In creating its universal audience of generalized and neutralized
readers, critical pluralism excludes from consideration as merely acci-
dental all matters of "gender, race, class position, sexuality, nationality,
and material interests" (62). By concentrating solely upon the episte-
mological dimensions of reading, theorists elide "precisely the critical
role of the resisting newreaders, black literary critics, marxist literary
critics, feminist literary critics, and others, who . . . [expose] the interests that ground 'standard meanings'" (42). In addition, contemporary
pluralism lives with a contradiction at its heart, because while claiming to include all views it finds itself committed to "*essential exclusions,
in particular, the exclusion of . . . marxist theory . . .* because marxism
itself theorizes the necessity, indeed, the inevitability, of exclusions"
(62–63).

After explaining that in her use of the term, "pluralism has relatively little to do with an individual critic's lack of dogmatism or his
tolerance of diverse views" (2), she examines its intonations not only,
as one might expect, in writings of pluralism's explicit advocates, E. D.
Hirsch and Wayne Booth, but also, more surprisingly, in those of its
explicit opponents — Stanley Fish, Paul de Man, and Fredric Jameson — all of whom ultimately elide "historical explanation" with "a
general, normative model. For Hirsch, this model is logical, for Booth,
ethical, for Fish, rhetorical, in the sense of polemical. . . . From the
perspective of pluralist practice, then, de Man's rigid distinction
between the linguistic and the extralinguistic . . . is merely routine"
(187). According to Rooney, therefore, "the pluralist may be a partisan
of *any* faction within the critical field, from intentionalist to feminist,
myth critic to marxist, so long as she practices (and of course preaches)
a contentious criticism founded on the theoretical possibility of universal or general persuasion. Pluralism, then, is not a practical commitment to methodological eclecticism, but an ensemble of discursive

practices constituted and bounded by a problematic of general persuasion" (2).

Does the critique of critical pluralism in *Seductive Reasoning* pertain
to hypertext? Is this a medium whose inclusiveness neutralizes the
politically suspect? I do not believe it is. Rooney's critique of pluralism
can apply to hypertext and the politics it implies only insofar as one
assumes that the simple fact of inclusion in some way appropriates
and thereby defuses Marxist, theocratic, or other exclusivist and exclu-
sionist positions. Of course, one might think considering the possibility that an information technology or medium could have such an
effect absurd. True, as we have already observed, book technology
provides one of the earliest instances of the combination of capitalist
investment, assembly-line work, and mass production. But who would
consider that print technology appropriates or expropriates Marx by
disseminating his ideas? The idea seems absurd, in part because the
media biases of this information technology toward fixity, multiplicity,
and rationalized clarity do not seem to intersect in a meaningful way
with the possibility of appropriation or modification. In contrast,
hypertext intervenes at the level of discursive practice. The simple
fact of linking, as we have seen, radically changes the way texts exist,
particularly in relation to one another. Linking and other aspects
of hypertextuality prevent one from avoiding the issue of inclusion
and exclusion. Including a lexia, an image, or a sound within a particular hypertext environment makes it appear experientially closer to
others; it appears close to other texts and more included in the totality
than would, say, placing a separate book within a library make it
appear in relation to the other volumes. In addition, linking and reader
control both might seem to have the potential of permitting someone
with a different or opposing ideology to appropriate a radical text
by attaching materials that contradict, misinterpret, or otherwise
infringe upon it.

The main reason I think hypertext does not appropriate alien
points of view, and thereby exclude them under the guise of pretend-
ing to include them, lies in the presence of the (politically) responsible,
active reader: because the reader chooses his or her own reading
paths, the responsibility lies with the reader. In linking and following
links lie responsibility — political responsibility — since each reader
establishes his or her own line of reading. This conception of the
reader's political responsibility matches Rooney's description of an

active, constructionist reader who takes responsibility for what she reads. Rooney herself credits Althusser with recognizing that "Marx founds a radical theory and practice of reading by refusing the ideology of 'innocent' *reading* which makes a written discourse the immediate transparency of the true, and the real discourse of a voice" (44).[18] So, one may add, do hypertext systems.

Many of Rooney's other points also seem to mesh with hypertextuality and its implications for politics and critical theory, one of the most obvious of which is her attraction to a "theoretical emphasis on the cut, the break" that led her, she explains, to "a politics of anti-pluralisms" (14). Similarly, her poststructuralist conception of self and selfhood parallels the effects we have observed in hypertext environments and therefore should have the same anti-pluralist implications. In her chapter on Fish she points out that "any theoretical account of the subject as an effect of language, a matrix of discontinuous codes that speak the 'individual,' discredits everything pluralism seeks to preserve" (137). Since hypertext diffuses selfhood and authorship at the same time that it unites these functions to other elements of textuality, it also implicitly discredits pluralist ideology.

Perhaps the most single important emphasis that Rooney shares with this discussion of hypertextuality (as well as with Ryan, Rorty, Hayden White, and others) is her deep suspicion of centrality and its flatteries. *Seductive Reasoning* therefore sets out to "delineate as sharply as possible the structure of a hegemonic pluralism, a discourse of power, of the center, or (as pluralists like to think) of the mainstream" (4). She therefore praises those "strains of feminist criticism" that have remained wary of "the blandishments of general persuasion" and quotes Gayatri Spivak's warning: "Pluralism is the method employed by the *central* authorities to neutralize opposition by seeming to accept it. The gesture of pluralism on the part of the *marginal* can only mean capitulation to the center" (242). Since hypertext destabilizes the very conception of a permanent center, or the center as any but a traveling focus of one's attention, it resists such co-option.

The Politics of Access

Mixed with the generally democratic, even anarchic tendencies of hypertext is another strain that might threaten to control the most basic characteristics of this information medium. Readers in hypertext obviously have far more control over the order in which they read individual passages than do readers of books, and to a large extent the reader's experience also defines the boundaries of the text and even the identity of the author, if one can conveniently speak of such a unitary figure in this kind of dispersed medium.

The use of hypertext systems involves four kinds of access to text and control over it: reading, linking, writing, and networking. Access to hypertext begins with the technology required to read and produce hypertext, and this technology has only recently begun to become available. Once it becomes widespread enough to serve as a dominant, or at least major, form of publication, issues of the right and power to use such technology will be multiplied.

One can easily envision reading a text for which one has only partial permission, so that portions of it remain forbidden, out of sight, and perhaps entirely unknown. An analogy from print technology would be having access to a published book but not to the full reports by referees, the author's contract, the manuscript before it has undergone copyediting, and so on. Conventionally, we do not consider such materials to be *part of* the book. Electronic linking has the potential, however, radically to redefine the nature of the text, and since this redefinition includes connection of the so-called main text to a host of ancillary ones (that then lose their ancillary-ness), issues of power immediately arise. Who controls access to such materials — the author, the publisher, or the reader?

Linking involves the essence of hypertext technology. One can expect that in the future all hypertext systems will offer the capacity that the Brown University/IRIS Intermedia system does to create links to texts over which others have editorial control. This ability to make links to lexias in which one does not possess the right to make verbal or other changes has no analogy in the world of print technology. One effect of this kind of linking is to create an intermediate realm between the writer and the reader, thus further blurring the distinction between these roles.

When discussing the educational uses of hypertext, one immediately encounters the various ways that reshaping the roles of reader and author quickly reshapes those of student and teacher, for this information medium enforces several kinds of collaborative learning. Granting students far more control over their reading paths than does book technology obviously empowers students in a range of ways,

onc of which is to encourage active explorations by readers and another
of which is to enable students to contextualize what they read. Pointing to such empowerment, however, leads directly to questions about
the politics of hypertext.

Hypertext demands the presence of many blocks of text that can
be linked to one another. Decisions about relevance and inclusion
obviously bear heavy ideological freight, and hypertext's very emphasis
upon connectivity means that excluding any particular bit of text
from the metatext places it comparatively much further from sight
than would be the case in print technology. When every connection
requires a particular level of effort, particularly when physical effort is
required to procure a copy of a work, availability and accessibility
become essentially equal, as they are for the skilled reader in a modern
library. When, however, some connections require no more effort
than does continuing to read the same text, *un*connected texts are
experienced as lying much farther off and availability and accessibility
become very different matters.

In addition to having the right to read and link lexias, one can also
have the right to create lexias and to link one's own text to those
created by others. The individual book is the basic unit of print text.
Hypertext has mini- and macrounits — that is, the individual lexias and
the entire system that comprises all the texts in the system, or at least
in a particular discipline or subject area. Here, as in almost every
other aspect of hypertext, we encounter crucial issues of status and
power. Since books already have a physically fixed, separate existence,
they exist in an isolation that only individual acts of intellection and
memory violate, though to be sure culture consists precisely in sharing
such acts among its constituent members. Hypertext facilitates this
sharing, but again the blurred distinction between author and reader
and the questions of inclusion or exclusion from the metatext become
issues of concern.

Complete hypertextuality requires gigantic information networks
of the kind now being planned and created. The vision of hypertext as
a means of democratic empowerment depends ultimately upon the
individual reader-author's access to these networks. As Norman Meyrowitz admits, "Down deep, we all think and believe that hypertext
is a vision that sometime soon there will be an infrastructure, national
and international, that supports a network and community of knowledge linking togcthcr myriad types of information for an enormous

variety of audiences."[19] The person occupying the roles of reader and author must have access to information, which in practice means access to a network. For the writer this access to a network becomes essential, for in the hypertext world access to a network is itself publication.

Considered as an information and publication medium, hypertext presents in starkest outline the contrast between availability and accessibility. Texts can be available somewhere in an archive, but without cataloguing, support personnel, and opportunities to visit that archive, they remain unseen and unread. Since hypertext promises to make materials living within a hypertext environment much easier to obtain, it simultaneously threatens to make any not present seem even more distant and more invisible than absent documents are in the world of print. The political implications of this contrast seem clear enough: gaining access to a network permits a text to exist *as a text* in this new information world. Lyotard, who argues that knowledge "can fit into the new channels, and become operational, only if learning is translated into quantities of information," predicts that "anything in the constituted body of knowledge that is not translatable in this way will be abandoned and that the direction of new research will be dictated by the possibility of its eventual results being translatable into computer language" (*Postmodern Condition*, 4). Antonio Zampolli, an Italian computational linguist and the recent president of the Association of Literary and Linguistic Computing, warns about this problem when he suggests an analogy between the Gutenberg revolution and what he terms the *informatization* of languages: "Languages which have not been involved with printing, have become dialects or have disappeared. The same could happen to languages that will not be 'informatized'" — transferred to the world of electronic text storage, manipulation, and retrieval.[20] As Lyotard and Zampolli suggest, individual texts and entire languages that do not transfer to a new information medium when it becomes culturally dominant will become marginalized, unimportant, virtually invisible.

Although a treatise on poetry, horticulture, or warfare that existed in half a dozen manuscripts may have continued to exist in the same number of copies several centuries after the introduction of printing, it lost power and status, except as a unique collector's item, and became far harder to use than ever before. Few readers cared to locate, much less make an inconvenient, costly, and possibly dangerous trip to peruse an individual manuscript when relatively far cheaper printed books existed close at hand. As habits and expectations of reading changed during the transition from manuscript to print, the experience of reading texts in manuscript changed in several ways. Although retaining the aura of unique objects, texts in manuscript appeared scarcer, harder to locate, and more difficult to read in comparison with books. Moreover, as readers quickly accustomed themselves to the clarity and uniformity of printed fonts, they also tended to lose or find annoying certain reading skills associated with manuscripts and certain of their characteristics, including copious use of abbreviations that made the copyist's work easier and faster. Similarly, book readers who had begun to take tables of contents, pagination, and indices for granted found locating information in manuscripts particularly difficult. Finally, readers in a culture of print who have enjoyed the convenience of abundant maps, charts, and pictures soon realized that they could not find certain kinds of information in manuscripts at all.

In the past, transitions from one dominant information medium to another have taken so long — millennia with writing and centuries with printing — that the surrounding cultures adapted gradually. Those languages and dialects that did not make the transition remained much the same for a long time but gradually weakened, were attenuated, or even died out because they could not do many of the things printed languages and dialects could do. Because during the early stages of both chirographic and typographic cultures much of the resources were devoted to transferring texts from the earlier to the current medium, these transitions were masked somewhat. The first centuries of printing, as McLuhan points out, saw the world flooded with versions of medieval manuscripts in part because the voracious, efficient printing press could reproduce texts faster than authors could write them. This flood of older work had the effect of thus using radically new means to disseminate old-fashioned, conservative, and even reactionary texts.

We can expect that many of the same phenomena of transition will repeat themselves, though often in forms presently unexpected and unpredictable. We can count on hypertext and print existing side by side for some time to come, particularly in elite and scholarly culture; and when the shift to hypertext makes it culturally dominant, it will appear so natural to the general reader-author that only specialists will notice the change or react with much nostalgia for the way things used to be. Whereas certain inventions, such as vacuum cleaners and dishwashers, took almost a century between their initial development and commercial success, recent discoveries and inventions, such as the laser, have required less than a tenth that time to complete the same process.[21] This acceleration of the dispersal of technological change suggests that the transition from print to electronic hypertext, if it comes, will therefore take far less time than did earlier transitions.

The history of print technology and culture also suggests that if hypertext becomes culturally dominant, it will do so by enabling large numbers of people either to do new things or to do old things more easily. Furthermore, one suspects that such a shift in information paradigms will see another version of what took place in the transition to print culture: an overwhelming percentage of the new texts created, like Renaissance and later how-to-do-it books, will answer the needs of an audience outside the academy and hence will long remain culturally invisible and objects of scorn, particularly among those segments of the cultural elite who claim to know the true needs of "the people."

The active readers hypertext creates can meet their needs only if they can find the information they want, and to find that information they must have access to networks. Similarly, authors cannot fully assume the authorial function if they cannot place their texts into a network. The following section provides a scenario that embodies some of the darker implications of a future hypertext author's attempt to gain access to the Net. Appropriately, an earlier electronic version of "Ms. Austen's Submission" appeared (was "published"?) in *IF*, an electronic periodical edited by Gordon Howell in Edinburgh and from there disseminated internationally on computer networks.

Ms. Austen's Submission

She knew that some like to make their Submissions in the privacy of their own living quarters. Other fragile souls, who had to work themselves up to such an important act, made theirs on the spur of the moment by making use of a foneport they encountered while away from home. Austen, however, had decided to do it the traditional way, the right way, as she thought of it, or perhaps, she had admitted to herself, it was just that she found such older forms comforting. At any rate, she had risen early, bathed, put on her best outfit, treated herself to an elegant breakfast at Rive Gauche, the restaurant frequented by would-be's, and then made her way to the Agency of Culture, outside of whose main portal she now stood.

Taking several deep, careful breaths to remain calm, she entered the forbidding building and sought the elevator that would take her to the eighty-ninth floor of the west tower. She found herself alone in the elevator for the last half of her ascent, and superstitiously taking anything she encountered as an omen, she wondered if that meant that she was to be one of the lucky ones who would rise fast and alone, one of those few who would make it. As the elevator eased to a halt and its bronze-colored doors slid back, she automatically stepped out of the elevator; but before proceeding down the long corridor, she carefully checked the number of the floor, though, like any other Apprentice Author, she had recognized it immediately. Smiling wryly at the way her nervous hesitation masked itself as a traveler's caution, Austen began an inner harangue that she sometimes carried on for hours at a time. "Come on, you know this is the right floor, and you recognized it immediately. Jane, you can recite the names of the worthies whose portraits line the halls, since they haven't changed in a hundred years. They certainly haven't since your disastrous last visit. There's Shakespeare, Homer, Dante, the first three on the left, and Woolf, Dickinson, Johnnes, and all the rest on the right."

Arriving at the end of the corridor, Austen paused, took a deep breath, and opened the door marked "Submissions." Now that she was here, she began to worry that perhaps she had been too hasty. Perhaps her story was not quite ready. Maybe she had better go home and let it sit for a few days or maybe a week. Her mouth was dry, so dry she licked her lips several times without much effect. "Relax," she told herself. "There's no sense in waiting any longer. You know it's the best thing you've ever done; you can feel it in your bones, and you knew this was the one as soon as it began to take shape last week. Besides," she added, "it's only your second Submission. If something crazy happens and it is not accepted, you still have one more."

Deciding that this was no time to hesitate, the young woman stepped firmly up to the central console, pressed her palm against the recognition pad, plugged in her Authorpad, and said in a voice that was slightly deeper and more hoarse than usual, "I, Jane Austen, Apprentice Author, would like to make a Submission."

"Thank you, Ms. Austen," a rich alto voice answered. "This is your second Submission. Are you fully aware that if this one is not accepted, you have only a single opportunity remaining?"

"I am."

"Please press the white button to make your Submission."

She had promised herself that, win or lose, she would make her Submission like a true Author. She would not close her eyes, take a deep breath, or mumble any prayers. She would just press the white button that had been pressed by so many thousands of fingers before her and would be pressed by so many thousands after.

Austen tried to summon courage by recalling how full of confidence and how eager to complete her Submission draft she had been yesterday. In fact, when the clerk at the writing bureau, a man in his sixties who always wore an old-fashioned ill-fitting suit, had looked in her direction, she had left her chair in the waiting room and headed directly toward the door even before he called her name. "Fourteen, Ms. Austen," he said in his sad, thin voice, when she looked back at him before opening the door to the workrooms. Silently counting the rooms on her right—"one, two, three, four"—she made her way to number fourteen, which she recognized immediately as one of the newly reconditioned units. Pressing her hand against the recognition pad that would charge her time in the workroom to her personal account at CenterBank, Austen waited until the door opened and then, full of barely repressed excitement, entered the little chamber that would be her working place for the next four hours, unslung the case containing her Authorpad, and proceeded to open its battered light blue case. Glancing at the portable writer that had been hers since the Agency of Culture had assigned it to her six years ago when she declared for authorship as a career, Austen plugged it into the narrow shelf before her and seated herself in the authorship chair, which immediately shaped itself to her back and sides.

"Welcome, Ms. Austen," she heard slightly behind her and to her left—that's where the sound always seemed to emanate from in this unit, she recalled. "Today we can offer you a fine selection of environment suitable for inspiration or editorial activities. First, we have Off Puerto Rico, 25 June, a calm seascape whose quiet waves many have found most suitable, and which Andros van Hulen, the recent winner of the Prix de Rome, used while composing the crucial third chapter of his brilliant prose epic. Second, you might like to work within Far Himalayas, 1 August, a bare, chilling setting far from human and other distractions. The third environment that is new since your last session is entitled Jungle Vista, Amazon Basin, 3 February, which, in contrast to the other new offerings, seethes with energy and strange life forms and is well worth the supplementary fee. Several of our young authors," the huckstering machine continued, "have already worked with it and claim that the reluctant work produced within this surround is simply wonderful."

"Thank you, Surround, but today I think I need something better known, more familiar. Please let me have Browning's study, personalized version no. 32-345B." Immediately, the narrow confines of her cramped workunit appeared to shift until she found herself seated at a large oak work table covered with manuscript and leather-covered rectangular solids in a walnut-paneled room the likes of which had not existed for several hundred years. She had no idea who this Robert Browning had been or even what kind of work he had created— whether it was, say, adventure tales or erotic epics—but she had felt at home in his work room since she first came upon it while idly browsing through infrequently used scenarios. Austen felt the temperature of the air around her drop slightly as Surround changed it to match the qualified realism that marked her own personalized version of this ancient writer's workplace.

Turning on her Authorpad model 73.2 automatically called up the last wordfile she had entered before going to sleep a very few hours before. Austen had caught fire late yesterday afternoon, and unwilling to spare attention or energy for anything else, she had composed until her latest tale—her best, she knew—arrived at the conclusion for which she had been searching. Anxious lest the passages that seemed so perfect before she had returned home and thrown herself down on her rumpled sheets and slept at last would now appear awkward and imprecise, she nervously rubbed her left hand over her mouth and cheek. She had waited long for this one, so long that she was terrified lest she had deluded herself into thinking, as all beginners must, that she had a winner. No, she was certain. This time her Submission would move the Agency to promote her from Apprentice Author Class 1C to Author.

Like all those many thousands of student and apprentice authors, she had wasted far too much creative energy, she knew, dreaming of making it. She wanted the enormously greater convenience of having her own workunit at home, of course, and like everyone else, she naturally wanted the stipend that came with promotion as well. And the status of being a real Author and not one of the hangers-on, the would-be's, so many of whom eventually dropped out of the struggle and ended their days as clerks or worse, well, that was wonderful, to be sure. But it was publication, gaining access to the literary network, that made it all worthwhile.

Sure, it wasn't much, not like achieving the status of Mass Author or even Serious Author, but it was a first step, the one that allowed and encouraged her to take others. Some legendary Apprentice Authors had made it real big. Why, not more than two or three years ago, she remembered, a young man had shot out of obscurity, scored big with a Mass Novel about the last war that had made international network where it had been picked up and used for videos throughout the world. There was even one of those weird pop fairy-tale versions in New Delhi, and the French had taken it, dividing the main character into six states of consciousness or moods, and creating a phantasmagoria that made the art channels.

Today she felt hopeful, energetic, sure that she would make it to the network. Moods are funny, she thought, for not more than a week ago she had felt crushed beneath the base of this massive pyramid that stretched from students, authors-in-training, and would-be authors to fully accredited practitioners and from them upward to the minor and major Mass Authors, and above them, in turn, to the Serious ones, whose works would be allowed to exist for one hundred years after their death. And, then, way off in the distance, at the peak of this pyramid, there were the Canonical Authors, those whose works had lasted and would be allowed to last, those whose works could be read and were even taught in schools to those who didn't want to be writers.

She knew how difficult creating something new had proved. And she certainly had learned the hard way that there were no easy shortcuts to success. In particular, she remembered with embarrassment how she had tried to crash through the gates of success with a little piece on a young author struggling to succeed, and she still squirmed when she remembered how Evaluator, the Agency of Culture's gateway computer, had responded to her first Submission with an extreme boredom and superior knowledge born of long experience,

"Ah, yes, Ms. Austen, a story on a young author, another one. Let's see, that's the eighth today—one from North America, one from Europe, two from Asia, and the rest from Africa, where that seems a popular discovery of this month. Your ending, like your concentration on classroom action and late night discussions among would-be authors, makes this a clear example of Kunstlerroman type 4A.31. Record this number and check the library, which at the last network census has 4,245 examples, three of which are canonical, 103 Serious Fiction, and the remainder ephemera.

"Your submission has been erased, and the portions of your Authorpad memory containing it have been cleared, thus allowing you to get on with more promising work. Thank you for your submission. Good day, Apprentice Author Austen."

That, she thought, must be her most painful memory, but another concerning her attempt at truly original creativity rivaled it. A year before the first incident, which took place this past November, she had decided that she had been relying too much on the Authorpad's tie-ins to the Agency's plot, character, and image generators. No, she promised, she would be her own woman, and though she had found it difficult working without the assistance of that friendly voice that made suggestions and allowed her to link instantly to source texts and abundant examples, she had forced herself to slog on, hour after hour, confident that she would return the craft of authorship to its past glories, the glories of the BackTime when computers had not offered their friendly assistance and authors, so it was rumored, actually created heavy things called books (though how one was supposed to store or even read them she wasn't quite certain). She remembered her chagrin when the Practice Evaluator at school, which was programmed to emulate the Agency's official one, pointed out how sadly derivative her contribution had turned out to be. When she emphasized how she had composed it entirely "on her own"—that was the phrase she used—the knowing voice commanded, "Look, Austen," and then before she realized what the evaluator was doing, the scene vanished from her Surround, replaced by sets of flow charts, concept maps, and menus, some of which bore labels like "Parallels to Plots of Submitted Work" or "Forty-One Types of Novels about Young Authors." She found herself particularly embarrassed to discover that even the title of which she was so proud, "A Portrait of the Artist as a Young Man," had already been used by an obscure twentieth-century author who resided in the distant reaches of the canon.

Worst, she had had to listen, this time forced to pay close attention, to another lecture on the foolish egotism of would-be authors. She had taken all the requisite courses in literary theory, naturally, and now Evaluator was accusing her of theoretical naiveté and ideological illiteracy. Her main problem, she had to admit, was that she had such a firm sense of herself, such a firm conviction that she existed apart, different, that she found the Culture Agency's emphasis on inevitable creation uncongenial, and well, yes, threatening as well. It all went back, the machine was reminding her, to language, the condition of all intelligence, whether human, artificial, or combination of the two. "All of us, Apprentice Austen, use it to communicate our thoughts and to shape our reality, but although you speak ComEnglish, you do not create it, even though no one may ever have combined those words that you use at this instant in precisely that way before. In fact, as your teachers have reminded you so many times, the thoughtful Author confronts the fact that language speaks her as much as she speaks language. And since literature is but another level of language and linguistically organized codes, you cannot assume that you are in sole control of the stories you produce. Your job as an author, Ms. Austen, involves recombinations and possible discoveries, not origins, not originations. An author is a weaver of tapestries and not a sheep producing wool fibre."

Austen learned her lesson, she felt sure, and this story would be the one to realize all that potential her teachers had seen so many years earlier.

■ ■ ■ ■ ■ ■ ■

Austen pressed the white button, transmitting her story from the Authorpad to Evaluator in the legally required act of Submission. She thereupon stepped back and waited. Slightly more than seven seconds later, Evaluator's melodious womanly voice, now warmer and more enthusiastic than before, announced, "Congratulations, Author Austen, your story has been accepted. It will appear this Thursday on the regional network and we predict solid interest. Please check the official reviews and abstract that will be circulated on this date in order to provide author's confirmation of the abstract. Additional congratulations are in order, Ms. Austen: Requests have just been received for translation rights from Greater Germany, Nepal, and Japan."

■ ■ ■ ■ ■ ■

Austen lifted her finger to press the white button that would transmit her story from the Authorpad to Evaluator in the legally required act of Submission. She placed her finger near the white button, paused a second, and then another. Slowly unplugging her Authorpad, she left the cell, and holding herself rigid by sheer force of will, walked briskly back toward the elevator.

■ ■ ■ ■ ■ ■

Austen pressed the white button, transmitting her story from the Authorpad to Evaluator in the legally required act of Submission. She was still seated, eyes shut and holding her breath, when less than ten seconds later, Evaluator announced, "Congratulations, Author Austen, your story has been accepted for a collaborative fiction! Your text will mingle with those of eleven other authors, only two of them brand new like yourself. That is quite an honor, I must say. Would you like to learn the identities of your collaborators?"

■ ■ ■ ■ ■ ■

Austen pressed the white button, transmitting her story from the Authorpad to Evaluator in the legally required act of Submission. She had not time to remove her index finger from the button, when the firm motherly voice of Evaluator gently announced, "I am sorry, Ms. Austen. Your Submission is not accepted. Please try not to be upset. At another time, your work might have been admitted to the Net, but this past week has seen an unusual number of texts submitted. If you find yourself in need of a tranquilizing agent now or something to help you sleep later, I am authorized to prescribe one at your local pharmacia."

Several years after writing the above speculative fiction, I encountered Gordon Wu's review of Paula Milne's *Earwig*. According to Wu's description, in Milne's play a "feminist novelist in need of money" works on "soap operas plotted by a committee of tired hacks working for a television network. Their success is judged by a computer, EARWIG, which projects audience ratings for their scripts."[22] When I first wrote my description of a future author's experience of trying to publish her work, I thought Ms. Austen's new world of publishing as a dystopia, though one, of course, that takes the form of extrapolating strands found in contemporary England and America. However, after reading Richard Ohmann's account of the relations that obtain among authors, publishers, advertisers, reviewers, and leading periodicals in contemporary America, I wonder if machines could do worse.[23] Then, of course, I recalled Ulmer's observation that machine intelligence necessarily reproduces someone's ideology. . . .

Access to the Text and the Author's Right (Copyright)

Access to a network implies access to texts "on" that network, and this access raises the issue of who has the right to have access to a text — access to read it as well as to link to it. Problems and possibilities come with the realization that authorship as it is conventionally understood is a convention. Conceptions of authorship relate importantly to whatever information technology currently prevails, and when that technology changes or shares its power with another, the cultural construction of authorship changes, too, for good or ill. A related problem concerns the fate of authorial rights. Michael Heim has pointed out that, "as the model of the integrated private self of the author fades, the rights of the author as a persistent self-identity also become more evanescent, more difficult to define. If the work of the author no longer carries with it definite physical properties as a unique original, as a book in a definite form, then the author's rights too grow more tenuous, more indistinct" (*Electric Language*, 221). If the author, like the text, becomes dispersed or multivocal, how does society fairly assign legal, commercial, and moral rights?

A second problem derives from the nature of virtual textuality, any example of which by definition exists only as an easily copiable and modifiable version — as a derivative of something else or as what Baudrillard would call a simulacrum. Traditional conceptions of literary property derive importantly from ideas of original creation, and these derive in turn from the existence of multiple copies of a printed text that is both fixed and unique. Electronic text processing changes, to varying degrees, all aspects of the text that had made conceptions of authorial property practicable and even possible. Heim correctly warns that the outmoded concept of "proprietary rights based on the possession of an original creation no longer permits us to adapt ourselves to a world where the technological basis of creative work makes copying easy and inevitable," and that to protect creativity we "must envision a wholly new order of creative ownership" (170). As Steven W. Gilbert testified before a congressional committee, technology already both extends conventional conceptions of intellectual property and makes its protection difficult and even inconceivable:

It may soon be technically possible for any student, teacher, or researcher to have immediate electronic access from any location to retrieve and manipulate the full text (including pictures) of any book, sound recording, or computer program ever published—and more. When almost any kind of "information" in almost any medium can now be represented and processed with digital electronics, the range of things that can be considered "intellectual property" is mind-boggling. Perhaps the briefest statement of the need to redefine terms was made by Harlan Cleveland in the May/June 1989 issue of *Change* magazine: "How can 'intellectual property' be 'protected'? The question contains the seed of its own confusion: it's the wrong verb about the wrong noun."[24]

Attitudes toward the correct and incorrect use of a text written by someone else depend importantly upon the medium in which that text appears. "To copy and circulate another man's book," H. J. Chaytor reminds us, "might be regarded as a meritorious action in the age of manuscript; in the age of print, such action results in law suits and damages."[25] From the point of view of the author of a print text, copying, virtual textuality, and hypertext linking must appear wrong. They infringe upon one person's property rights by appropriating and manipulating something over which another person has no proper rights. In contrast, from the point of view of the author of hypertext, for whom collaboration and sharing are of the essence of "writing," restrictions on the availability of text, like prohibitions against copying or linking, appear absurd, indeed immoral, constraints. In fact, without far more access to (originally) printed text than is now possible, true networked hypertextuality cannot come into being.

Difficult as it may be to recognize from our position in the midst of the transition from print to electronic writing, "it is an asset of the new technology," as Gilbert reminds us, "not a defect, that permits users to make and modify copies of information of all kinds — easily, cheaply, and accurately. This is one of the fundamental powers of this technology and it cannot be repressed" ("Information Technology," 18). Therefore, one of the prime requisites for developing a fully empowering hypertextuality is to improve, not technology, but laws concerning copyright and authorial property. Otherwise, as Meyrowitz warns, copyrights will "replace ambulances as the things that lawyers chase" ("Hypertext," 24). We do need copyright laws protecting intellectual property, and we shall need them for the foreseeable future. Without copyright, society as a whole suffers, for without such protection authors receive little encouragement to publish their work. Without copyright protection they cannot profit from their work, or they can profit from it only by returning to an aristocratic patronage system. Too rigid copyright and patent law, on the other hand, also harms society by permitting individuals to restrict the flow of information that can benefit large numbers of people.

Hypertext demands new classes or conceptions of copyright that protect the rights of the author while permitting others to link to that author's text. Hypertext, in other words, requires a new balancing of rights belonging to those entities whom we can describe variously as primary versus secondary authors, authors versus reader-authors, or authors versus linkers. Although no one should have the right to modify or appropriate another's text any more than one does now, hypertext reader-authors should be able to link their own texts or those by a third author to a text created by someone else, and they should also be able to copyright their own link sets should they wish to do so. A crucial component in the coming financial and legal reconception of authorship involves developing schemes for equitable royalties or some other form of payment to authors. We need, first of all, to develop some sort of usage fee, perhaps of the kind that ASCAP levies when radio stations transmit recorded music; each time a composition is broadcast the copyright owner earns a minute sum that adds up as many "users" employ the same information — an apposite model, it would seem, for using electronic information technology on electronic networks.

Gilbert warns us that we must work to formulate new conceptions of copyright and fair use, since "under the present legal and economic conventions, easy use of the widest range of information and related services may become available only to individuals affiliated with a few large universities or corporations" ("Information Technology," 14). Thus dividing the world into the informationally rich and informationally impoverished, one may add, would produce a kind of techno-feudalism in which those with access to information and information technology would rule the world from electronic fiefdoms. William Gibson, John Shirley, and other practitioners of cyberpunk science fiction have convincingly painted pictures of a grim future, much like that in the movie *Blade Runner*, in which giant multinational corporations have real power and governments play with the scraps left over. Now is the time to protect ourselves from such a future. Like many others concerned with the future of education and electronic information technology, Gilbert therefore urges that we develop *"new economic mechanisms to democratize the use of information, and economic mechanisms beyond copyright and patent.* It would be a tragedy if the technology that offers the greatest hope for democratizing information became the mechanism for withholding it. We must make information accessible to those who need it. . . . Any pattern that resembles information disenfranchisement of the masses will become more obviously socially and politically unacceptable" (17–18; emphasis in original).

Most of the discussions of copyright in the electronic age that I have recently encountered fall into two sharply opposing camps. Those people, like Gilbert, who consider issues of authorial property from the vantage point of the hypertext reader or the user of electronic text and data emphasize the need for access to them and want to work out some kind of equitable means of assigning rights, payment, and protection to all parties. Their main concern, nonetheless, falls upon rights of access. Others, mostly representatives of publishers, often representatives of university presses, fiercely resist any questioning of conventional notions of authorship, intellectual property, and copyright as if their livelihoods depended upon such resistance, as indeed they well might. They argue that they wish only to protect authors and that without the system of refereed works that controls almost all access to publication by university presses, standards would plummet, scholarship would grind to a halt, and authors would not benefit financially as they do now. These arguments have great power, but it must be noted that commercial presses, which do not always use referees, have published particularly important scholarly contributions and that even the most prestigious presses sometimes invite thesis advisors to read the work of their own students or have scholars evaluate the manuscripts of their close friends. Nonetheless, publishers do make an important point when they claim that they fulfill an important role by vetting and then distributing books, and one would expect them to retain such roles even when their authors begin to publish their texts on networks.

Although almost all defences of present versions of copyright I have encountered clearly use the rights of the author or society in large part as a screen to defend commercial interests, one issue, that of the author's moral rights, is rarely discussed, certainly not by publishers. As John Sutherland explains in "Author's Rights and Transatlantic Differences," Anglo-American law treats copyright solely in terms of property. "Continental Europe by contrast enshrines moral right by statute. In France and West Germany the author has the power to withdraw his or her work after it has been (legally) published — something that would be impossible in Britain or the United States without the consent of the publisher. . . . In [France and West Germany], publishers who acquire rights to the literary work do not 'own it,' as do their Anglo-American counterparts. They merely acquire the right to 'exploit' it."[26] The occasion for Sutherland's article raises important questions about rights of the hypertext as well as the print author. In 1985 an American historian, Francis R. Nicosia, published *The Third Reich and the Palestine Question* with the University of Texas Press, which subsequently sold translation rights to Duffel-Verlag, a neo-Nazi publisher whose director "is (according to Nicosia) identified by the West German Interior Ministry as the publisher of the *Deutscher Monatschefte*, a publication that, among other matters, has talked about 'a coming Fourth Reich in which there will be no place for anti-Fascists. The path to self-discovery for the German

people will be over the ruins of the concentration camp memorials.'"
Believing that an association with Duffel-Verlag will damage his
personal and professional reputation, the author has complained vig-
orously about his American publisher's treatment of his book.
Traditional Anglo-American law permits the author no recourse in
such situations, but Sutherland points out that "on October 31, 1988,
Ronald Reagan signed into law America's ratification of the Berne
Convention," which grants the author moral rights including that
which prevents a publisher from acting in ways "prejudicial to his
honour and reputation."

The question arises, would an author whose text appears on a
hypertext system find that text protected more or less than a comparable print author? At first glance, one might think that Nicosia would
find himself with even fewer rights if his work appeared as a hypertext, since anyone, including advocates of a Fourth Reich, could link
comments and longer texts to *The Third Reich and the Palestine Question*. Such an answer is, I believe, incorrect for two reasons. First,
in its hypertext version Nicosia's monograph would not appear isolated
from its context in the way its print version does. Second (and this is
really a restatement of my previous point), a hypertext version would
permit the author to append his objections and any other materials
he wished to include. Linking, in other words, has the capacity to
protect the author and his work in a way impossible with printed volumes. Allowing others to link to one's text therefore does not sacrifice
the author's moral rights.

An Open-ended Conclusion; or, The Dispatch Comes to an End

As my readers will no doubt have observed, this book is simultaneously an enthusiastic hard sell, a prophecy, a grim warning, and a report from the front. Above all, it is an invitation to make connections. Take it, then, as a plea to link up very different areas of endeavor — contemporary critical and literary theory and late-twentieth-century state-of-the-art computing — that supposedly have little in common. Contemporary theory can illuminate the design and implementation of hypertext, and hypertext in turn offers theory an empirical laboratory, a means of practice, refinement, and extension, a space, in other words, in which to test imaginings.

One of the most interesting and exciting things about hypertext appears in the way it offers us a means of looking a short way into one or more possible futures, an electronic Pisgah Sight, as it were, a vision of the future that we ourselves will probably not reach. Equally important, it permits another glance, a re-vision of aspects of our past and present, because even a brief experience of reading and writing in a hypertext environment denaturalizes and demystifies the culture of the printed book. The strangeness, the newness, and the difference of hypertext permit us, however transiently and however ineffectively, to de-center many of our culture's assumptions about reading, writing, authorship, and creativity.

Electronic hypertext, the latest extension of writing, raises many questions and problems about culture, power, and the individual, but it is no more (or less) natural than any other form of writing, which is the greatest as well as the most destructive of all technologies.

Notes

Chapter 1
Hypertext and
Critical Theory

1. Here, right at the beginning, let me assure my readers that although I urge that Barthes and Derrida relate in interesting and important ways to computer hypertext, I do not take them — or semiotics and poststructuralism, or, for that matter, structuralism — to be essentially the same.

2. J. David Bolter, *Writing Space* (Hillsdale, N.J.: Lawrence Erlbaum, 1990), 143.

3. Roland Barthes, *S/Z* (Paris: Éditions du Seuil, 1970), 11–12; *S/Z*, trans. Richard Miller (New York: Hill and Wang, 1974), 5–6. Subsequent references are to the English translation.

4. Michel Foucault, *The Archeology of Knowledge*, trans. A. M. Sheridan Smith (New York: Harper Colophon, 1976), 23.

5. Theodor H. Nelson, *Literary Machines* (Swarthmore, Pa.: self-published, 1981), 0/2. [Pagination begins with each section or chapter, thus 0/ 2 = prefatory matter, page 2/.]

6. Nicole Yankelovich, Norman Meyrowitz, and Andries van Dam, "Reading and Writing the Electronic Book," *IEEE Computer* 18 (October 1985): 18.

7. See, for example, Jacques Derrida, *La Dissémination* (Paris: Éditions de Seuil, 1972), 71, 108, 172, 111; *Dissemination*, trans. Barbara Johnson (Chicago: University of Chicago Press, 1981), 96, 63, 98, 149. Subsequent references are to the English translation.

8. Gregory L. Ulmer, *Applied Grammatology: Post(e)-Pedagogy from Jacques Derrida to Joseph Beuys* (Baltimore: Johns Hopkins University Press, 1985), 58.

9. Jacques Derrida, "Signature Event Context," *Glyph 1: Johns Hopkins Textual Studies* (Baltimore: Johns Hopkins University Press, 1977), 185. Quoted by Ulmer, *Applied Grammatology*, 58–59.

10. Jacques Derrida, *Speech and Phenomena*, trans. David B. Allison (Evanston, Ill.: Northwestern University Press, 1973), 131.

11. Thaïs E. Morgan, "Is There an Intertext in This Text?: Literary and Interdisciplinary Approaches to Intertextuality," *American Journal of Semiotics* 3 (1985): 1–2.

12. Mikhail Bakhtin, *Problems of Dostoevsky's Poetics*, ed. and trans. Caryl Emerson (Minneapolis: University of Minnesota Press, 1984), 18.

13. I am thinking of Richard Rorty's description of edifying philosophy as a conversation: "To see keeping a conversation going as a sufficient aim of philosophy, to see wisdom as consisting in the ability to sustain a conversation,

is to see human beings as generators of new descriptions rather than beings one hopes to be able to describe accurately. To see the aim of philosophy as truth — namely, the truth about the terms which provide ultimate commensuration for all human inquiries and activities — is to see human beings as objects rather than subjects, as existing *en-soi* rather than as both *pour-soi* and *en-soi*, as both described objects and describing subjects" (*Philosophy and the Mirror of Nature* [Princeton: Princeton University Press, 1979], 378). To a large extent, Rorty can be thought of as the philosopher of hypertextuality.

14. George P. Landow, *Victorian Types, Victorian Shadows: Biblical Typology and Victorian Literature, Art, and Thought* (Boston: Routledge and Kegan Paul, 1980).

15. Examples include *GodSpeed Instant Bible Search Program*, from Kingdom Age Software in San Diego, California, and the Dallas Seminary CD-Word Project, which builds upon Guide, a hypertext system developed by OWL (Office Workstations Limited) International. See Steven J. DeRose, "Biblical Studies and Hypertext," in *Hypermedia and Literary Studies*, ed. Paul Delany and George P. Landow (Cambridge: MIT Press, 1991), 185–204.

16. Jorge Luis Borges, "The Aleph," in *The Aleph and Other Stories, 1933–1969*, trans. Norman Thomas di Giovanni (New York: Bantam, 1971), 13: "In that single gigantic instant I saw millions of acts both delightful and awful; not one of them amazed me more than the fact that all of them occupied the same point in space, without overlapping or transparency. What my eyes beheld was simultaneous, but what I shall now write down will be successive, because language is successive. . . . The Aleph's diameter was probably little more than an inch, but all space was there, actual and undiminished. Each thing (a mirror's face, let us say) was infinite things, since I saw it from every angle of the universe."

17. Jacques Derrida, "Structure, Sign, and Play in the Discourse of the Human Sciences," in *The Structuralist Controversy: The Languages of Criticism and the Sciences of Man* (Baltimore: Johns Hopkins University Press, 1972), 251.

18. Vannevar Bush, "As We May Think," *Endless Horizons* (Washington, D.C.: Public Affairs Press, 1946), 16–38. This essay first appeared in *Atlantic Monthly* 176 (July 1945): 101–8.

19. Vannevar Bush, "Memex Revisited," in *Science Is Not Enough* (New York: William Morrow, 1967), 75–101.

20. Elizabeth L. Eisenstein, *The Printing Press as an Agent of Change: Communications and Cultural Transformations in Early-Modern Europe* (Cambridge: Cambridge University Press, 1980), 116.

21. Jean Baudrillard, *Simulations*, trans. Paul Foss, Paul Patton, and Philip Beitchman (New York: Semiotext(e), 1983), 115. In *Writing Space*, Bolter ex-

plains some of these costs: "Electronic text is the first text in which the elements of meaning, of structure, and of visual display are fundamentally unstable. Unlike the printing press, or the medieval codex, the computer does not require that any aspect of writing be determined in advance for the whole life of a text. This restlessness is inherent in a technology that records information by collecting for fractions of a second evanescent electrons at tiny junctions of silicon and metal. All information, all data, in the computer world is a kind of controlled movement, and so the natural inclination of computer writing is to change" (31).

22. Terry Eagleton's explanation of the way ideology relates the individual to his or her society bears an uncanny resemblance to the conception of the virtual machine in computing: "It is as though society were not just an impersonal structure to me, but a 'subject' which 'addresses' me personally — which recognizes me, tells me that I am valued, and so makes me by that very act of recognition into a free, autonomous subject. I come to feel, not exactly as though the world exists for me alone, but as though it is significantly 'centred' on me, and I in turn am significantly 'centred' on it. Ideology, for Althusser, is the set of beliefs and practices which does this centring" (*Literary Theory: An Introduction* [Minneapolis: University of Minnesota Press, 1983], 172).

23. Michael Heim, *Electric Language: A Philosophical Study of Word Processing* (New Haven: Yale University Press, 1987), 10–11.

24. Brian L. Hawkins, "Campus-wide Networking at Brown University," *Academic Computing* 3 (January 1989): 32–33, 36–39, 44, 46–49.

25. For a description of existing networks, see Tracy LaQuey, "Networks for Academics," *Academic Computing* 4 (November 1989): 32–34, 39, 65. For a description of the proposed National Research and Education Network, see Albert Gore, "Remarks on the NREN," *EDUCOM Review* 25 (Summer 1990): 12–16; and Susan M. Rogers, "Educational Applications of the NREN," *EDUCOM Review* 25 (Summer 1990): 25–29.

26. Barbara Herrnstein Smith, "Narrative Versions, Narrative Theories," in *On Narrative*, ed. W. J. T. Mitchell (Chicago: University of Chicago Press, 1980), 223.

27. Michel Foucault, *The Order of Things: An Archeology of the Human Sciences* (New York: Vintage, 1973), 75.

28. Heinz R. Pagels, *The Dreams of Reason: The Computer and the Rise of the Sciences of Complexity* (New York: Bantam, 1989), 50.

29. See Eagleton, *Literary Theory*, 14, 33, 78, 104, 165, 169, 173, 201.

30. Pierre Machery, *A Theory of Literary Production*, trans. Geoffrey Wall (London: Routledge and Kegan Paul, 1978), 268. Emphasis added.

31. Fredric Jameson, *The Political Unconscious: Narrative as a Socially Symbolic Act* (Ithaca, N.Y.: Cornell University Press, 1981), 27.

32. Fredric Jameson, *Marxism and Form: Twentieth-Century Dialectical Theories of Literature* (Princeton: Princeton University Press, 1971), x.

33. J. Hillis Miller, "Literary Theory, Telecommunications, and the Making of History," in *Conference Papers from the International Conference on Scholarship and Technology in the Humanities*, Elvetham Hall, England, May 1990, 1.

34. J. Hillis Miller, *Fiction and Repetition* (Cambridge: Harvard University Press, 1982), 126.

35. J. Hillis Miller, "The Critic as Host," in Harold Bloom, Paul de Man, Jacques Derrida, Geoffrey H. Hartman, and J. Hillis Miller, *Deconstruction and Criticism* (London: Routledge and Kegan Paul, 1979), 223.

36. Jacques Derrida, *Of Grammatology*, trans. Gayatri Chakravorty Spivak (Baltimore: Johns Hopkins University Press, 1976), 10.

37. Gregory Ulmer pointed this fact out to me during our conversations at the October 1989 Literacy Online conference at the University of Alabama in Tuscaloosa.

38. Alvin Kernan, *Printing Technology, Letters and Samuel Johnson* (Princeton: Princeton University Press, 1987), 49.

39. Roger Chartier, "Religious Uses," in *The Culture of Print: Power and the Uses of Print in Early Modern Europe*, ed. Roger Chartier, trans. Lydia G. Cochrane (Princeton: Princeton University Press, 1987), 139. Chartier bases his remarks in part on Marie-Elizabeth Ducreux, "Reading unto Death: Books and Readers in Eighteenth-Century Bohemia," also in *The Culture of Print*, 191–230.

Chapter 2
Reconfiguring the
Text

1. A primitive form of hypertext appears whenever one places an electronic text on a system that has capacities for full-text retrieval or a built-in reference device, such as a dictionary or thesaurus. For example, I am writing the manuscript of this book on an Apple Macintosh II, and I am using a word-processing program called Microsoft Word; my machine also runs On Location, a program that quickly locates all occurrences of an individual word or phrase, provides a list of them, and, when requested, opens documents containing them. Although somewhat clumsier than an advanced hypertext system, this program provides the functional analogue to some aspects of hypertext.

2. Paul Delany and John K. Gilbert, "HyperCard Stacks for Fielding's *Joseph Andrews*: Issues of Design and Content," in *Hypermedia and Literary Studies*, ed. Paul Delany and George P. Landow (Cambridge: MIT Press, 1991), 287–

98. *The Dickens Web*, a corpus of Intermedia documents focused on *Great Expectations* (1990) available from the Institute of Research in Information and Scholarship at Brown University, differs from Delany's project in not including the primary text.

3. Steven J. DeRose, *CD Word Tutorial: Learning CD Word for Bible Study* (Dallas: CD Word Library, 1990), 1, 117–26.

4. See Paul D. Kahn, "Linking together Books: Experiments in Adapting Published Material into Intermedia Documents," *Hypermedia* 1(1989): 111–45.

5. When I first used *intratextuality* in an article some years ago to refer to such referential and reverberatory relations within a text or within a metatext conceived as a "work," I mistakenly believed I had coined the term. So did my editor, who was not enthusiastic about the coinage. But we were both wrong: Tzvetan Todorov used it in "How to Read" (1969), which appears in *The Poetics of Prose*, trans. Richard Howard (Ithaca, N.Y.: Cornell University Press, 1977), 242.

6. Walter Benjamin, "The Work of Art in the Age of Mechanical Reproduction," in *Illuminations*, ed. Hannah Arendt, trans. Harry Zohn (New York: Schocken, 1969), 237.

7. See Rhoda L. Flaxman, *Victorian Word Painting and Narrative: Toward the Blending of Genres* (Ann Arbor, Mich.: UMI Research Press, 1987); and Elizabeth K. Helsinger, *Ruskin and the Art of the Beholder* (Cambridge: Harvard University Press, 1982).

8. The *In Memoriam* web, which contains a graphic overview of the poem's sources and analogues, also permits one to read the poem along axes provided by Tennyson's use of individual authors.

9. Mireille Rosello of the University of Illinois in Urbana has created both HyperCard and Intermedia prototypes of such a hypertext version of *S/Z* (1989). I would like to thank her for kindly sharing it with me at an early stage of development.

10. See Stuart Moulthrop, "Reading from the Map: Metonymy and Metaphor in the Fiction of 'Forking Paths,'" in *Hypermedia and Literary Studies*, ed. Delany and Landow, 119–32. Another fiction that calls for translation into hypertext is "The Babysitter," by Robert Coover, which appears in his 1969 collection of short stories, *Pricksongs and Descants*. For Coover's recent interest in hypertextuality, see chapter 3 of this book.

11. IBM mainframe computers running the CMS (Conversational Monitor System) operating system call each user's electronic mailbox or message center the "reader."

12. See Ronald F. Weissman, "From the Personal Computer to the Scholar's Workstation," *Academic Computing* 3 (October 1988): 10–14, 30–34, 36, 38–41; and Steven R. Lerman, "UNIX Workstations in Academia: At the Crossroads," *Academic Computing* 3 (October 1988): 16–18, 51–55.

13. Kenneth Utting and Nicole Yankelovich, "Context and Orientation in Hypermedia Networks," *ACM Transactions on Information Systems* 7 (1989): 58–84, which surveys various attempted solutions to the problems of hypertext orientation and provides illustrations of the three stages in the development of Intermedia's dynamic hypergraph.

14. Intermedia 4.0, which saw completion in time for the conference Hypertext '89 in November 1989, includes full-text searching, a feature that promises to change readers' habits of working with materials on Intermedia. Since it has not yet been used in the Intermedia classroom at Brown, I concentrate above on features in use for several iterations of my survey course.

15. J. David Bolter (*Writing Space*, 63–81) provides an excellent survey of visual elements in writing technologies from hieroglyphics to hypertext. The periodical *Visible Language*, which began publication in 1966, contains discussions of this subject from a wide variety of disciplines ranging from the history of calligraphy and educational psychology to book design and human-computer interaction.

16. In discussing Barthes's *Elements of Semiology*, Annette Lavers exemplifies the usual attitude toward nonalphanumeric information when she writes that Barthes's notion of narrative "acknowledges the fact that literature is not only 'made of words' but also of representational elements, although the latter can of course only be conveyed in words" (*Roland Barthes: Structuralism and After* [Cambridge: Harvard University Press, 1982], 134). That pregnant "of course" exposes conventional assumptions about textuality.

17. See Robert Suckale, *Studien zu Stilbildung und Stilwandel de Madonnenstatuen der Ile-de-France zwischen 1230 und 1300* (Munich, 1971).

18. Tom McArthur, *Worlds of Reference: Lexicography, Learning and Language from the Clay Tablet to the Computer* (Cambridge: Cambridge University Press, 1986), 69.

19. Edward W. Said, *Beginnings: Intention and Method* (New York: Columbia University Press, 1985), 3.

20. Jacques Derrida, "Living On," trans. James Hulbert, in *Deconstruction and Criticism* (London: Routledge and Kegan Paul, 1979), 83–84.

21. Gérard Genette, "Stendhal" (1968), in *Figures of Literary Discourse*, trans. Alan Sheridan (New York: Columbia University Press, 1982), 147.

22. Walter J. Ong, *Orality and Literacy: The Technologizing of the Word* (London: Methuen, 1982), 136.

Chapter 3
Reconfiguring the
Author

1. Michael Heim, *Electric Language: A Philosophical Study of Word Processing* (New Haven: Yale University Press, 1987), 221.

2. William R. Paulson, *The Noise of Culture: Literary Texts in a World of Information* (Ithaca, N.Y.: Cornell University Press, 1988), 139.

3. Jean-François Lyotard, *The Postmodern Condition: A Report on Knowledge*, trans. Geoff Bennington and Brian Massumi (Minneapolis: University of Minnesota Press, 1984), 15.

4. Michel Foucault, "What Is an Author?" in *Language, Counter-Memory, Practice: Selected Essays and Interviews*, trans. Donald F. Bouchard and Sherry Simon (Ithaca, N.Y.: Cornell University Press, 1977), 119.

5. Heinz Pagels, *The Dreams of Reason: The Computer and the Rise of the Sciences of Complexity* (New York: Bantam, 1989), 92.

6. Claude Lévi-Strauss, *The Raw and the Cooked: Introduction to a Science of Mythology: I*, trans. John and Doreen Weightman (New York: Harper and Row, 1969), 12. Lévi-Strauss's observation in a note on the same page that "the Ojibiwa Indians consider myths as 'conscious beings, with powers of thought and action'" has some interesting parallels to remarks by Pagels on the subject of quasi-animate portions of neural nets: "Networks don't quite so much compute a solution as they settle into it, much as we subjectively experience our own problem solving. . . . There could be subsystems within supersystems — a hierarchy of information and command, resembling nothing so much as human society itself. In this image the neuron in the brain is like an individual in society. What we experience as consciousness is the 'social consciousness' of our neuronal network" (126, 224).

7. Lévi-Strauss also employs this model for societies as a whole: "Our society, a particular instance in a much vaster family of societies, depends, like all others, for its coherence and its very existence on a network — grown infinitely unstable and complicated among us — of ties between consanguineal families" (*The Scope of Anthropology*, trans. Sherry Ortner Paul and Robert A. Paul [London: Jonathan Cape, 1967], 33).

8. Said in fact prefaces this remark by the evasive phrase, "it is quite possible to argue," and since he nowhere qualifies the statement that follows, I take it as a claim, no matter how nervous or half-hearted.

9. See Cliff McKnight, John Richardson, and Andrew Dillon, "Journal Articles as a Learning Resource: What Can Hypertext Offer?" in *Designing Hypertext/Hypermedia for Learning*, ed. David H. Jonassen and Heinz Mandl (Heidelberg: Springer-Verlag, 1990), 16.1–14.

10. J. J. Hertz, ed., *The Pentateuch and Haftorahs*, 2nd ed. (London: Soncino Press, 1962), 668.

11. Norman Meyrowitz, "Hypertext—Does It Reduce Cholesterol, Too?" in *Vannevar Bush and the Mind's Machine: From Memex to Hypertext*, ed. James M. Nyce and Paul D. Kahn (San Diego: Academic Press, 1991).

12. Kenneth Morrell, "Teaching with *HyperCard.* An Evaluation of the Computer-Based Section in Literature and Arts C-14: The Concept of the Hero in Hellenic Civilization," Perseus Project Working Paper 3 (Cambridge: Department of Classics, Harvard University, 1988).

13. Jolene Galegher, Carmen Egido, and Robert E. Kraut, "Patterns of Contact and Communication in Scientific Research Collaboration," in *Intellectual Teamwork*, ed. Jolene Galegher, Carmen Egido, and Robert E. Kraut (Hillsdale, N.J.: Lawrence Erlbaum, 1990), 151.

14. According to the scientists that Galegher, Egido, and Kraut studied, people in these fields work collaboratively not only to share material and intellectual resources but also because "working with another person was simply more fun than working alone. They also believed that working with another improved the quality of the research product, because of the synthesis of ideas it afforded, the feedback they received from each other, and the new skills they learned. In addition to these two major motives, a number of our respondents collaborated primarily to maintain a preestablished personal relationship. In a relationship threatened by physical separation, the collaboration provided a reason for keeping in touch. Finally, some researchers collaborated for self-presentational or political reasons, because they believed that working with a particular person or being in a collaborative relationship per se was valuable for their careers. Of course, these motives are not mutually exclusive" ("Patterns of Contact," 152).

15. For a classical statement of the historicizing elements in humanistic study, see Erwin Panofsky, "The History of Art as a Humanistic Discipline," *Meaning in the Visual Arts: Papers in and on Art History* (Garden City, N.Y.: Doubleday Anchor, 1955), 1–25.

16. Lisa Ede and Andrea Lunsford, *Singular Texts/Plural Authors: Perspectives on Collaborative Writing* (Carbondale: Southern Illinois University Press, 1990), ix–x.

17. The large number of individuals credited with authorship of scientific papers—sometimes more than one hundred—produces problems, too, as does the practice of so-called honorary authorship, according to which the head of a laboratory or other person of prestige receives credit for research whose course he or she may not have followed and about which he or she may know very little. In this latter case problems arise when the names of such scientists of reputation serve to authenticate poor quality or even falsified re-

search. See Walter W. Stewart and Ned Feder, "The Integrity of Scientific Literature," *Nature* 15 (1987): 207–14; cited by Ede and Lunsford.

18. Marshall McLuhan, *The Gutenberg Galaxy: The Making of Typographic Man* (Toronto: University of Toronto Press, 1962), 229–33.

19. James H. Coombs, Anne Scott, George P. Landow, and Arnold Sanders, eds., *A Pre-Raphaelite Friendship: The Correspondence of William Holman Hunt and John Lucas Tupper* (Ann Arbor, Mich.: UMI Research Press, 1986).

20. Tora K. Bikson and J. D. Eveland, "The Interplay of Work Group Structures and Computer Support," in *Intellectual Teamwork*, ed. Galegher, Egido, and Kraut, 286. The authors add that "the frequency and spontaneity of interactions equally facilitate task and social exchange."

21. In addition to McLuhan and Bolter, see Elizabeth L. Eisenstein, *The Printing Press as an Agent of Change: Communications and Cultural Transformations in Early-Modern Europe* (Cambridge: Cambridge University Press, 1980).

22. *The Dickens Web: User's and Installation Guide* (Providence, R.I.: Institute for Research in Information and Scholarship, 1990), 5.

23. Joseph D. Novak and D. Bob Gowin, *Learning How to Learn* (New York: Cambridge University Press, 1984).

24. Paul D. Kahn, Julie Launhardt, Krzysztof Lenk, and Ronnie Peters, "Design Issues of Hypermedia Publications: Issues and Solutions," in *EP90: Proceedings of the International Conference on Electronic Publishing, Document Manipulation, and Typography*, ed. Richard Furuta (Cambridge: Cambridge University Press, 1990), 107–24.

Chapter 4
Reconfiguring
Narrative

1. Aristotle, *Poetics*, trans. Ingram Bywater, in *The Basic Works*, ed. Richard McKeon (New York: Random House, 1941), 1462.

2. Dorothy Lee, "Lineal and Nonlineal Codifications of Reality," in *Symbolic Anthropology: A Reader in the Study of Symbols and Meanings*, ed. Janet L. Dolgin, David S. Kemnitzer, and David M. Schneider (New York: Columbia University Press, 1977), 151–64, argues that the language of Trobriand Islanders reveals that they "do not describe their activity lineally; they do no dynamic relating of acts; they do not use even so innocuous a connective as *and*" (157). According to Lee, they do not use causal connections in their descriptions of reality, and "where valued activity is concerned, the Trobrianders do not act on an assumption of lineality at any level. There is organization or rather coherence in their acts because Trobriand activity is patterned activity. One act within this pattern gives rise to a preordained cluster of acts." Lee presents the analogy that, in knitting a sweater, the "ribbing at the bottom does not *cause* the making of the neckline" (158). Similarly, "a Trobriander

does not speak of roads either as connecting two points or as *running from point to* point. His paths are self-contained, named as independent units; they are not *to* and *from*, they are *at*. And he himself is *at*; he has no equivalent for our *to* or *from*" (159). Appropriately, therefore, when an inhabitant of the Trobriand Islands "relates happenings, there is no developmental arrangement, no building up of emotional tone. His stories have no plot, no lineal development, no climax" (160), and this absence of what we mean by narrativity relates directly to the fact that "to the Trobriander, climax in history is abominable, a denial of all good, since it would imply not only the presence of change, but also that change increases the good; but to him value lies in sameness, in repeated pattern, in the incorporation of all time within the same point" (161). Lee, incidentally, does not claim that the people of the Trobriand Islands cannot perceive linearity, just that it possesses solely a negative value in their culture and it is made difficult to use by their customs and language. If one accepts the accuracy of her translations of Trobriand language and her interpretations of Trobriand culture, one can see that what Lee calls nonlineal thought based on the idea of clustering differs significantly from both linear and multilinear thought. Placed upon the spectrum constituted by Trobriand culture at one extreme and Western print culture at the other, hypertextuality appears only a moderate distance from other Western cultural patterns. Lee's description of Trobriand structuration by cluster, however, does possibly offer means of creating forms of hypertextual order.

3. Barbara Herrnstein Smith, "Narrative Versions, Narrative Theories," in *On Narrative*, ed. W. J. T. Mitchell (Chicago: University of Chicago Press, 1980), 225.

4. Hayden White, "The Value of Narrativity in the Representation of Reality," in *On Narrative*, ed. Mitchell, 1–2.

5. Lyotard also proposes that "the decline of narrative can be seen as an effect of the blossoming of techniques and technologies since the Second World War, which has shifted emphasis from the ends of action to its means; it can also be seen as an effect of the redeployment of advanced liberal capitalism after its retreat under the protection of Keynesianism during the period 1930–60, a renewal that has eliminated the communist alternative and valorized the individual enjoyment of goods and services" (37–38). His use of "can be seen as" suggests that Lyotard makes less than a full commitment to these explanations.

6. Robert Coover, "Endings," unpublished typescript of notes for a talk delivered at a May 1990 conference in Macerata, Italy, on the future of the novel.

7. William Dickey, "Poem Descending a Staircase: Hypertext and the Simultaneity of Experience," in *Hypermedia and Literary Studies*, ed. Delany and Landow, 147.

8. Paul Ricoeur, *Time and Narrative*, trans. Kathleen McLaughlin and David Pellauer, 2 vols. (Chicago: University of Chicago Press, 1984), 1: 67.

9. Barbara Herrnstein Smith, *Poetic Closure: A Study of How Poems End* (Chicago: University of Chicago Press, 1968), 99–100.

10. Brian McHale, *Postmodernist Fiction* (New York: Methuen, 1987), 219.

11. Robert Coover, "He Thinks the Way We Dream," *New York Times Book Review* (20 November 1989), 15. Ricoeur makes a similar point: "On the one hand, the episodic dimension of a narrative draws narrative time in the direction of the linear representation of time. . . . The configurational dimension, in its turn, presents temporal features directly opposed to those of the episodic dimension" (*Time and Narrative*, 1:67).

12. Penelope Lively, *Moon Tiger*, 1st ed. 1987 (New York: Harper and Row, 1989), 2.

13. Robert Coover, *Pricksongs and Descants: Fictions* (New York: New American Library, 1970), 206–39.

14. Dickey, "Poem Descending a Staircase," in *Hypermedia and Literary Studies*, ed. Delany and Landow, 147.

15. Hypertext is not the first information technology to make closure difficult. In *Writing Space*, Bolter reminds us that "the papyrus scroll was poor at suggesting a sense of closure" (85).

16. Gérard Genette, *Figures of Literary Discourse*, trans. Alan Sheridan (New York: Columbia University Press, 1982), 165.

17. J. Hillis Miller, *Versions of Pygmalion* (Cambridge: Harvard University Press, 1990), 127, 130.

18. See Wolfgang Köhler, *Gestalt Psychology: An Introduction to New Concepts in Modern Psychology* (New York: Liveright, 1947); and E. H. Gombrich, *Art and Illusion: A Study in the Psychology of Pictorial Representation*, 2nd ed. (New York: Pantheon, 1961).

19. The term *prosopopoeia*, Miller explains, describes "the ascription to entities that are not really alive first of a *name*, then of a face, and finally, in a return to language, of a voice. The entity I have personified is given the power to respond to the name I invoke, to speak in answer to my speech. Another way to put this would be to say that though my prosopopoeia is a fact of language, a member of the family of tropes, this tends to be hidden because the trope is posited a priori" (5).

20. The phrase "structuralist study of plot" is from Jonathan Culler, *Structuralist Poetics: Structuralism, Linguistics and the Study of Literature* (Ithaca, N.Y.: Cornell University Press, 1975), 207. For Propp, see Vladimir Propp, "Fairy Tale Transformations" (1928), trans. C. H. Stevens, in *Readings in Russian*

Poetics: Formalist and Structuralist Views, ed. Ladislav Matejka and Krystyna Pomorska (Cambridge: MIT Press, 1971), 94–114; and *Morphology of the Folktale* (Bloomington: Indiana Research Center in Anthropology, 1958). See also Robert Scholes, *Structuralism in Literature: An Introduction* (New Haven: Yale University Press, 1974), 59–141.

Chapter 5
Reconfiguring
Literary Education

1. Gary Marchionini, "Evaluating Hypermedia-Based Learning," in *Designing Hypertext/Hypermedia for Learning*, ed. Jonassen and Mandl, 355.

2. John L. Leggett, John L. Schase, and Charles J. Kacmar, "Hypertext for Learning," in *Designing Hypertext*, ed. Jonassen and Mandl, 27.

3. We have been observing ways that hypertext embodies literary theory; it also instantiates related pedagogical theory. The hypertextual reader-author, for instance, matches R. A. Schoaf's claim that "every reader, in fact, from the beginning student to the seasoned professional, is also a writer, or more accurately a rewriter — and must be aware of that" ("Literary Theory, Medieval Studies, and the Crisis of Difference," in *Reorientations: Critical Theories and Pedagogies*, ed. Bruce Henricksen and Thaïs Morgan [Urbana: University of Illinois Press, 1990], 80).

4. David H. Jonassen and R. Scott Grabinger, "Problems and Issues in Designing Hypertext/Hypermedia for Learning," in *Designing Hypertext*, ed. Jonassen and Mandl, 4, 7.

5. Philippe C. Duchastel, "Discussion: Formal and Informal Learning with Hypermedia," in *Designing Hypertext*, ed. Jonassen and Mandl, 139.

6. Terry Mayes, Mike Kibby, and Tony Anderson, "Learning about Learning from Hypertext," in *Designing Hypertext*, ed. Jonassen and Mandl, 229.

7. Rand J. Spiro, Walter P. Vispoel, John G. Schmitz, Ala Samarapungavan, and A. E. Boerger, "Knowledge Acquisition for Application: Cognitive Flexibility and Transfer in Complex Content Domains," in *Executive Control Processes in Reading*, ed. B. K. Britton and S. McGlynn (Hillsdale, N.J.: Lawrence Erlbaum, 1987), 187.

8. Brook Thomas, "Bringing about Critical Awareness through History in General Education Literature Courses," in *Reorientations*, ed. Henricksen and Morgan, 229.

9. Jolene Galegher and Robert E. Kraut, "Technology for Intellectual Teamwork: Perspectives on Research and Design," in *Intellectual Teamwork*, ed. Galegher, Egido, and Kraut, 9.

10. John G. Blair, *Modular America: Cross-Cultural Perspectives on the Emergence of an American Way of Life* (New York: Greenwood Press, 1988), 11, 20: "The modularity in question emerges when the Americans take something the Europeans had always considered as a whole, namely undergraduate education, and break it up into small, self-contained and implicitly recombinable units

commonly called course credits or credit hours. . . . The implications of the new system show up most clearly in the new artifact to which they give rise: the student transcript. . . . The transcript, by tracing one person's passage through the curriculum, is an additive record bounded by the number of credits required for graduation. Equivalence of parts dictates that a course is a course is a course, though locally defined restraints on combinability (majors, distribution requirements, prerequisites, and the like) may sometimes lead a student to accumulate more credits than the minimum required for graduation." A full hypertext version of the present book would, at this point, link the reader to the entire text of Blair's book (most likely through a section or chapter that, in turn, would link to the entire text) and also to the enormous body of internal reports produced in recent decades by individual American colleges and universities discussing the results of such modular approaches.

11. Joseph E. McGrath, "Time Matters in Groups," in *Intellectual Teamwork*, ed. Galegher, Egido, and Kraut, 38.

12. That part of the Intermedia development plan funded by the Annenberg/CPB Project included an intensive three-year evaluation, which was carried out by a team of ethnographers who attended, taped, and analyzed all class meetings and who conducted frequent surveys of and interviews with students during the two years before the introduction of the hypertext component and for the year following. Many of my observations on conventional education and on the effects of hypertext upon it derive from their data and from conversations with Professor Peter Heywood, a participant in the project. See William O. Beeman, Kenneth T. Anderson, Gail Bader, J. Larkin, A. P. McClard, Patrick McQuillan, and Mark Shields, *Intermedia: A Case Study of Innovation in Higher Education* (Providence, R.I.: Office of Program Analysis/Institute for Research in Information and Scholarship, 1988).

13. *Context 32* and other Intermedia webs contain materials created by my students in six iterations of English 32 (the survey course), two of English 61 (Victorian poetry), one each of English 137 (Anglo-American nonfiction) and English 263 (graduate seminar in Victorian poetry), plus a handful of undergraduate and graduate independent research projects that include Graham Swift's fiction (Barry J. Fishman); World War I, technology, and literature (Thomas G. Bowie); the semiotics of emblem literature (Gary Weissman); Italian Renaissance cultural history and an anthropological approach to women's fashion, 1700 to the present (Shoshana M. Landow); contemporary postcolonial fiction (Melissa Culross); and selected authors from the Women Writers Project (Elizabeth Soucar).

14. Peter Whalley, "Models of Hypertext Structure and Models of Learning," in *Designing Hypertext*, ed. Jonassen and Mandl, 66.

15. George P. Landow, "Course Assignments Using Hypertext: The Example of Intermedia," *Journal of Research on Computing in Education* 21 (1989): 349–65.

16. Gary Putka, "New Kid in School: Alternative Exams," *Wall Street Journal*, November 16, 1989, B1, surveys changing national attitudes toward testing and provides several instances of alternative approaches that stress critical thinking.

17. Marchionini, "Evaluating Hypermedia-Based Learning," in *Designing Hypertext*, ed. Jonassen and Mandl, 356.

18. I wish to thank the students in my graduate seminar in Victorian literature—Maryanne Ackershoek, Chatchai Atsavapranee, Mark Gaipa, Laura Henrickson, Helen Kim, and Mark McMorriss—for their contributions to the *In Memoriam* project.

19. Six students, thirty percent of the class, composed their documents directly on Intermedia, rather than on typewriters or personal computers in clusters or in their own rooms.

20. The essays from the second semester include Melinda Barton, "Soyinka as a Romantic"; Jonathan Clough, "Jonathan Swift's Influences on Soyinka with Reference to 'Gulliver'"; Andrew Colcord Curtis, "Notions of Progress in Swift's *Waterland* and Soyinka's 'When Seasons Change'"; Mary Jane Ebert, "Soyinka's Drama"; Andrew Frumovitz, "Religion, the Earth, and the City in the Drama and Poetry of Wole Soyinka," *"The Swamp Dwellers," "The Trials of Brother Jero,"* and "Soyinka's 'Ujamaa'"; Jonathan Protass, "Soyinka's Battle against Insanity in *The Man Died*"; Abra Reid, "Christianity and Yoruba: The Fusing of Influences in Wole Soyinka'a Work"; Rob Rosenthal, "Swift and Soyinka as Satirists"; Anujeet Sareen, "Wole Soyinka and A. D. Hope"; Leslie Stern, "Soyinka's Use of the Yoruba Conception of Man"; Emily Steiner, "Changes in African Poetry" and "Soyinka's Roots and the Oral Tradition"; Valerie Steinberg, "Wole Soyinka's 'Gulliver' and the Perils of Vision"; Karen van Ness, "The Nigerian Elections of 1965"; Amelia Warren, "Soyinka's 'Gulliver' and *Gulliver's Travels*," "Wole Soyinka: 'The Critic and Society: Barthes, Leftocracy, and Other Mythologies'"; and Kelley Wilson, "The Test of Idealism in *The Man Died*."

21. Gerald L. Bruns, "Canon and Power in the Hebrew Scriptures," in *Canons*, ed. Robert von Hallberg (Chicago: University of Chicago Press, 1984), 67.

22. See George P. Landow, *The Aesthetic and Critical Theories of John Ruskin* (Princeton: Princeton University Press, 1971); and *Victorian Types, Victorian Shadows*.

23. Hugh Kenner, "The Making of the Modernist Canon," in *Canons*, ed. von Hallberg, 371. Writing in terms of the broadest canon, that constituted by the concept of literature and the literary, Eagleton observes: "What you have defined as a 'literary' work will always be closely bound up with what you consider 'appropriate' critical techniques: a 'literary' work will mean, more or less, one which can be usefully illuminated by such methods of enquiry" (*Literary Theory*, 80).

24. Toril Moi, *Sexual/Textual Politics: Feminist Literary Theory* (London: Methuen, 1985), 78.

25. Reed Way Dasenbrock, "What to Teach When the Canon Closes Down: Toward a New Essentialism," in *Reorientations*, ed. Henricksen and Morgan, 67.

26. Richard Ohmann, "The Shaping of a Canon: U.S. Fiction, 1960–1975," in *Canons*, ed. von Hallberg, 385–86.

27. In 1968, for example, Random House, which purchased seventy-four pages of advertising to Harper's twenty-nine, "had nearly three times as many books mentioned in the feature 'New and Recommended' as Doubleday or Harper, both of which published as many books as the Random House group" (381). Ohmann also points out "it may be more than coincidental" that in the same year in the *New York Review of Books*, founded by a Random House vice president, "almost one-fourth of the books granted full reviews . . . were published by Random House (again, including Knopf and Pantheon) — more than the combined total of books from Viking, Grove, Holt, Harper, Houghton Mifflin, Oxford, Doubleday, Macmillan, and Harvard so honored; or that in the same year one-fourth of the *reviewers* had books in print with Random House and that a third of those were reviewing other Random House books, mainly favorably; or that over a five-year period more than half the regular reviewers (ten or more appearances) were Random House authors" (383).

28. According to Hugh Kenner: "Since Chaucer, the domain of English literature had been a country, England. Early in the 20th century its domain commenced to be a language, English" ("Making of the Canon," 366).

1. From this point Lyotard continues, "Technology is therefore a game pertaining not to the true, the just, or the beautiful, etc., but to efficiency: a technical 'move' is 'good' when it does better and/or expends less energy than another."

2. Paul Saenger, "Books of Hours and the Reading Habits of the Later Middle Ages," in *The Culture of Print: Power and the Uses of Print in Early Modern Europe*, ed. Roger Chartier, trans. Lydia G. Cochrane (Princeton: Princeton University Press, 1987), 155.

3. Alvin Kernan, *Printing Technology, Letters and Samuel Johnson* (Princeton: Princeton University Press, 1987), 3.

4. Terry Eagleton, *Criticism and Ideology: A Study in Marxist Literary Theory* (London: NLB, 1976), 44–63. Although Eagleton never cites McLuhan or other students of the history of information technology, he several times compares manuscript and print cultures within the context of Marxist theory; see 47–48, 51–52.

5. Michael Ryan, *Marxism and Deconstruction: A Critical Articulation* (Baltimore: Johns Hopkins University Press, 1982), 60. Ryan also offers an oddly limited description of technology when he writes: "Technology is the human mind working up the natural world into machines. And, as I have argued, it is motivated by the desire of a class of subjects — capitalists — to maintain power over another class of subjects — workers" (92). The problems with this statement include, first, the fact that Ryan confuses "capitalists" with "owners of production," even though he makes clear elsewhere that what he calls the Leninist tradition also relies upon heavy technology; and second, such a bizarrely narrow definition apparently restricts technology to heavy machinery, thereby omitting both everything before the Industrial Revolution and everything in the electronic and atomic age other than old-fashioned rust-belt manufacturing. The context makes difficult determining whether it is Ryan's dislike of technology or capitalism that leads him to such an obsolete definition.

6. Elizabeth Eisenstein makes a particularly astute point when discussing arguments about the role of print technology in radical social change during the Reformation: "Given the convergence of interests among printers and Protestants, given the way that the new media implemented older evangelical goals, it seems pointless to argue whether material or spiritual, socio-economic or religious 'factors' were more important in transforming Western Christianity. Not only do these dichotomies seem to be based on spurious categories, but they also make it difficult to perceive the distinctive amalgam which resulted from collaboration between diverse pressure groups." One does not have to espouse pluralism to recognize that Marxist analyses could easily incorporate evidence provided by Eisenstein.

7. Mayes, Kibby, and Anderson, "Learning about Learning from Hypertext," in *Designing Hyperptext*, ed. Jonassen and Mandl, 228.

8. Nelson also points out: "Tomorrow's hypertext networks have immense political ramifications, and there are many struggles to come. Many vested interests may turn out to be opposed to freedom . . . for rolled into such designs and prospects is the whole future of humanity and, indeed, the future of the past and the future of the future — meaning the kinds of future that become forbidden, or possible" (3/19).

9. Lynn T. White, *Medieval Technology and Social Change* (Oxford: Clarendon Press, 1963).

10. In *The Gutenberg Galaxy*, 216, McLuhan quotes Harold Innis, *The Bias of Communication* (Toronto: University of Toronto Press), 29: "The effect of the discovery of printing was evident in the savage religious wars of the sixteenth and seventeenth centuries. Application of power to communication industries hastened the consolidation of vernaculars, the rise of nationalism, revolution, and new outbreaks of savagery in the twentieth century."

11. In print this thrust appears with particular clarity in the radically new discovery that the best way to preserve information lies in disseminating large numbers of copies of a text containing it rather than keeping it secret; see Eisenstein, 116.

12. Professor Ulmer made these comments in the course of the 1988 University of Alabama conference entitled Literacy Online.

13. George P. Landow, "Hypertext in Literary Education, Criticism, and Scholarship," *Computers and the Humanities* 23 (1989): 173. This essay, first distributed in 1987 as an IRIS technical paper, also appeared in an abbreviated version as "Changing Texts, Changing Readers: Hypertext in Literary Education, Criticism, and Scholarship," in *Reorientations,* ed. Henricksen and Morgan, 133–61.

14. Ryan, whose prose clots and stutters at this point, explains: "The deconstructive rewriting of the classical dialectic removes the justification for the conservative marxist model of a linearly evolutionary and finalistically resolutive progress to socialism, while implicitly furthering a politics predicated upon a more realistic assessment of the antagonistic forces and irreducible differences that characterize capitalist social and productive relations" (43).

15. Rorty continues on the same page: "The edifying philosophers are thus agreeing with Lessing's choice of the *infinite striving for* truth over 'all of Truth.' For the edifying philosopher the very idea of being presented with 'all of Truth' is absurd, because the Platonic notion of Truth itself is absurd."

16. Karl Popper, *The Open Society and Its Enemies* (Princeton: Princeton University Press, 1963), argues that Plato developed his conceptions of humanity, society, and philosophy in reaction to the political disorder of his time. Plato's "theory of Forms or Ideas," according to Popper, has three main functions within his thought: (1) as a methodological device that "makes possible pure scientific knowledge"; (2) as a "clue" to a theory of change, decay, and history; and (3) as the basis of an historicist "social engineering" that can arrest social change (30–31). Popper argues that Plato bases his ideal state on Sparta, "a slave state, and accordingly Plato's best state is based on the most rigid class distinctions. It is a caste state. The problem of avoiding class war is solved, not by abolishing classes, but by giving the ruling class a superiority which cannot be challenged" (46). Popper, who attacks him for providing the ultimate ideological basis of fascism, claims that in *The Republic* Plato "used the term 'just' for a synonym for 'that which is in the interest of the best state.' And what is in the interest of the best state? To arrest all change, by the maintenance of a rigid class division and class rule. If I am right in this interpretation, then we should have to say that Plato's demand for justice leaves his political programme at the level of totalitarianism" (89).

17. Ellen Rooney, *Seductive Reasoning: Pluralism as the Problematic of Contemporary Literary Theory* (Ithaca, N.Y.: Cornell University Press, 1989), 1–2.

222

18. Instead of such politically naive innocent readings, the active reader produces "symptomatic" readings, which "disclose an unacknowledged problematic" (*Seductive Reasoning*, 241). Following Althusser, she observes that "to propose a 'symptomatic' reading of any text is to claim a different position vis-à-vis that text, a new relation, which enables a heretofore unthinkable reading" (12). She locates the "symptomatic moment of pluralist discourse," for example, at the point "when the theoretical problem of the position of the reader is displaced, rewritten as a question of logic, ethics, or rhetoric. To interrogate the status of the general audience is to risk discovering the interests of readers as a theoretical limit to persuasion, and this is a possibility pluralists must consistently evade, whatever their other critical commitments" (2).

19. Norman Meyrowitz, "Hypertext — Does It Reduce Cholesterol, Too?" in *Vannevar Bush and the Mind's Machine*, ed. Nyce and Kahn, 2.

20. Antonio Zampolli, "Computational Linguistics and Linguistic Research," in *Conference Papers*, 43–44. Zampolli credits a personal communication from B. Quemada as the source of this analogy.

21. See Sigfried Giedeon, *Mechanization Takes Command: A Contribution to Anonymous History* (New York: Norton, 1969).

22. Gordon Wu, "Soft Soap," *Times Literary Supplement*, 20–26 July 1990, 777.

23. Richard Ohmann, "The Shaping of a Canon: U.S. Fiction, 1960–1975," in *Canons*, ed. von Hallberg, 377–401.

24. Steven W. Gilbert, "Information Technology, Intellectual Property, and Education," *EDUCOM Review* 25 (Spring 1990): 16.

25. H. J. Chaytor, *From Script to Print* (Cambridge, England: Heffer and Sons, 1945), 1. Cited by McLuhan (*The Gutenberg Galaxy*, 87) and credited on the previous page as "a book to which the present one owes a good deal of its reason for being written."

26. John Sutherland, "Author's Rights and Transatlantic Differences," *Times Literary Supplement*, 20–26 May 1990, 554. Sutherland quotes E. W. Plowman and L. C. Hamilton's explanation (in *Copyright: Intellectual Property in the Information Age* [London: Routledge and Kegan Paul, 1980]) that in France and Germany moral rights include "the rights to determine the manner of dissemination, to ensure recognition of authorship, to prohibit distortion of the work, to ensure access to the original or to copies of the work, and to revoke a license by reason of changed convictions against payment of damages." This and all subsequent quotations from this article in the main text come from page 554.

Bibliography

Printed Materials   Accame, Lorenzo. *La Decostruzione e il Testo.* Florence: G. C. Sansoni, 1976.

Akscyn, Robert M., Donald L. McCracken, and Elise Yoder. "KMS: A Distributed Hypermedia System for Managing Knowledge Organizations." *Communications of the ACM* 31 (1988): 820–35.

Althusser, Louis. *For Marx.* Translated by Ben Brewster. London: Verso, 1979.

Auerbach, Nina. *Woman and the Demon: The Life of a Victorian Myth.* Cambridge: Harvard University Press, 1982.

Bakhtin, Mikhail. *Problems of Dostoevsky's Poetics.* Edited and translated by Caryl Emerson. Minneapolis: University of Minnesota Press, 1984.

Barrett, Edward, ed. *Text, ConText, and Hypertext: Writing with and for the Computer.* Cambridge: MIT Press, 1988.

Barthes, Roland. "Authors and Writers." In *A Barthes Reader,* edited by Susan Sontag, 185–93. New York: Hill and Wang, 1982.

———. *The Eiffel Tower and Other Mythologies.* Translated by Richard Howard. New York: Hill and Wang, 1979.

———. *Elements of Semiology.* Translated by Annette Lavers and Colin Smith. London: Jonathan Cape, 1967.

———. *Mythologies.* Translated by Annette Lavers. New York: Hill and Wang, 1972.

———. *Sade, Fourier, Loyola.* Translated by Richard Miller. New York: Hill and Wang, 1976.

———. *S/Z.* Paris: Éditions du Seuil, 1970. *S/Z.* Translated by Richard Miller. New York: Hill and Wang, 1974.

———. *Writing Degree Zero.* Translated by Annette Lavers and Colin Smith. London: Jonathan Cape, 1967.

Baudrillard, Jean. *The Ecstasy of Communication.* Translated by Bernard and Caroline Schutze and edited by Sylvère Lotringer. New York: Semiotext(e), 1988.

———. *Fatal Strategies.* Translated by Philip Beitchman and W. G. J. Niesluchowski. New York: Semiotext(e)/Pluto, 1990.

———. *Simulations.* New York: Semiotext(e), 1983.

Beeman, William O., Kenneth T. Anderson, Gail Bader, James Larkin, Anne P. McClard, Patrick McQuillan, and Mark Shields. *Intermedia: A Case Study of*

Bibliography *Innovation in Higher Education.* Providence, R.I.: Office of Program Analysis, Institute for Research in Information and Scholarship, 1988.

Benjamin, Walter. *Illuminations.* Edited by Hannah Arendt and translated by Harry Zohn. New York: Schocken, 1969.

Berger, Peter L., and Thomas Luckmann. *The Social Construction of Reality: A Treatise in the Sociology of Knowledge.* Garden City, N.Y.: Doubleday, 1966.

Blair, John G. *Modular America: Cross-Cultural Perspectives on the Emergence of an American Way of Life.* New York: Greenwood Press, 1988.

Bloom, Harold, Paul de Man, Jacques Derrida, Geoffrey H. Hartman, and J. Hillis Miller. *Deconstruction and Criticism.* London: Routledge and Kegan Paul, 1979.

Bolter, J. David. "Beyond Word Processing: The Computer as a New Writing Space." *Language & Communication* 9 (1989): 129–42.

———. *Turing's Man: Western Culture in the Computer Age.* Chapel Hill: University of North Carolina Press, 1984.

———. *Writing Space: The Computer in the History of Literacy.* Hillsdale, N.J.: Lawrence Erlbaum, 1990.

Borges, Jorge Luis. *The Aleph and Other Stories, 1933–1969.* Translated by Norman Thomas di Giovanni. New York: Bantam, 1971.

———. *Other Inquisitions, 1937–1952.* Translated by Ruth L. C. Simms. New York: Washington Square Press, 1966.

Brennan, Elaine. "Using the Computer to Right the Canon: The Brown Women Writers Project." *Brown Online: A Journal of Computing in Academic Settings* 2 (1989): 7–13.

Bush, Vannevar. "As We May Think." *Atlantic Monthly* 176 (July 1945): 101–8.

———. *Endless Horizons.* Washington, D.C.: Public Affairs Press, 1946.

———. "Memex Revisited." In *Science Is Not Enough*, 75–101. New York: William Morrow, 1967.

Chartier, Roger. *The Cultural Uses of Print in Early Modern France.* Translated by Lydia G. Cochrane. Princeton: Princeton University Press, 1987.

———. *The Culture of Print: Power and the Uses of Print in Early Modern Europe.* Translated by Lydia G. Cochrane. Princeton: Princeton University Press, 1987.

———. "Meaningful Forms." Translated by Patrick Curry. *Liber* 1 (1989): 8–9.

Chatman, Seymour. *Story and Discourse: Narrative Structure in Fiction and Film.* Ithaca: Cornell University Press, 1978.

Bibliography

Clement, Richard W. "Italian Sixteenth-Century Writing Books and the Scribal Reality in Verona." *Visible Language* 20 (1986): 393–412.

Collaud, G., J. Monnard, and J. Pasquier-Boltuck. *Untangling Webs: A User's Guide to the Woven Electronic Book System.* Fribourg, Switzerland: University of Fribourg (IAUF), 1989.

Conklin, E. Jeffrey. "Hypertext: An Introduction and Survey." *IEEE Computer* 20 (1987): 17–41.

Coombs, James H. "Hypertext, Full Text, and Automatic Linking." SIGIR 90 (technical report). Providence, R.I.: Institute for Research in Information and Scholarship, 1990.

Coover, Robert. "Endings: Work Notes." Manuscript, 1990.

———. "He Thinks the Way We Dream." *New York Times Book Review* (20 November 1988): 15.

———. *Pricksongs and Descants.* New York: New American Library, 1969.

Crane, Gregory. "Redefining the Book: Some Preliminary Problems." *Academic Computing* 2 (February 1988): 6–11, 36–41.

Culler, Jonathan. *Framing the Sign: Criticism and Its Institutions.* Norman: University of Oklahoma Press, 1988.

———. *On Deconstruction: Theory and Criticism after Structuralism.* Ithaca: Cornell University Press, 1982.

———. *The Pursuit of Signs: Semiotics, Literature, Deconstruction.* Ithaca: Cornell University Press, 1981.

———. *Structuralist Poetics: Structuralism, Linguistics, and the Study of Literature.* Ithaca: Cornell University Press, 1975.

Delany, Paul, and George P. Landow, eds. *Hypermedia and Literary Studies.* Cambridge: MIT Press, 1991.

DeRose, Steven J. *CD Word Tutorial: Learning CD Word for Bible Study.* Dallas: CD Word Library, 1990.

Derrida, Jacques. *De la Grammatologie.* Paris: Les Éditions de Minuit, 1967. *Of Grammatology.* Translated by Gayatri Chakravorty Spivak. Baltimore: Johns Hopkins University Press, 1976.

———. *La Dissemination.* Paris: Éditions du Seuil, 1972. *Dissemination.* Translated by Barbara Johnson. Chicago: University of Chicago Press, 1981.

———. "Structure, Sign, and Play in the Discourse of the Human Sciences." In *The Structuralist Controversy: The Languages of Criticism and the Sciences of Man*, edited by Richard A. Macksey and Eugenio Donato. Baltimore: Johns Hopkins University Press, 1972.

Bibliography

———. *Writing and Difference.* Translated by Alan Bass. Chicago: University of Chicago Press, 1978.

Eagleton, Terry. *Criticism and Ideology: A Study in Marxist Theory.* London: NLB, 1976.

———. *Literary Theory: An Introduction.* Minneapolis: University of Minnesota Press, 1983.

Ede, Lisa, and Andrea Lunsford. *Singular Texts/Plural Authors: Perspectives on Collaborative Writing.* Carbondale: Southern Illinois University Press, 1990.

Eisenstein, Elizabeth L. *The Printing Press as An Agent of Change: Communications and Cultural Transformations in Early-Modern Europe.* Cambridge: Cambridge University Press, 1980.

Fishman, Barry J. "The Works of Graham Swift: A Hypertext Thesis." Honors thesis, Brown University, 1989.

Flaxman, Rhoda L. *Victorian Word Painting and Narrative: Toward the Blending of Genres.* Ann Arbor, Mich.: UMI Research Press, 1987.

Foelsche, Otmar K. E. "Hypertext-like Environments in HyperCard: The Beginning Phase of the Brown, Dartmouth, Harvard Language Workstation Project." Hanover: Dartmouth College Language Resource Center, 1989.

Foster, Hal, ed. *The Anti-Aesthetic: Essays on Postmodern Culture.* Port Townsend, Wash.: Bay Press, 1983.

Foucault, Michel. *The Archeology of Knowledge and the Discourse on Language.* Translated by A. M. Sheridan Smith. New York: Harper and Row, 1976.

———. *The Order of Things: An Archeology of the Human Sciences.* New York: Vintage, 1973.

———. "What Is an Author?" In *Language, Counter-Memory, Practice: Selected Essays and Interviews,* translated by Donald F. Bouchard and Sherry Simon, 113–38. Ithaca: Cornell University Press, 1977.

Friedlander, Larry. "The Shakespeare Project: Experiments in Multimedia Education." *Academic Computing* 2 (May/June 1988): 26–29, 66–68.

Frow, John. *Marxism and Literary History.* Cambridge: Harvard University Press, 1986.

Galegher, Jolene, Carmen Egido, and Robert Kraut, eds. *Intellectual Teamwork.* Hillsdale, N.J.: Lawrence Erlbaum, 1990.

Gatlin, Lila L. *Information Theory and the Living System.* New York: Columbia University Press, 1972.

Geertz, Clifford. *Works and Lives: The Anthropologist as Author.* Stanford: Stanford University Press, 1988.

Bibliography

Genette, Gérard. *Figures of Literary Discourse.* Translated by Alan Sheridan. New York: Columbia University Press, 1982.

———. *Narrative Discourse: An Essay in Method.* Translated by Jane E. Lewin. Ithaca: Cornell University Press, 1980.

Gibson, William. *Burning Chrome.* New York: Ace, 1987.

———. *Mona Lisa Overdrive.* New York: Bantam, 1988.

———. *Neuromancer.* New York: Ace, 1984.

Giedion, Sigfried. *Mechanization Takes Command: A Contribution to Anonymous History.* New York: Norton, 1969.

Gilbert, Sandra M., and Susan Gubar. *The Madwoman in the Attic: The Woman Writer and the Nineteenth-Century Imagination.* New Haven: Yale University Press, 1984.

Gilbert, Steven W. "Information Technology, Intellectual Property, and Education." *EDUCOM Review* 25 (Spring 1990): 14–20.

Gombrich, E. H. *Art and Illusion: A Study in the Psychology of Pictorial Representation.* 2nd ed. New York: Pantheon, 1961.

Gore, Albert. "Remarks on the NREN." *EDUCOM Review* 25 (Summer 1990): 12–16.

Greene, Gayle, and Coppélia Kahn, eds. *Making a Difference: Feminist Literary Criticism.* London: Methuen, 1985.

Griest, Guinevere L. *Mudie's Circulating Library and the Victorian Novel.* Bloomington: Indiana University Press, 1970.

Hawkins, Brian L. "Campus-wide Networking at Brown University." *Academic Computing* 3 (January 1989): 32–33, 36–39, 44, 46–49.

Heim, Michael. *Electric Language: A Philosophical Study of Word Processing.* New Haven: Yale University Press, 1987.

Helsinger, Elizabeth K. *Ruskin and the Art of the Beholder.* Cambridge: Harvard University Press, 1982.

Henricksen, Bruce, and Thaïs Morgan, eds. *Reorientations: Critical Theories and Pedagogies.* Urbana: University of Illinois Press, 1990.

Hertz, J. J., ed. *The Pentateuch and Haftorahs.* 2nd ed. London: Soncino Press, 1962.

Howard, Alan. "Hypermedia and the Future of Ethnography." *Cultural Anthropology* 3 (1988): 304–15.

Huyssen, Andreas. *After the Great Divide: Modernism, Mass Culture, and Postmodernism.* Bloomington: Indiana University Press, 1987.

Bibliography   Institute for Research in Information and Scholarship (IRIS). *The Dickens Web: User's and Installation Guide.* Providence, R.I.: IRIS, 1990.

Institute for Research in Information and Scholarship (IRIS). *Linking the Continents of Knowledge: A Hypermedia Corpus for Discovery and Collaborative Work in the Sciences, Arts, and Humanities.* Providence, R.I.: IRIS, 1988.

Intermedia: From Linking to Learning. 27-minute video. Directed by Deborah Dorsey. Cambridge Studies and the Annenberg/Corporation for Public Broadcasting Project, 1986.

IRIS Intermedia System Administrator's Guide: Release 3.0. Providence, R.I.: Institute for Research in Information and Scholarship, 1989.

IRIS Intermedia User's Guide: Release 3.0. Providence, R.I.: Institute for Research in Information and Scholarship, 1989.

Ivins, William M. *Prints and Visual Communication.* New York: DaCapo, 1969.

Jameson, Fredric. *Marxism and Form: Twentieth-Century Dialectical Theories of Literature.* Princeton: Princeton University Press, 1971.

————. *The Political Unconscious: Narrative as a Socially Symbolic Act.* Ithaca: Cornell University Press, 1981.

Johnson, Barbara. *A World of Difference.* Baltimore: Johns Hopkins University Press, 1987.

Jonassen, David H. "Hypertext Principles for Text and Courseware Design." *Educational Psychologist* 21 (1986): 269–92.

————. "Information Mapping: A Description, Rationale and Comparison with Programmed Instruction." *Visible Language* 15 (1981): 55–66.

Jonassen, David H., and Heinz Mandl, eds. *Designing Hypertext/Hypermedia for Learning.* Heidelberg: Springer-Verlag, 1990.

Jones, Loretta L., Jennifer L. Karloski, and Stanley G. Smith. "A General Chemistry Learning Center: Using the Interactive Videodisc." *Academic Computing* 2 (September 1987): 36–37, 54.

Joyce, Michael. "Siren Shapes: Exploratory and Constructive Hypertexts." *Academic Computing* 3 (November 1988): 10–14, 37–42.

Kahn, Paul D. "Isocrates: Greek Literature on CD Rom." In *CD ROM: The New Papyrus: The Current and Future State of the Art*, edited by Steve Lambert and Suzanne Ropiequet. Redmond, Wash.: Microsoft Press, 1986.

————. "Linking together Books: Experiments in Adapting Published Material into Intermedia Documents." *Hypermedia* 1 (1989): 111–45.

Kahn, Paul D., Julie Launhardt, Krzysztof Lenk, and Ronnie Peters. "Design Issues of Hypermedia Publications: Issues and Solutions." In *EP 90: Interna-*

Bibliography *tional Conference on Electronic Publishing, Document Manipulations, and Typography*, edited by Richard Furuta, 107–24. Cambridge: Cambridge University Press, 1990.

Kahn, Paul D., and Norman Meyrowitz. "Guide, HyperCard, and Intermedia: A Comparison of Hypertext/Hypermedia Systems." Technical Report no. 88-7. Providence, R.I.: Institute for Research in Information and Scholarship, 1987.

Kermode, Frank. *The Sense of an Ending: Studies in the Theory of Fiction.* New York: Oxford University Press, 1967.

Kernan, Alvin. *Printing Technology, Letters and Samuel Johnson.* Princeton: Princeton University Press, 1987.

Kerr, Stephen T. "Instructional Text: The Transition from Page to Screen." *Visible Language* 20 (1986): 368–92.

King, Kenneth M. "Evolution of the Concept of Computer Literacy." *EDU-COM Bulletin* 20 (1986): 18–21.

Köhler, Wolfgang. *Gestalt Psychology: An Introduction to New Concepts in Modern Psychology.* New York: Liveright, 1947.

Kuhn, Thomas S. *The Structure of Scientific Revolutions.* 2nd ed. Chicago: University of Chicago Press, 1970.

Lacan, Jacques. *The Language of the Self: The Function of Language in Psychoanalysis.* Translated by Anthony Wilden. Baltimore: Johns Hopkins University Press, 1968.

Landow, George P. "Course Assignments in Hypertext: The Example of Intermedia." *Journal of Research on Computing in Education* 21 (1989): 349–65.

———. "Hypertext and Collaborative Work: The Example of Intermedia." In *Intellectual Teamwork*, edited by Jolene Galegher, Carmen Egido, and Robert Kraut, 407–28. Hillsdale, N.J.: Lawrence Erlbaum, 1990.

———. "Hypertext in Literary Education, Criticism, and Scholarship." *Computers and the Humanities* 23 (1989): 173–98.

———. "The Rhetoric of Hypermedia: Some Rules for Authors." *Journal of Computing in Higher Education* 1 (1989): 39–64.

———. *Victorian Types, Victorian Shadows: Biblical Typology and Victorian Literature, Art, and Thought.* Boston: Routledge and Kegan Paul, 1980.

LaQuey, Tracy. "Networks for Academics." *Academic Computing* 4 (November 1989): 32–34, 39, 65.

Larson, James A. "A Visual Approach to Browsing in a Database Environment." *IEEE Computer* 19 (1986): 62–71.

Bibliography

Lavers, Annette. *Roland Barthes: Structuralism and After.* Cambridge: Harvard University Press, 1982.

Learning How to Write Means Learning How to Think. Cupertino, Calif.: Apple Computers, 1989.

Lee, Dorothy. "Lineal and Nonlineal Codifications of Reality." In *Symbolic Anthropology: A Reader in the Study of Symbols and Meanings*, edited by Janet L. Dolgin, David S. Kemnitzer, and David M. Schneider, 151–64. New York: Columbia University Press, 1977.

Leitch, Vincent B. *Deconstructive Criticism: An Advanced Introduction.* New York: Columbia University Press, 1983.

Lerman, Steven R. "UNIX Workstations in Academia: At the Crossroads." *Academic Computing* 3 (October 1988): 16–18, 51–55.

Lévi-Strauss, Claude. *The Raw and the Cooked: Introduction to a Science of Mythology: I.* Translated by John and Doreen Weightman. New York: Harper and Row, 1969.

———. *The Scope of Anthropology.* Translated by Sherry Ortner Paul and Robert A. Paul. London: Jonathan Cape, 1967.

Lyotard, Jean-François. *The Postmodern Condition: A Report on Knowledge.* Translated by Geoff Bennington and Brian Massumi. Minneapolis: University of Minnesota Press, 1984.

Machery, Pierre. *A Theory of Literary Production.* Translated by Geoffrey Wall. London: Routledge and Kegan Paul, 1978.

Matejka, Ladislav, and Krystyna Pomorska, eds. *Readings in Russian Poetics: Formalist and Structuralist Views.* Cambridge: MIT Press, 1971.

Matejka, Ladislav, and Irwin R. Titunik, eds. *Semiotics of Art: Prague School Contributions.* Cambridge: MIT Press, 1976.

McArthur, Tom. *Worlds of Reference: Lexicography, Learning and Language from the Clay Tablet to the Computer.* Cambridge: Cambridge University Press, 1986.

McClintock, Robert. "On Computing and the Curriculum." *SIGCUE Outlook* (Spring/Summer 1986): 25–41.

McCorduck, Pamela. *Machines Who Think: A Personal Inquiry into the History and Prospects of Artificial Intelligence.* New York: W. H. Freeman, 1979.

McHale, Brian. *Postmodernist Fiction.* New York: Methuen, 1987.

McKnight, John Richardson, and Andrew Dillon. "The Authoring of HyperText Documents." Loughborough, England: Loughborough University of Technology/HUSAT Research Centre, 1988.

Bibliography

McLuhan, Marshall. *The Gutenberg Galaxy: The Making of Typographic Man.* Toronto: University of Toronto Press, 1962.

McQuillan, Patrick. "Computers and Pedagogy: The Invisible Presence." Providence, R.I.: Office of Program Analysis, Institute for Research in Information and Scholarship, 1988.

Meyrowitz, Norman. "Hypertext — Does It Reduce Cholesterol, Too?" In *Vannevar Bush and the Mind's Machine: From Memex to Hypertext,* edited by James M. Nyce and Paul D. Kahn. San Diego: Academic Press, 1991.

———. "Intermedia: The Architecture and Construction of an Object-Oriented Hypermedia System and Applications Framework." *OOPSLA '86 Proceedings,* 186–201. Portland, Oreg., 1986.

———. "The Link to Tomorrow." *Unix Review* 8 (1990): 58–67.

Miller, J. Hillis. *Fiction and Repetition: Seven English Novels.* Cambridge: Harvard University Press, 1982.

———. "Literary Theory, Telecommunications, and the Making of History." *Conference Papers from the International Conference on Scholarship and Technology in the Humanities.* Sponsored by the British Library, the British Academy, and the American Council of Learned Societies, Elvetham Hall, England, May 1990.

———. *Versions of Pygmalion.* Cambridge: Harvard University Press, 1990.

Millett, Kate. *Sexual Politics.* Garden City, N.Y.: Doubleday, 1970.

Minsky, Marvin. *The Society of Mind.* New York: Simon and Schuster, 1986.

Mitchell, W. J. T., ed. *On Narrative.* Chicago: University of Chicago Press, 1980.

Moers, Ellen. *Literary Women.* New York: Oxford University Press, 1985.

Moi, Toril. *Sexual/Textual Politics: Feminist Literary Theory.* London: Methuen, 1985.

Morgan, Thaïs E. "Is There an Intertext in This Text?: Literary and Interdisciplinary Approaches to Intertextuality." *American Journal of Semiotics* 3 (1985): 1–40.

Morrell, Kenneth. "Teaching with *HyperCard.* An Evaluation of the Computer-based Section in Literature and Arts C-14: The Concept of the Hero in Hellenic Civilization." Perseus Project Working Paper 3. Cambridge: Department of Classics, Harvard University, 1988.

Moulthrop, Stuart. "Empires of Signs: Hypertext and the Politics of Interpretation." Manuscript, 1988.

Bibliography Murray, Oswyn. "The Word Is Mightier than the Sword." *Times Literary Supplement* (16–22 June 1989): 655.

Nelson, Theodor H. *Computer Lib/Dream Machines.* Seattle, Wash.: Microsoft Press, 1987.

———. *Literary Machines.* Swarthmore, Pa.: Self-published, 1981.

Nielsen, Jakob. "The Art of Navigating through Hypertext." *Communications of the ACM* 33 (1990): 296–310.

———. "Three Medium-sized Hypertexts on CD-ROM." Working Paper JN-1989–7.2. Lyngby: Technical University of Denmark, 1989.

———. "Trip Report: CHI '88: ACM Conference on Computer-Human Interaction." Lyngby: Technical University of Denmark, 1988.

———. "Trip Report: *Hyper Hyper:* Developments across the Field of Hypermedia. BCS Workshop, London." Lyngby: Technical University of Denmark, 1989.

———. "Trip Report: Hypertext II, York." Lyngby: Technical University of Denmark, 1989.

Novak, Joseph D., and D. Bob Gowin. *Learning How to Learn.* New York: Cambridge University Press, 1984.

Nyce, James M., and Paul Kahn. "Innovation, Pragmatism, and Technological Continuity: Vannevar Bush's Memex." *Journal of the American Society for Information Science* 40 (1989): 214–20.

Ong, Walter J. *Orality and Literacy: The Technologizing of the Word.* London: Methuen, 1982.

———. *Rhetoric, Romance, and Technology: Studies in the Interaction of Expression and Culture.* Ithaca: Cornell University Press, 1971.

Pagels, Heinz R. *The Dreams of Reason: The Computer and the Rise of the Sciences of Complexity.* New York: Bantam, 1989.

Panofsky, Erwin. *Meaning in the Visual Arts: Papers in and on Art History.* Garden City, N.Y.: Doubleday Anchor, 1955.

Paulson, William R. *The Noise of Culture: Literary Texts in a World of Information.* Ithaca: Cornell University Press, 1988.

Pavič, Milorad. *Dictionary of the Khazars: A Lexicon Novel in 100,000 Words.* Translated by Christina Pribicevic-Zoric. New York: Knopf, 1988.

Peckham, Morse. *Man's Rage for Chaos: Biology, Behavior, and the Arts.* New York: Shocken, 1967.

Bibliography   Perkins, D. N. "The Fingertip Effect: How Information-Processing Technology Shapes Thinking." *Educational Researcher* (August/September 1985): 11–17.

Perseus: An Interactive Curriculum on Ancient Greek Civilization. 3 vols. Cambridge: Harvard University, 1988.

Popper, Karl. *The Open Society and Its Enemies.* Princeton: Princeton University Press, 1963.

Provenzo, Eugene F. *Beyond the Gutenberg Galaxy: Microcomputers and the Emergence of Post-Typographic Culture.* New York: Teachers College Press, 1986.

Ricoeur, Paul. *Time and Narrative.* Translated by Kathleen McLaughlin and David Pellauer. 2 vols. Chicago: University of Chicago Press, 1984.

Rogers, Susan M. "Educational Applications of the NREN." *EDUCOM Review* 25 (Summer 1990): 25–29.

Rooney, Ellen. *Seductive Reasoning.* Ithaca: Cornell University Press, 1990.

Rorty, Richard. *Philosophy and the Mirror of Nature.* Princeton: Princeton University Press, 1979.

Ruthven, K. K. *Feminist Literary Studies: An Introduction.* Cambridge: Cambridge University Press, 1985.

Ryan, Michael. *Marxism and Deconstruction: A Critical Articulation.* Baltimore: Johns Hopkins University Press, 1982.

Said, Edward W. *Beginnings: Intention and Method.* New York: Columbia University Press, 1985.

Schmitz, Ulrich. "Automatic Generation of Texts without Using Cognitive Models: Television News." In *The New Medium: ALLC-ACH 90 Book of Abstracts,* 191–95. Siegen, Germany: University of Siegen, Association for Literary and Linguistic Computing, and the Association for Computers and the Humanities, 1990.

———. *Postmoderne Concierge: Die "Tagesschau." Wortwelt und Weltbild der Fernsehnachtrichten.* Opladen, Germany: Westdeutscher Verlag, 1990.

Scholes, Robert. *Structuralism in Literature: An Introduction.* New Haven: Yale University Press, 1974.

———. *Textual Power: Literary Theory and the Teaching of English.* New Haven: Yale University Press, 1985.

Scholes, Robert, and Robert Kellogg. *The Nature of Narrative.* New York: Oxford University Press, 1966.

Bibliography

Schor, Naomi. *Breaking the Chain: Women, Theory, and French Realist Fiction.* New York: Columbia University Press, 1985.

Showalter, Elaine. *A Literature of Their Own: British Women Novelists from Brontë to Lessing.* Princeton: Princeton University Press, 1977.

Smith, Barbara Herrnstein. *Poetic Closure: A Study of How Poems End.* Chicago: University of Chicago Press, 1968.

Smith, Tony C., and Ian H. Witten. "A Planning Mechanism for Generating Story Text." In *The New Medium: ALLC-ACH 90 Book of Abstracts,* 201–4. Siegen, Germany: University of Siegen, Association for Literary and Linguistic Computing, and the Association for Computers and the Humanities, 1990.

Spacks, Patricia Meyer. *The Female Imagination.* New York: Alfred A. Knopf, 1975.

Spiro, Rand J., Richard L. Coulson, Paul J. Felktovich, and Daniel K. Anderson, "Cognitive Flexibility Theory: Advanced Knowledge Acquisition in Ill-structured Domains." In *Program of the Tenth Annual Conference of the Cognitive Science Society.* Hillsdale, N.J.: Lawrence Erlbaum, 1988.

Spiro, Rand J., Walter P. Vispoel, John G. Schmitz, Ala Samarapungavan, and A. E. Boerger. "Knowledge Acquisition for Application: Cognitive Flexibility and Transfer in Complex Content Domains." In *Executive Control Processes in Reading,* edited by B. K. Britton and S. McGlynn, 177–99. Hillsdale, N.J.: Lawrence Erlbaum, 1987.

Steigler, Marc. "Hypermedia and Singularity." *Analog Science Fiction* (January 1989): 52–71.

Steinberg, S. H. *Five Hundred Years of Printing.* 2nd ed. Baltimore: Penguin, 1961.

Suckale, Robert. *Studien zu Stilbildung und Stilwandel de Madonnenstatuen der Ile-de-France zwischen 1240 und 1300.* Munich: University of Munich, 1971.

Sutherland, John. "Author's Rights and Transatlantic Differences." *Times Literary Supplement* (25–31 May 1990): 554.

Timpe, Eugene F. "Memory and Literary Structures." *Journal of Mind and Behavior* 2 (1981), 293–307.

Todorov, Tzvetan. *The Poetics of Prose.* Translated by Richard Howard. Ithaca: Cornell University Press, 1977.

Ulmer, Gregory L. *Applied Grammatology: Post(e)-Pedagogy from Jacques Derrida to Joseph Bueys.* Baltimore: Johns Hopkins University Press, 1985.

Utting, Kenneth, and Nicole Yankelovich, "Context and Orientation in Hypermedia Networks." *ACM Transactions on Information Systems* 7 (1989): 58–84.

Bibliography

von Hallberg, Robert, ed. *Canons*. Chicago: University of Chicago Press, 1984.

Weissman, Ronald F. E. "From the Personal Computer to the Scholar's Workstation." *Academic Computing* 3 (October 1988): 10–14, 30–34, 36, 38–41.

Wilson, Kathleen S. "Palenque: An Interactive Multimedia Optical Disc Prototype for Children." Working Paper no. 2. New York: Center for Children and Technology, Bank Street College of Education, 1986.

Wittgenstein, Ludwig. *Philosophical Investigations*. 3rd ed. Translated by G. E. M. Anscombe. New York: Macmillan, 1968.

Wu, Gordon. "Soft Soap." *Times Literary Supplement* (20–26 July 1990): 777.

Yankelovich, Nicole, George P. Landow, and David Cody. "Creating Hypermedia Materials for English Literature Students." *ACM SIGCUE Outlook* 19, no. 3–4 (1987): 12–25.

Yankelovich, Nicole, Norman Meyrowitz, and Stephen Drucker. "Intermedia: The Concept and the Construction of a Seamless Information Environment." *IEEE Computer* 21 (1988): 81–96.

Yankelovich, Nicole, Norman Meyrowitz, and Andries van Dam. "Reading and Writing the Electronic Book." *IEEE Computer* 18 (October 1985): 15–30.

Zimmer, Carl. "Floppy Fiction." *Discover* (November 1989): 34–36.

Electronic Materials

CD Word: The Interactive Bible Library. Environment: Specially amplified Guide. Dallas: CD Word Library, 1990.

The Dickens Web. Developer: George P. Landow. Editors: Julie Launhardt and Paul D. Kahn. Environment: Intermedia 3.5. Providence, R.I.: Institute for Research in Information and Scholarship, 1990.

Exploring the Moon. Developers: Katie Livingston, Jayne Aubele, and James Head. Editors Paul D. Kahn and Julie Launhardt. Environment: Intermedia 3.5. Providence, R.I.: Institute for Research in Information and Scholarship, 1988.

Joyce, Michael. *Afternoon*. Environment: Storyspace Beta 3.3. Jackson, Mich.: Riverrun Limited, 1987.

Moulthrop, Stuart. *Forking Paths: An Interaction after Jorge Luis Borges*. Environment: Storyspace Beta 3.3 Jackson, Mich.: Riverrun Limited, 1987.

Perseus 1.0b1: Interactive Sources and Studies on Ancient Greek Civilization. (Beta pre-release version.) Developers: Gregory Crane and Elli Mylonas. Environment: HyperCard. Washington, D.C.: Annenberg/Corporation for Public Broadcasting Project, 1990.

Bibliography   Seid, Tim. *Interpreting Manuscripts.* Environment: HyperCard. Providence, R.I.: Privately published, 1990.

Winter, Robert. *CD Companion to Beethoven Symphony No. 9: A HyperCard/CD Audio Program.* Environment: HyperCard. Santa Monica, Calif.: Voyager, 1989.

Index